CW00727095

RUSSIAN AT HEART

RUSSIAN AT HEART

Sonechka's Story

Olga *&* John Hawkes

To Barbara + Robin
Best wishes & many thanks.

Olga Soca-Hawk
& John

14/9/2010.

WILY PUBLICATIONS

Published by
Wily Publications Ltd
302 Lake Terrace Road
Shirley
Christchurch 8061
New Zealand
Email: jjhaworth@xtra.co.nz
www.wily.co.nz

Text copyright © 2009 Olga and John Hawkes
Photographs copyright © 2009 Olga Hawkes
First published 2009

The authors have asserted their moral rights in the work.

This book is copyright. Except for the purposes of fair reviewing,
no part of this publication (whether it be in any eBook, digital,
electronic or traditionally printed format or otherwise) may
be reproduced or transmitted in any form or by any means,
electronic, digital or mechanical, including CD, DVD, eBook,
PDF format, photocopying, recording, or any information storage
and retrieval system, including by any means via the internet or
World Wide Web, or by any means yet undiscovered, without
permission in writing from the publisher. Infringers of copyright
render themselves liable to prosecution.

ISBN 978-0-9582923-3-7

Cover and page design by Quentin Wilson
Page layout by Antoinette Wilson
Printed by Sunny Young Printing Ltd, Taiwan

CONTENTS

To my mother,
Sonechka.

ACKNOWLEDGEMENTS

I cannot thank my mother and Aunt Dora enough for writing their priceless memoirs all those years ago. I am also indebted to them for sharing their reminiscences in conversations with me. Their exceptional lives form the basis of this book.

I am most grateful for my sister Margarita's recollections of her childhood and adolescence in Shanghai and for giving us many of the photographs in this book. Only now do I fully appreciate why it continues to be painful for her to recall how our family suffered in Shanghai.[1]

I am also grateful for the photographs given me by my ninety-four-year-old cousin Katherine, in Paris, and the family stories she has shared with me.

Without my husband John's encouragement and his love of history, especially Russian, this book would never have been written.

We owe a special debt of gratitude to the writer and historian Jenny Haworth, our publisher and editor. Without her this book would probably not have seen the light of day.

We would like to thank all the many friends and acquaintances worldwide who have contributed to this joint writing venture.

In Christchurch: the journalist and linguist Robin Munro, Jenny's assistant editor, and Quentin Wilson for the skilfull layout of the work. Other people in New Zealand who have helped include: Barbara Arnold, Tatiana Blagova, Archpriest Vladimir Boikov, David Elworthy, John Goodliffe, Helen Lamont, Mary Newton, Elizabeth Robertson, Anna Rogers, Professor Richard Rowe, Joe Studholme, Dr Barrie Tait, Kathryn Taylor, Father Arkadi Trashkov, Lorraine Willis.

In Australia: Dai Baker, Tatiana Fedukowicz, Natasha and Frank Fuller, Mila and Val Kraft, Metropolitan Hilarion and Archimandrite Alexis Rosentool, Alex Saranin, Katya and Peter Tatarinoff, Wolfgang Troeger.

In North America: Elaine and Tony Avdienko, Marvin Lyons, Boris and Nikolai Massenkoff, Dr Alexander Studeimeister.

In England: Peter and Sue Adams, John Bayfield, Kay Bellinger, Katya Burova, Professor Robin Carrell and Susan Carrell, Rebecca and Greg Stock, Jason Tilney, Richard Wildman.

In Paris: Michel and Margit Farrugia's hospitality, over many years, deserves a special mention. They have given us books and introductions to people relevant to our work. Our other life-long French friends, Nina Soldatenkoff (née Guilsher), my bridesmaid, and her husband Father Nikolai, who live in the Bourgogne, and Madeleine and Maurice Knoertzer in Bordeaux, have been equally generous with their hospitality and input.

In 2002 we had the good fortune to meet Susan Hine, who lives and works in Shanghai. On our second visit, in 2006, Susan introduced us to Tess Johnson, a long-time resident. Until her retirement she worked at Shanghai's American consulate. Tess is renowned for her knowledge of history and architecture in Shanghai's former French Concession. She gave us a wonderful insight into my birthplace and where I lived as a child, enhanced by the purchase of her impressive illustrated books.

In deference to the express wishes of several members of my family who are featured in this book, I have changed their names.

PREFACE

I have wanted to write *Russian at Heart*, my mother's story, for many years. Shortly after Sonechka, my mother, died in 1974, Margarita, my sister, sent me our mother's notebook memoirs, written in Russia and Shanghai. At the time we were living in England, where John was the consultant rheumatologist at Bedford Hospital. With our three young children and John's evening private specialist practice, I had little time for anything else. Furthermore, I found it painful to read what my thirteen-year-old mother had endured as a destitute orphan in revolutionary Russia and subsequently during the Civil War and under the Bolshevik regime. From time to time I would glance at these memoirs, hold them to my breast, and then replace them in the drawer.

Knowing what my mother had suffered, from what she told me and her memoirs, it upsets me that articles, books and films continue to portray the White Russian Diaspora, especially in Shanghai, in such a poor light. The White Russian women in Shanghai are mostly depicted as prostitutes and the White Russian men as drunken good-for-nothings. *Russian at Heart* highlights the harsh realities of the plight of my parents' generation: stateless and stranded exiles, shunned by the world. Yet these ignored or abhorred White Russians, against almost insurmountable odds, created a dynamic self-help community in Shanghai. Only a minority were prostitutes and good-for-nothings.

Having read many books about the White Russian Diaspora, I was disheartened that I had no formal writing training. How could I possibly write about Sonechka's life or convey that her dream of fleeing Bolshevik Russia was considered a foolish fantasy?

It was not until 1999, after my husband John had retired from his job in England, that I read my mother's memoirs in their entirety and translated them for him. The poignant plea she made: 'I hope that someone someday will read this and know what I suffered', brought tears to John's eyes. This cry from the heart further fired my determination to write Sonechka's story.

The alien Bolshevik ideology that was foisted on the hapless Russian people so nearly destroyed historic Russia and its soul. It was White Russians like my parents in the Diaspora who maintained the traditional Russian values. This flame, tended for so long by the Diaspora, has now been relit in the Motherland.

John and I hope that Sonechka's story will give the reader an insight into what it means to be 'Russian at Heart'.

– Olga Hawkes,
New Zealand, 2009

PEOPLE IN SONECHKA'S LIFE

BALK FAMILY

Lev Balk	Sonechka's father, born 1874
Anastasia Balk	Sonechka's mother, born 1876

BALK CHILDREN

Sasha	born 1894
Liza	born 1898
Mishka	born 1900
Sonechka	born 1904

OTHER BALK FAMILY MEMBERS

Aunt Olya	Anastasia's elderly aunt
Lydia	Lev's second wife
Gregory	Lydia's distant cousin
Aunt Frosya	Anastasia's sister
Uncle Fyodor	Aunt Frosya's husband
Aunt Eva	Anastasia's sister
Vera	Uncle Fyodor's sister
Alexander	Vera's husband
Pavel	Liza's husband
Sofia	Liza and Pavel's daughter

BALK HOUSEHOLD STAFF

Glasha	cook
Semyon	handyman/gardener

PAVEL'S ALMA ESTATE

Shura Ryzhkov	resident commissar
Stepanov	resident commissar
Nikolai Zhukov	commissar and Sonechka's first love
Leonid Ivanov	commissar
Katya	Sonechka's roommate
Volodya	youth who courts Sonechka

MOSCOW AND LENINGRAD

Valentina	wardrobe mistress at a Moscow theatre
Zhenya	Balk family friend, Leningrad

TRANS-SIBERIAN TRAIN FLIGHT

David and Esther	Jewish husband and wife
Miriam, Sara, Rachel	David and Esther's daughters
Ivan	commissar

HARBIN

Nina	boarding house landlady
Gregory	Nina's nephew
Olya	acrobat staying at the boarding house
Mr Gibbes	tutor to the Tsar's children

VLADIMIR'S FAMILY

Emil Rossi	Vladimir's father, born 1839
Sofia Rossi	Vladimir's mother (née Rousseau), born 1866
Dora	Vladimir's sister, born 1892
Vladimir	born 1894
Dorothea Rousseau	Vladimir's grandmother (nee von Meltzer)
Gertruda Rossi	Mother of Karlo Rossi, renowned dancer
Karlo Rossi	renowned St Petersburg architect and town planner
Vera, Vasya and Kolya	Dora and Vladimir's cousins and playmates
Andrei	Dora's husband
Mlle Louise	French governess

SHANGHAI

Margarita	Sonechka and Vladimir's daughter, born 1930
Olga	Sonechka and Vladimir's daughter and co-author of this book, born 1942
Lara	Sonechka's friend
Gustav	Lara's husband
Peter and Alexander	Lara and Gustav's twins
Maria Nikolayevna	Lara's mother
Mary	Lara's Eurasian salon assistant
Duncan Kerr	Sonechka and Sasha's benefactor
Cynthia and Gerald Parsons	Lara's English friends
Angus Kerr	Duncan's nephew
Masha and Nadya	Sonechka's Russian friends
Nikolai Bibikov	Vladimir's friend and Olga's godfather
Father Nikodim	Russian Orthodox priest and friend of Rossi family
Bishop John	Russian Orthodox priest (canonised as St John of Shanghai and San Francisco, 1994)
Boris Aprelev	Vladimir's friend from St Petersburg
Wolfgang	Lara's boyfriend

EVENTS RELEVANT TO
RUSSIAN AT HEART

1904   Trans-Siberian Railway completed, reaching Vladivostok via
        Manchuria.
        Japan attacks Russian fleet at Port Arthur. Start of Russo-Japanese
        War.

1905   Japan defeats Russian army at Mukden and Russia's Baltic fleet at
        Battle of Tsushima.
        Revolutionaries rampage throughout Russia.

1911   China's Manchu dynasty relinquishes power.

1912   Dr Sun Yat-sen becomes first President of Chinese Republic.

1913   Tercentenary of Imperial Russia's Romanov dynasty.

1914   First World War starts.
        St Petersburg renamed Petrograd.
        Battle of Tannenberg.

1916   Peasant mystic Rasputin assassinated.
        Second completion date of the Trans-Siberian Railroad, the Amur
        Railway to Vladivostok, wholly within Russian territory.

1917   February Russian Revolution.
        Tsar Nicholas abdicates.
        October Bolshevik counter-revolution overthrows the
        Provisional Government.

1918   Bolsheviks abolish Constituent Assembly.
        Russian Civil War starts.
        Brest-Litovsk Treaty.
        Bolsheviks cede large part of Russian territory to Germans.
        Russia ceases fighting Germany and her Axis allies.
        Tsar Nicholas II and his family murdered at Yekaterinburg.
        First World War ends.

1919   Lenin creates Bolshevik propaganda organ the Communist
International (Comintern).
Treaty of Versailles.
Japan takes possession of Germany's former Chinese territories.

1920   White Army defeated in European Russia.

1921   Famine in Russia.
Massive American aid saves millions of Soviet lives.
Lenin launches his New Economic Policy (NEP).

1922   Union of the Soviet Socialist Republics (USSR).
Benito Mussolini becomes Prime Minister of Italy.

1924   Lenin dies.
Petrograd renamed Leningrad.
Johnson-Reed Immigration Act, United States.

1925   Chinese protestors shot during Shanghai's May 30 Nanking
Road Incident.

1927   Chiang Kai-shek, hand-in-glove with Chinese Green Gang boss Du,
kills Shanghai communists.

1928   Stalin's first Five-Year Plan.

1929   Wall Street Crash. Start of Great Depression.

1931   Japan invades Manchuria.

1932   Japan attacks Chinese section of northern Shanghai.

1933   Hitler becomes Chancellor of Germany.
Franklin D. Roosevelt inaugurated President of the United States.

1934   Japan appoints Pu Yi, former emperor of China, the puppet emperor of
Manchukuo (formerly Manchuria).

1937   Japan occupies half of China including Chinese sections of Shanghai.

1938   Munich Agreement.

1939   Soviet Union and Germany sign Non-Aggression Pact.
Germany invades western half of Poland.
Britain and France declare war on Germany.
Soviet Union invades eastern half of Poland.

1940	Germany defeats France. Marshal Petain's Vichy France. Shanghai's French Concession governed by Vichy France.
1941	Germany invades Soviet Union. Japan attacks Pearl Harbour. America declares war on Japan. Shanghai's International Settlement occupied by Japan. Hitler declares war on America.
1942	Singapore, Britain's greatest-ever military defeat. Japan begins internment of allies in Shanghai.
1943	German Sixth Army and its Axis allies surrender at Stalingrad. Britain, America and France relinquish their extraterritorial rights in China.
1944	D-Day allied invasion of Europe. Paris is liberated. Vichy France collapses.
1945	Churchill, Roosevelt and Stalin's Yalta Conference. Roosevelt dies. Germany surrenders. Atomic bombs dropped on Nagasaki and Hiroshima. Japan surrenders. Americans occupy Shanghai.
1946	Civil war rages in China.
1948	Stalin's Berlin blockade intensifies Cold War.
1949	Communist leader Mao Zedong defeats nationalist leader Chiang Kai-shek.
1950	United States Senator Joseph McCarthy's anti-communist crusade.

The Balk family, Crimea, 1909. *From left*: Liza (11); Sonechka's mother, Anastasia; Sasha (15); Sonechka (5); Sonechka's father, Lev; Mishka (9).

CHAPTER ONE

On the night of June 2, 1924, my mother, nineteen-year-old Sofia Lvovna Balk, known as Sonechka, fled Moscow on the Trans-Siberian Railway. She was bound for China.

In Shanghai, freed from the clutches of the Bolsheviks, Sonechka became an exile, longing to return to her pre-revolutionary Motherland. Her faith in God and her memories of an idyllic childhood in the Crimea proved to be a great solace throughout her life-long exile.

Sonechka used to recall basking in the sun on the veranda of her family home in the Crimean resort town, Alushta. She was cooled by a gentle breeze drifting in from the Black Sea.

Her earliest recollections were of sitting on the steps of the veranda surrounded by a profusion of flowers whose fragrance filled the air. Here she listened to the soothing sound of her *mamochka* (diminutive of mother) playing the piano. Papa would be sitting close by in an ancient carved rocking chair, savouring a pungent Turkish cigarette.

Madly in love, Sonechka's parents, Lev Alexandrovich and Anastasia Nikolayevna, had eloped in their late teens. Anastasia's parents were outraged and disinherited her. However, in 1904, the year of Sonechka's birth, Anastasia had the good fortune to inherit a gracious property set in extensive grounds in Alushta. She and Lev converted it into a luxurious pension. The summer months brought an influx of lodgers, mainly escapees from the stifling heat of St Petersburg and Moscow. Besides the scenery and historic sites, these summer guests came to enjoy the sea air and gentle climate. The house burst at its seams with these loyal holidaymakers. They enjoyed Lev's animated stories, in particular his tales of fearsome bandits who had once inhabited the nearby mountains.

Sonechka often recalled how her papa would take their guests on pleasure trips in the family's rather grand but faded landau, a horse-drawn carriage, along the beautiful Tauride coast, known as Russia's Riviera. As a special treat, she was allowed to join these tours, which were enlivened by her papa's commentaries. Bright and festive villas built by the nobility lined the route as did a number of exotic palaces perched on cliff tops with their underground grottos, galleries and labyrinths. Sonechka was fascinated by the remnants of fortresses built by the Crimea's many different rulers, including Greeks, Romans, Persians, Mongols, Tartars, Turks, Venetians and Russians.

During these tours the guests would listen, enchanted, to her papa reciting poems by Pushkin and Lermontov. Alushta had earlier paid tribute to Pushkin, the Shakespeare of Russian literature, by erecting an elegant, life-size, commemorative statute of him. The Tauride coast also inspired Anton Chekhov, Maxim Gorky and Leo Tolstoy, who had been an artillery officer in the Crimean War in the 1850s. Crimea was a Mecca not only for renowned writers, but also for many others in the world of arts, including painters, musicians and actors who either lived there or stayed for long periods.

Anastasia supervised the household, the paying guests, and the extended family. Sonechka was the youngest of four children. Mikhail, known as Mishka, Yelizaveta, known as Liza and Alexander, known as Sasha, were respectively four, six, and ten years older than her. Sonechka adored her big brother, Sasha. In her eyes, he was the cleverest of boys. She loved creeping silently into the room when a guest sat for Sasha to paint their portrait. These portraits, it was said, revealed their inner souls. As Sonechka grew older, Sasha let her accompany him on his painting expeditions. She would sit for hours watching him paint, marvelling at how he caught on canvas the subtle changes of light and shadow at dawn and dusk as they played across the nearby mountains and sea. He told her of his secret wish to one day gain a place at St Petersburg's Royal Academy of Art. She recalled how Anastasia proudly displayed Sasha's works of art in her study.

Lev, who had inherited an extensive library, encouraged the family to read. From an early age, my mother loved reading. She devoured the accounts of Tom Sawyer and Huckleberry Finn's lives. Their adventures made her want to visit America to see the great Mississippi River with its famed riverboats. As she grew older her yearning to travel increased, inspired by reading Jules Verne and Pushkin, while Sir Walter Scott awakened her romantic imagination.

Towards the end of each summer season the family staged a play. Nearly everyone in the household participated. Friends and neighbours and most of the local inhabitants looked forward to this yearly spectacle. Aged six, Sonechka was delighted with her first role, even if it was only a small part. It was an introduction to an art form that would forever fascinate her.

Chekhov was one of the family's favourite playwrights. He had lived in Yalta, 40 kilometres from Alushta, from 1899 to 1904 when he wrote 'The Three Sisters' and 'The Cherry Orchard'. He was born in Taganrog on the Sea of Azov, which borders the Crimean Peninsula.

During rehearsals Lev revelled in the role of director, which he carried out with great panache. His booming voice could be heard reverberating throughout the house. Sasha displayed his artistic skills in painting wonderful stage sets. The play took most of August to produce. Each year, Lev went to great lengths to persuade Anastasia to take part in the play, but to no avail. Fixing her bewitching, deep violet-blue eyes on him, she would murmur, 'Levushka, someone has to remain sane in this household,' or words to that effect.

The adventurous Mishka seemed incapable of keeping out of trouble. One summer's afternoon he lured Sonechka down to the pond built by their *dedushka* (grandfather), located in an overgrown part of their extensive garden. Mishka and his gang of mischievous playmates made this pond the focal point of their secret hideaway. Holding her hand he guided her through dense undergrowth towards what he described as 'the promised land of Robinson Crusoe'.

On reaching a steep mound, a clearing appeared that led to the fabled pond. 'Look!' he exclaimed, grinning with pride. 'We've built a swing on this overhanging branch at the edge of our pond.' He then jumped onto the wooden seat and got Sonechka to push him higher and higher.

She begged him to let her have a turn. He paused, looked around, and said, 'I can only let you have a short ride because we don't allow girls to come here.' Having hoisted her onto the seat, he then propelled her forwards with a mighty shove, shouting out, 'For heaven's sake, hold on tight!' How she loved the sensation of flying through the air. Suddenly, she felt herself falling. Unable to keep hold of the swing ropes, she pitched head first into the pond. Mishka plunged into the water and dragged her out. Soaked and covered in mud, but uninjured, she returned home with the chastened Mishka. Besides banning him from playing in the pond area, their parents had him copy out pages and pages of verse.

During the winters at Alushta, Glasha, the cook, often said to Sonechka, 'Come into the kitchen and play by the *pechka* (a large stove).' From morning till night there was always something baking in its great oven.

Glasha liked reminiscing about the 'good old days' when *dedushka* ruled the household. A generous host, he presided over frequent large gatherings of family and friends. Sonechka recalled how Glasha, pausing for effect and sighing in despair, would say, 'Whatever happened to the old-fashioned hospitality practised by Nikolai Dmitriyevich (*dedushka*). His doors were always open to neighbours and visitors. Alas, today the guests must pay! *Ah, Bozhe moi, Bozhe moi!* (Oh, my God, Oh my God!) What's the world coming to?'

She would then turn to the icon corner of the kitchen, lit by a *lampada* (oil lamp), and cross herself.

Sonechka recalled how Liza and papa often engaged in animated and, at times, acrimonious discussions on a wide range of subjects. Disdainful of Liza, Glasha would call her '*nasha molodaya barinya*' (our young madam).

Aunt Olya (Olga), an elderly aunt of Sonechka's mother lived with them. A great beauty in her day, she married Andrei Ignatyevich, the owner of a large estate in the Simferopol region managed by a German agent. Each autumn, they went 'for the season', first to St Petersburg and then on to Europe, returning home for the traditional Easter family reunions. Andrei, who liked to gamble, was well known in Baden Baden and other glamorous European spas and holiday towns. They did this for twenty years, until, as Lev liked to say, with a dismissive shrug of the shoulders, 'the money ran out'.

The petite, elegant Aunt Olya would sit on the veranda in the afternoons sipping her tea at an elegant table dominated by a magnificent silver samovar. Irrespective of the weather she always wrapped herself in a shawl or two. Comfortably settled in her armchair, she would engage in conversation with whoever was within earshot.

Sonechka loved listening to her reminiscing about St Petersburg's fabulous balls and troika sleigh rides along the city's frozen Neva River. Aunt Olya had met Andrei Ignatyevich, a dashing young guards officer, in St Petersburg. After a whirlwind romance they were married and went to live on his estate. Their greatest disappointment was that both their children died in infancy.

Once the summer guests had departed, life at their home took on an altogether different character. Lev supervised the harvest of the fruit trees and olive groves, while Glasha, mama and Aunt Olya bottled the preserves. Around the time of Sonechka's birthday in early October, they picked mushrooms in the neighbouring wooded slopes; it was a popular activity. The innumerable basket loads were either pickled or laid out to dry on the flat rooftop of the large building next to the kitchen.

The rhythm of the house slowed down even more during the winter months. By Moscow and St Petersburg standards, the Tauride coast winters were mild. Even so, the family spent much of the winter in the dining room, where a large fireplace kept them warm. The treasured samovar would occupy a prominent position on the dining table.

After supper, Aunt Olya produced one of a variety of handicrafts from her distinctive sewing basket and recommenced whatever she had been doing the previous evening. Lev read out loud from a newspaper, a passage from a recently published book or from a collection of poems. Anastasia mended garments or did similar handiwork. Sasha and Liza enjoyed these witty conversations. Lev tried hard to involve Mishka in these discussions, but to no avail. The practical Mishka, who loved action, had no interest in politics, literature or the arts. Though much of what was said passed over Sonechka's head, she enjoyed listening and learned a lot, while playing with Marusya, her favourite doll.

Anastasia always put Sonechka to bed and they would pray together. Brought up in a deeply religious family, Anastasia wanted her children to base their lives on Christ's teachings and would read Sonechka the life of the saint of the day, from 'Lives of the Saints'. By the time Sonechka was eight she knew the lives of most of the important Russian Orthodox saints and their respective feast days.

The family followed the Russian Orthodox tradition of naming the newborn child after the saint of the day. Though Sonechka was born on 1 October, her mother decided to call her Sofia, despite St Sofia's feast day falling on September 30. Of the several diminutives of Sofia available, the family thought Sonechka the most appropriate. Birthdays were not celebrated in Imperial Russia. Instead, Name Days, the saints' feast days, were observed.

With their extended family there were many Name Day celebrations throughout the year. On these occasions Lev made a great fuss of the person's special day. Glasha baked the traditional family *krendel* (a rich yeast cake mixture made with eggs, milk, honey, raisins and nuts). She also cooked a favourite dish for dinner. If the Name Day fell during the Great Lent[2], the fifty-day period before the Orthodox Church Easter, they went without the scrumptious *krendel*. Dairy products, meat and eggs were forbidden during Lent.

Despite the solemnity of Passion Week, the household took on a festive mood. On the Monday Glasha and her helpers began spring cleaning not only the house, but also all the outer buildings. This ended on Wednesday. On Thursday, known as *Velikii Chetverg* (Holy Thursday), Glasha with her troupe of household retainers went to the local *banya* (a type of Turkish bathhouse).

That night the household attended the local village church for the Holy Thursday service, where there were readings from the twelve gospels.

Sonechka did not attend this service until aged eight when, together with the family and other worshippers, she stood solemnly holding a lighted candle, listening to the readings. As instructed, she held her candle as upright as she could to prevent the candle wax dripping on the floor. She felt very grown up. At the end of the long service her mama placed her lighted candle in a glass lantern so that she could carry it home without the flame being extinguished by the wind. The long procession of worshippers wending their way with their sacred lights could be seen from afar.

On arriving home, her papa raised his lighted candle above their main doorway and made the sign of the cross. This left a blackened cross which symbolised God's protection over the household during the coming year. The children did the same above their bedroom doorways. Sonechka recalled, with pride, how she managed, with her papa's help, to do her first doorway cross.

When they returned home, Glasha's food preparations for *Paskha* began in earnest. The specially milled flour, eggs and butter had been delivered that morning. With the raisins weighed and the almonds chopped, Glasha called on the Lord's help before preparing the yeast dough. Turning to the icon corner of the kitchen, she made the sign of the cross and murmured a prayer beseeching God to make this 'batch of *kulichi*' the best ever. She proceeded to bake the *kulichi* (a cylinder-shaped yeast bread containing candied fruit, almonds, and raisins) throughout the night and most of the next morning.

The memory of waking to the delicious smell of freshly baked *kulichi* wafting through the house remained forever with my mother. She recalled running to the kitchen, first thing in the morning, to see the mass of newly baked *kulichi* set out on the long table. In the afternoon she helped decorate the tops of the *kulichi* with white frosting, finishing with *Khristos Voskres* (Christ is Risen) made from raisins. Each child was given a small *kulich*, which they placed in a basket with the decorated painted eggs ready to be taken to the church for the traditional blessing after the *Paskha* midnight service.

Sonechka recalled that Easter for another reason: Mishka accidentally set fire to Liza's dress during the *Paskha* midnight procession. The fifteen-year-old Liza, dressed in a lovely white frock made by Anastasia, was an attractive young woman with beautiful thick wavy hair reaching down to her waist. Holding lighted candles, the clergy, bearing icons, led the congregation in the procession around the outside of the church. Taking care not to stumble on the uneven footpath, Anastasia, Liza and Sonechka walked abreast, followed by Lev, Sasha and Mishka. The procession halted in front of the church's closed front door. On entering the church, Mishka tripped on the step. Suddenly,

Liza's hair and dress were alight. Lev's quick reaction to extinguish the flames with his overcoat saved the petrified Liza from being badly burned.

Each Easter Lev and Anastasia held the traditional 'open house' attended by both rich and poor dressed in their Sunday best. After the seven weeks of fasting, it was, for many, the highlight of their year. The Easter tables were awash with numerous meat dishes and many other delicacies, including the traditional *paskha* (curd cheese, eggs, sugar, cream, almonds and raisins).

Glasha was celebrated for her baking. Lev boasted that her *kulichi* and *paskha* could well grace the Tsar's table.

The parish priests were the first visitors to arrive to bless the house and Easter fare. Then, from midday onwards, the guests arrived. Anastasia and Aunt Olya, seated by the silver samovar, plied everyone with food and drink, making it difficult not to overindulge. Glasha, dressed in her best *sarafan* (traditional Russian peasant smock), and in a new kerchief, given each Easter by Anastasia, bustled about beaming. Humiliated by her singed hair Liza decided to forgo the Easter Day festivities.

Years later she told Sonechka how she hated having to kiss all and sundry, especially the elderly men from the village with their dirty beards. The traditional Easter greeting is to say, '*Khristos Voskrese*' (Christ is Risen), and then to kiss each other three times on the cheeks. For some, these festivities meant eating and drinking for several days: sampling the hospitality of the different households in the parish. Such was the importance of the *kulich* and *paskha* that households vied with one another to have the tastiest.

Apart from the joyous celebration of Christ's resurrection, Easter heralded the onset of spring with its profusion of blossoms. It also meant that before long Sonechka could enjoy the summer school holidays, playing on their sun-drenched property, listening to her papa's stories, reading and being with the guests.

That Easter, worried that her mama spent so much time in her bedroom during the afternoons, Sonechka expressed her concern to Glasha. Stroking Sonechka's head gently, Glasha whispered, 'Your *mamochka* is tired. Don't worry my little one, resting will, I'm sure, help her.'

CHAPTER TWO

With Anastasia's health continuing to deteriorate, that spring, Lev decided to employ a housekeeper to take over her duties. He chose Lydia Vladimirovna, a widow from Yalta, to fill this role. Her husband, a merchant, who had been much older than her, had died after twelve years of marriage, leaving her comfortably off. She seemed to enjoy the hustle and bustle of the household and maintained that it was a 'blessing' for her. From early on, Liza disliked her, as did Glasha, who would murmur under her breath, 'I've got to keep a watchful eye on this imperious *barinya's* (madam's) movements.'

That summer, 1913, Lev and Anastasia were delighted to receive an invitation from Alexander Pavlovich Balk to be his guests for the St Petersburg winter season. He was one of Lev's distinguished relations (Governor of St Petersburg at the time of the February 1917 revolution). Liza, who was just sixteen, accompanied them. Throughout that year there were numerous nationwide festivities celebrating the tercentenary of the House of Romanov. Anastasia and Liza pored over ladies' fashion journals, some from Paris, to get the latest mode. Anastasia got a renowned local seamstress to sew the outfits they would wear to the various functions in the imperial capital.

Early one autumn morning they set off for Yalta in a horse-drawn carriage which took them to Simferopol, where they boarded the train for Moscow. They spent two days in Moscow before catching another train for St Petersburg. This was a great adventure for Liza who had never ventured beyond the Tauride coast. Sonechka envied her. Unbeknown to Sonechka, her parents had another reason for going to the imperial capital. They were very concerned above Anastasia's deteriorating health. Lev wanted the best doctors in Russia to assess his wife's condition.

In Lev's absence, Aunt Olya and Lydia took charge of the household, and of Mishka and Sonechka. Mishka was about to start his second year at the local *gimnasia* (a high school preparing students for university) where, several months earlier, Liza had completed her studies with distinction. Sonechka was enjoying her primary school. Sasha had completed his first year at the Art Academy.

That October, just after her birthday, Sonechka came down with the mumps. The doctor confined her to bed, all alone, in a semi-darkened room. Sonechka missed the fun-loving Mishka and her mother's care. She devoured the letters from St Petersburg describing Liza's successful entry into the famed *beau monde*. Aunt Olya relived her youthful golden years through these letters, with their fascinating accounts of the wondrous world of imperial St Petersburg. She maintained that her St Petersburg coming-out ball was the finest of that season, during which, for weeks on end, she waltzed the evenings away with many gallant young suitors.

After the Romanov celebrations the New Year seemed full of promise for Russia, especially during the early summer of 1914. Nobody was aware that a terrible war was about to break out that would lead to revolution and civil war and would destroy virtually everything they held dear.

The family was consumed with concern about Anastasia, as the St Petersburg doctors had diagnosed her heart condition. Despite the medicines they prescribed, her shortness of breath and fatigue increased to such an extent that she and Lev came home in mid-January. Liza remained in St Petersburg.

On her return, Anastasia's condition got so bad that she spent most of the day confined to her bedroom. With the warmer weather, Lev moved her divan onto the veranda in the hope that the fresh air would help her.

After school Sonechka would rush home to be with Anastasia, who cherished these precious times with her youngest child. She dismissed any suggestion that they might be hastening her decline. Besides helping Sonechka with her schoolwork, she read to her from her favourite books and poets' works. She taught Sonechka to accept life's trials and tribulations as being God's will. Reflecting on her mother's ordeal, some years later, Sonechka had no doubt that her faith in God enabled her to bear her suffering with fortitude. As her darling *mamochka* grew weaker, a sad veil fell over the household. Anastasia spent hours in prayer and discussions with the family priest, Father Arseny, often with Lev in attendance. Occasionally Sonechka and Mishka joined in these prayers, which gave her mama great solace.

Liza returned from St Petersburg for Easter and, two months later, Sasha came home.

By mid-summer 1914 it seemed that the whole world was about to explode. It began with the assassination in Sarajevo of Crown Prince Franz Ferdinand, the heir to the Austro-Hungarian throne. Austria-Hungary subsequently declared war on Serbia, with Germany's Kaiser Wilhelm threatening war on everyone. In response, Tsar Nicholas II ordered the mobilisation of more than a million men. In the evenings, Lev read the latest news. Fervent discussions followed as to what Russia should or should not do. The adults hoped it would all be resolved peaceably and that Sasha would not have to go to war.

The hot-headed Mishka told Sonechka in confidence that, should war break out, he would run away and join up despite being well under age. With his mates, he staged mock battles down near the pond. By August the war had started. Anti-German feeling became intense. This hostility had built up for quite some time, and the capital was renamed Petrograd. The overwhelming defeat in late August of the Imperial Russian army at the battle of Tannenberg in East Prussia dispelled the generally held belief that Russia would be victorious by Christmas. Some historians think that this offensive saved Paris. Tens of thousands died with many more wounded and taken prisoner. Only belatedly did the Russians learn that their massive army was poorly equipped, inadequately clothed and made up mainly of untrained peasants, many mere boys, led by officers of whom only a small proportion were well trained.

Three days after Sonechka's tenth birthday her mother, Anastasia, passed away in her sleep. She was only thirty-eight years old.

Straightaway, Lydia took charge. She had the mirrors shrouded and ornaments put away. The seamstress was summoned to sew the mourning shroud for Anastasia and to ensure the family wore the appropriate attire. For two days before the funeral Anastasia's body was laid out in the dining room surrounded by family icons and lighted candles. Relatives and friends came, some from afar, to pay their respects. Most stayed on for the funeral. Lev, no longer the jovial host, was in deep mourning. When not with the mourners, he spent long periods alone in the library.

As the grief-stricken household prepared for the funeral an oppressive cloud descended upon the once happy home. Sonechka tried to comprehend why *Bozhenka* (a diminutive for God) had taken her *mamochka* away from her. During this time Sasha, tenderly holding Sonechka's hand, took her for a walk along the path of cypress trees at the back of their home. He explained how, on the day of the funeral, the angels would take their *mamochka's* soul to heaven where she would no longer suffer. He told Sonechka that before Anastasia died she made him promise to look after his little sister no matter what.

The night before the funeral Anastasia's coffin was taken to the church where the *Parastas* (a vigil service for the dead) was conducted. During the night nuns read from the Psalter (Book of Psalms) over the body until the funeral the next day. Family and friends attended the liturgy, followed immediately by the funeral service.

During these services Sonechka stood alongside the open coffin unable to take her eyes off the alabaster-like features of her mother's face. The intense smell of the incense mingled with the fragrant aroma of the mass of white flowers, mainly roses, covering the coffin, pervaded the church. Later, as the haunting funeral chant of *Vechnaya Pamyat* (Eternal Memory) accompanied the coffin to its final destination, Sonechka watched her distraught *papochka* bend down to kiss Anastasia's forehead for the last time. She was broken-hearted.

CHAPTER THREE

That winter an empty sadness pervaded the household. The loss of Anastasia affected everyone. In December, during Advent, Aunt Olya caught a chill that developed into pneumonia. When she died, Lydia became the new mistress of the samovar. With mounting resentment, Liza felt that, as the eldest daughter of the household, she should occupy this privileged position. Never before had my mother sensed such discord in the home.

Sasha left the Art Academy to join the army. By Christmas he was fighting somewhere in Poland.

Sonechka missed her *mamochka* desperately. Glasha was her sole confidante. Sharing her sorrow, Glasha would put her to bed and hear her prayers. Often, she curled up and fell asleep beside Sonechka. When Lydia found out about this she complained to Lev, who forbade Glasha to sleep in Sonechka's bed.

At the start of the 1915 summer only a few guests came to stay. Lydia, who was, by now, in complete charge, had Lev advertise for guests. One of them, Grigory Ippolitovich, boasted that he had spent time in prison for distributing pamphlets in Petrograd agitating for the overthrow of the Tsar. Tall, moustached and bespectacled, he claimed to be a distant relation of Lydia's. She endearingly called him Grisha, a diminutive of Grigory. Glasha hated him, maintaining that he was a German spy. As the news from the front got worse, Lev vehemently disagreed with Grigory's contention that defeat should be welcomed since it would allow Russia to become a socialist utopia.

Each morning at school Sonechka sang with great gusto the national anthem, 'God Save the Tsar'.

In Alushta, as elsewhere throughout the country, numerous fundraising bazaars and tea dances were held. Lev helped stage theatrical productions in Alushta to raise money for Mother Russia. Liza joined the war effort with her friends by attending first aid lectures at the local *lazaret* (infirmary) where among other tasks they wound bandages and knitted scarves for Russia's fighting sons. In addition, she learned how to use the typewriter. Everyone helped in their own way. Though he still mourned Anastasia, Lev gradually became his old self with a twinkle in his eye.

The defeat suffered at Brest-Litovsk in August 1915 stunned them all. It was one of many disastrous defeats at the hands of the Germans, who proceeded to conquer a large part of Russia's western empire. When Lev read out the accounts of the battles Sonechka and Mishka pinpointed them on a large wall map they had drawn. After the Brest-Litovsk battle the Tsar proclaimed, 'We must fight on till victory crowns our glory.' Soon afterwards he took personal charge of the army. Later, pictures in the newspapers showed the young Tsarevich, the heir to the throne, visiting the front with his father. Several of Mishka's older playmates were called up, further heightening his fervent desire to go to war. Lev vowed that if Mishka ran away he personally would find him and give him such a thrashing he wouldn't be good for anything.

Christmas that year was celebrated quietly with just a few neighbours. Liza and her friend Dasha organised an evening performance re-enacting Krylov's animal fables. Each chose their favourite fable role to recite. The costumes took several days to create. Dressed as a grasshopper, Sonechka recited the fable *Strekoza i Muravei* (*The Dragonfly and the Ant*). Even with Lev and Mishka's help, the designing and making of the wings took many hours. This pleasurable diversion in a world that seemed determined to destroy itself lifted everyone's spirits.

During this time they received a letter from Sasha. He was in a *lazaret*, somewhere on the Ukrainian front, making a good recovery from shrapnel wounds in his shoulder. They thanked God that he had not been killed or seriously wounded. They knew few families were unaffected by the war, with many having tragic stories to tell.

It infuriated Liza to hear Lydia address her papa as Levchik (another affectionate diminutive of Lev), and for him to call her Lydochka. Sonechka assumed that this was one of the reasons why Liza spent most evenings with friends in town. During the day Liza practised at home on the typewriter that Lev had given her for Christmas. Sonechka was amazed how quickly her fingers tapped away on the shiny metal keys. She would not let anyone touch her precious possession.

Once when Sonechka tried to use it, the keys got stuck and her fingers became blackened trying to free them up. Fully expecting Liza to accuse her of damaging her machine, she was greatly relieved when she made no mention of this matter. Liza's first job using her new skill was at the town hall, where she recorded the particulars of soldiers missing at the front.

By now Mishka was in his final year at the *gimnasia*. Though he wanted to be an engineer, he was still determined to join the army and fight the Germans. In mid-June 1916 jubilation greeted the news that General Alexei Brusilov had won a series of spectacular victories against the Austrians. Hundreds of thousands of prisoners were taken. There had been no word from Sasha for several months. Fearful he might have been killed, Liza tried desperately to find out at work what had happened to him. Nothing came of her inquiries.

That summer the same summer guests duly arrived. Grigory Ippolitovich had recently grown a goatee beard. Lev thought it made him a comic rather than a dignified figure, especially when he got worked up trying to convince him that only a radical socialist government could save Russia.

Early one morning Lev asked Liza, Sonechka and Mishka to meet him in the dining room. He came straight to the point, announcing that he and Lydia had made a most important decision. While Liza stood glaring at him he put an affectionate hand on Sonechka's shoulder and gently said, 'In these trying times, my little darling, you need motherly affection and guidance.' Liza let out an anguished cry and shot out of the room. She left so suddenly that Lydia, who must have been listening at the door, stumbled into the room. Bewildered, they all stared at one another. Lev, taking Lydia's hand in his, kissed it and ushered her onto the veranda.

That evening there was a celebratory dinner in honour of the betrothed couple. Wine and vodka flowed. Numerous speeches were given and toasts made. Liza was absent throughout. Later Sonechka learned that, after staying overnight with her friend Dasha, Liza went to live with their mother's sister, Aunt Frosya, and her husband, Fyodor, in Simferopol.

Dreading what Lydia might do, Sonechka hoped, up to the last moment, that the wedding would be cancelled. It was not to be. The marriage duly took place at the same church where her mama's funeral service had been held – a poignant reminder of how much she missed her. In fact, the only notable change in the household was that Grigory became part of the family, rather than a long-staying guest.

Sonechka noticed that her papa returned to being his familiar jovial self during Grigory's frequent absences. All the while she sensed her mama's presence. Oh, how she missed her.

For some time rumours had abounded concerning the evil influence said to be exerted on the royal family by Rasputin, the Siberian peasant mystic.

Though it was believed that only Rasputin could alleviate the Tsarevich's haemophilia, his assassination by several eminent courtiers, led by Prince Yusupov, was greeted with widespread relief. Many believed that his long-standing hold over the Tsarina, the Tsar and the court had left the country leaderless, with catastrophic consequences. This failure applied particularly to the war against Germany, Austro-Hungary and Turkey, in which more than six million Russian soldiers had been killed or wounded. To make matters even worse, by early 1917, there were critical shortages of most necessities in much of the country, with hunger fuelling widespread protests and strikes.

Though quite well informed about events in Russia during this period, most people still found it unbelievable when their revered 'little father', the Tsar of all Russia, was forced to abdicate in early March 1917 by alienated aristocrats, courtiers and generals. This humiliation took place at an obscure rail siding far from Petrograd in a temperature of minus 35 degrees. He named his brother, the Grand Duke Mikhail, to succeed him, but Mikhail refused to accept the role.

On his return to Petrograd, the Tsar and his family were placed under house arrest.

On the battlefronts, officers tried in vain to lead their poorly equipped and dispirited men, most of whom had fought continuously for three years. They were worn out like the rags that bound their feet. Incited by Russian revolutionaries, all they wanted was to go home. Meanwhile, in April the Germans spirited the Bolshevik leader, Lenin, back to Russia by rail in a sealed carriage from Switzerland. The Germans counted on Lenin, who had been living in exile, latterly in Switzerland, to foment a revolution that would take Russia out of the war.

Lev detested Lenin. He saw him as a zealot steeped in the works of Russian anarchists, European revolutionaries and philosophers, and especially the German philosophers Karl Marx and Friedrich Engels. It mystified Lev how so many privileged Russians found it 'fashionable' to support Lenin, since they themselves were his sworn enemy, the bourgeoisie, whom he had vowed to exterminate.

From now on politics dominated the home. Besides attending frequent political meetings in a nearby hall, Lydia and Grigory harangued everyone about the urgent need for a socialist Russia. They maintained that massive numbers of Russian soldiers had discarded their weapons and fled the battlefronts. They were ecstatic when Prince Lvov, the head of the Provisional Government, resigned but disgusted when another democrat, Alexander Kerensky, replaced him as prime minister. When they heard that their hero,

Lenin, had disappeared and his close colleague, Trotsky, had been arrested, they fell silent.

That summer Sonechka loved lying on an old cane divan in the garden, hidden from view by an umbrella of wisteria. Here she day-dreamed to her heart's content. In a household of adults who had little time for an over-imaginative twelve-year-old, reading became her all-consuming passion. Furthermore, it allowed her to escape the turmoil threatening to engulf them. Romantic fantasies filled her mind, fuelled by devouring such classics as Pushkin's great verse novel, *Yevgeny Onegin*. She shed tears of sympathy for the heartbroken Tatyana's unrequited love for the heartless Onegin. The characters in Sir Walter Scott's books came to life for her. She dreamt of living in a castle in the rugged, sparsely populated Highlands.

One day in late August, as Sonechka looked down their long, steep driveway, she saw a familiar figure labouring his way up towards her. It was Sasha. After weeks of walking, and jumping trains, he had finally come home. Lev couldn't believe his eyes. His firstborn had been spared and was back in the family fold. Many changes had taken place since he had left three years ago.

Sasha, who by then was an officer, had fled the front due to the wrath of his soldiers, fired up by Bolshevik propaganda. In normal times he would have been considered a deserter.

In the evenings Lev continued his newspaper readings, often with the whole household listening in stunned silence. It seemed that not a day passed without news of their beloved Russia collapsing in chaos. The stablehand's grandson had recently been killed, as had two of Mishka's friends. They wondered how it would all end. With hindsight, Sonechka had no doubt that these daily readings, with their ominous news, took their toll on her poor papa, who began to complain of severe chest pains. He was advised by the doctor to have peace and quiet. Grigory, who took it upon himself to read out the daily news in place of Lev, infuriated Sasha by proclaiming his radical socialist politics. Consequently, these readings ceased.

At the end of September, Kerensky announced that for their own protection, the Tsar and his family had been taken under guard to somewhere in Siberia. Meanwhile, the Germans were advancing on all fronts.

In early October, after a year's absence, Liza returned home. During her stay Lev regained some of his old vitality. Though happy to be reunited, foreboding continued to dominate their discussions concerning what the future might hold. Liza announced her intention to marry Pavel Konstantinovich, a friend of the family's whom she had got to know while living in Simferopol.

He was a forty-year-old widower with a grown family, who owned Alma, a large orchard estate near the river Alma. Lev, of course, wanted to meet his prospective son-in-law before giving his blessing. Mishka had completed his *gimnasia* education and was about to enter the engineering department of the Commercial School. Determined to make his own way in the world, an intense restlessness had replaced his youthful exuberance.

CHAPTER FOUR

October 25, 1917, was a momentous turning point for Russia. On this day, the newspapers, including the *Krymsky Vestnik* (Crimean Messenger), reported that a relatively small handful of Bolsheviks led by Lenin had overthrown Kerensky's multi-party Provisional Government when they occupied the Winter Palace. Soon after, the Bolsheviks abolished the democratically elected Constitutional Assembly and declared war on all other political parties. This persecution was enforced by Lenin's secret police, the dreaded Cheka[3] (forerunner of the KGB). The Bolshevik slogan 'Peace, Bread, Land and All Power to the Soviets', though a dreadful lie, proved to be powerful propaganda that mesmerised many.

In no time, Lenin instigated peace talks with Germany. Lev and Sasha were appalled that millions of Russians had laid down their lives defending their country against the Germans only for it to be torn apart within by a far greater enemy, the Bolsheviks. A Volunteer Army, created in the Don Cossack region in southern Russia, which evolved into the White Army, proved to be the only effective opposition to the Bolsheviks. This anti-Bolshevik force was made up of men drawn from every section of society and political persuasion. The fiercely proud Cossacks, who had defended Imperial Russia's southern borders since Catherine the Great's reign, constituted the other half of the White Army. These Cossacks realised that the Bolsheviks would abolish their treasured freedoms, including the ownership of the land that they farmed, making them serfs once again in all but name.

Both my mother's brothers joined the Volunteer Army in the Don Cossack region. On the day of their departure the whole household bowed their heads in prayer as Lev blessed each of his sons with the icons of St George and St Nicholas. Sonechka was terrified she might never see Sasha and Mishka again. With tear-filled eyes, she bid them farewell. For Mishka, war was a game. The battle-weary Sasha knew it to be brutal, but necessary to preserve their way of life.

The ranks of the White Army rapidly swelled, rising to a peak of well over 100,000 men, with units fighting in most parts of the country. Lev dolefully mused that Imperial Russia had fallen, 'like an old tree falls, rotted at heart by weather and time'. He had nightmares concerning the fate of his sons.

Her father often spoke of how much he missed Anastasia and conceded that he had wronged Sonechka by remarrying. He thought that Lydia's close relationship with Grigory belied her contention that she was not a revolutionary. It was about that time that Sonechka noticed that Lydia had moved out of Lev's bedroom into a room at the other end of the house near Grigory.

In the evenings, after Lev had checked Sonechka's homework, they discussed articles in the newspapers. It worried Lev that the fanatical and single-minded Bolsheviks controlled both Moscow and Petrograd, the heart of the country. In contrast, the thin lines of communication of the disparate White Army were spread across the length and breadth of the enormous Russian empire – one sixth of the world's landmass – making co-ordination of its individual units virtually impossible. The token support given to the White Army by some dozen nations, including Britain, France, America and Japan, proved disastrous for the anti-Bolshevik cause. It meant that many persons, who would otherwise not have supported the Bolsheviks, fought for them against the White Army in defence of their Motherland.

Rumour ruled supreme. Concerned with what might become of Sonechka should anything happen to him, Lev showed her the deeds to the house, railroad share certificates and papers to do with money and valuables held in the bank. In the library he had hidden a small quantity of gold. He explained that should inflation make money worthless these valuables could be used as barter for food and essentials. It upset her to hear him speak in this way.

On February 10, 1918, Lenin signed the infamous Brest-Litovsk Treaty, which ceded a third of European Russia, including the Crimea, to Germany. Though incensed to be under the heel of the Germans without a fight, Lev conceded that they had restored law and order. To Lev and Sonechka's horror, they heard in August that the Bolsheviks had murdered the Tsar and his family in a cellar in Yekaterinburg. Lev saw this heinous crime as the final nail in Imperial Russia's coffin. He regretted that the Jewish sisters Fanny and Dora Kaplan had merely wounded Lenin in their recent assassination attempt. The diabolical Bolsheviks used this incident to justify their edict of mass terror, which led to the death of millions.

On returning from school one day Sonechka went into her father's room. Not wanting to disturb him she tiptoed towards the bed. Standing by his side, she sensed a deathly silence had replaced her father's gentle snore. Was her darling papa dead? In disbelief she kept caressing his lifeless hand. Finally convinced, she tenderly kissed his brow and knelt to pray for his departed soul.

Some time later Glasha found her there, motionless and drained of all emotion.

Sonechka's only solace was that both her papa and mama would now be reunited in heaven.

Lydia insisted on burying Lev quickly, without the traditional three days of mourning and the reading of prayers for the dead. Religion was a foolish bourgeois fantasy, she insisted. However, unbeknown to her, Glasha and Sonechka took turns that night reading the Psalter. The funeral service took place in such haste that relatives and friends, including Liza, who did not live nearby were unable to attend.

As when her mother died a profound sense of loss overwhelmed Sonechka. She had cried herself to sleep for weeks on end. Now there were no tears, only a feeling of emptiness.

Sonechka knew that her life had changed forever – she was a thirteen-year-old orphan, adrift in a disintegrating world.

After the funeral, to Sonechka's dismay, Lydia told her that she alone would deal with Lev's estate. The next day, when Sonechka returned home from the *gimnasia*, chaos confronted her. The contents of drawers and cupboards littered the floors the furniture was in disarray and the beds were stripped. Shocked, she rushed through to the kitchen hoping to find Glasha, all the while calling out her name. She then ran out into the backyard and called out for old Semyon, the handyman/gardener. From the far end of the yard she heard muffled cries coming from the garden storeroom. She unbolted the door and found Glasha and Semyon tied together back-to-back, tethered to a pillar. With difficulty she freed them both and removed their blindfolds. Semyon's battered face and Glasha's blood-clotted hair appalled her. She could not imagine how anyone could have been so brutal to these two elderly retainers.

It took several hours for Glasha and Semyon to come to their senses. Soon after Sonechka had left for school that morning, Grigory had arrived unexpectedly in a horse-drawn wagon at the back of the house. Wielding a revolver, he confronted Semyon in the backyard and proceeded to pistol-whip him. Hearing the old man scream, Glasha rushed to his aid, whereupon, she was felled by a blow to the head. Grigory and Lydia then dragged them both into the storeroom and trussed them up. They took virtually everything of value, including the property and bank papers that Sonechka had been shown by Lev. Even the jewellery bequeathed to her by her mama disappeared.

Semyon recovered quickly from his ordeal. Glasha, however, was far from her normal spirited self. For long periods, she sat in the icon corner of the kitchen, under the *lampada*, bemoaning their lot and beseeching the Holy Mother of God for help. There was no word from Liza. It became obvious to Sonechka that Lydia had not told Liza of Lev's death. In her distressed state, Glasha was unable to help Sonechka.

Several days later, an amiable looking middle-aged man with a prominent moustache, whom Sonechka did not recognise, arrived at their home. With a warm smile, he grasped her hand and introduced himself as Pavel Konstanti-novich, Liza's betrothed. He explained that he was in Alushta on business and had taken the opportunity to visit them. He was shocked that Lev had died and that Lydia had stripped the house. Concerned for Sonechka and Glasha's safety, he offered to take them to Aunt Frosya's in Simferopol, where Liza was living. For Sonechka, the prospect of a sanctuary in Simferopol helped offset her sadness at leaving her home.

The Mother of God had answered their prayers.

Though she missed the lush Tauride coastal vegetation, the rugged mountain pass with its majestic waterfalls and sheer cliff faces was awe-inspiring. Pavel told her stories about this part of the Crimea.

When they arrived in Simferopol, the capital of the Crimea, they saw many more German soldiers than on the Tauride coast. Pavel reassured them that, in accordance with the terms of the Brest-Litovsk Treaty, the German occupation forces were generally well behaved.

Several damaged buildings caught their eye. Silhouetted by the setting sun, they saw a Russian Orthodox Church. Its windows were smashed. Its door lay battered on the ground. Its broken crosses dangled from the damaged cupolas. Glasha and Sonechka were horrified to see this sacred house of God so defiled. Pavel explained that it had been one of the first buildings attacked by revolutionaries when Lenin seized power. The priests were beaten and dragged out of the church and denounced as 'enemies of the people'. Pavel did not know their fate.

Aunt Frosya's home was on the outskirts of the city, set back from the road in a mature garden with a barn at the back of the property. The longstanding friends, Pavel and Fyodor Nikolayevich, greeted one another heartily.

A grain merchant, Fyodor had married Frosya, Anastasia's sister. They had no children. Fyodor's two daughters from a previous marriage were both married. Whereas Frosya welcomed them, Fyodor was aloof, making it clear from early on, that they were a burden he could well do without. However, he tolerated Liza, no doubt because she was marrying Pavel and she brought home food given as payment for her secretarial job. Sonechka kept out of Fyodor's way as best she could. Thankfully, Glasha got on well with Frosya. They spent many hours together in the kitchen reminiscing about the good old days in Alushta, where Glasha had first come to work for the family as a fourteen-year-old, forty years ago. Unfortunately, it was a different story between Liza and Sonechka. To Liza, Sonechka remained a child. She mocked her at the slightest pretext and had Sonechka forever at her beck and call. To make matters worse they shared a bedroom. Mercifully, Liza spent most evenings with friends in town.

At the local *gimnasia* Sonechka met Rachel, a Jewish girl, who became her best friend. They shared a passion for the theatre, especially, the new craze of moving pictures. They would sit in a darkened hall, their eyes riveted to a rapid sequence of pictures projected onto a large screen portraying a melodramatic story with the piano providing the appropriate musical accompaniment. Girls with their boyfriends sat towards the back. Sonechka and Rachel made a point of sitting near the front, behind Sergei, the good-looking young pianist, whose deft touch enhanced the story's crises and emotional moments. Sighing and crying, they saw *Camille*, based on Alexandre Dumas' novel *The Lady of the Camellias*, several times. Just before the end, not wanting Sergei to see their tear-streaked cheeks and swollen eyes, they would tiptoe out of the hall. They then rushed to Rachel's home to reread the tragic parts in the story, taking turns playing the finale, the heart-breaking, couch-death scene.

Rachel's family lived above her father's jewellery shop. They were Karaite Jews who traced their ancestry way back to the time when the Crimea was part of the mighty Byzantine Empire. Both sides of Sonechka's family came to the Crimea from northern Germany during the eighteenth century. Their families were just two of the many different peoples that made up the exotic Crimean ethnic mix. Rachel's family, who were religious Jews, invited Sonechka for a meal. The welcoming glow of the candles, and the togetherness, brought back poignant memories of her family in Alushta when her mama was alive.

In late October the family received a letter from Sasha, from whom they had not heard since he left home with Mishka to join the Volunteer Army. He was fighting the Bolsheviks somewhere in the depths of Siberia. Sonechka thanked God that Sasha, her guardian, was alive and prayed that he would survive. However, her heart ached for her childhood playmate, Mishka. Sasha wrote that he had lost contact with him. Knowing Mishka as she did, Sonechka kept reassuring herself that, being resourceful, he too would be alive. Sonechka never learned his fate.

With the defeat of Germany in the World War, and the departure of their occupation forces by the end of 1918, the Crimea erupted in violent conflict. Until April 1919 the Crimean civil government, headed by the Karaite Jew Solomon Krym, tried but failed to restore peace and prosperity.

The once-abundant market stalls were empty. Hyperinflation made money worthless. Marauding gangs demanded food, clothing and valuables from the population, killing those who resisted them. These gangs included anti-Bolsheviks, ranging from monarchists to anarchists; Bolshevik supporters, known as Reds; local peasant guerrillas, known as Greens; Ukrainian nationalists and Crimean Tartars. People behaved like animals with no clear-cut battle lines.

During this turmoil, lasting some sixteen months, the part of the Crimea Sonechka was in endured some fourteen different changes of rule. Irrespective of their ideology, gangs targeted Jewish shops and premises. Sonechka was devastated to learn that one such gang had raided Rachel's father's shop. It was rumoured that the survivors had been rounded up and taken to the outskirts of the city and shot. Since Sonechka lost contact with Rachel she assumed that these monsters had murdered her.

Lenin issued a nationwide directive requisitioning food for the starving cities; this was where his bedrock of support, the industrial proletariat, lived. This had dire consequences. The Cheka ripped up floors and tore down walls in their search for hidden stores of food and valuables.

His savings worthless, Fyodor's hope of a secure and peaceful future had evaporated. Now his very survival was threatened. As a grain merchant he knew that it was inevitable his property would continue to be targeted, not just by the Cheka, but also by the marauding gangs. Furthermore, the Cheka had recently forcibly requisitioned the grain, food and valuables (vital for bartering), that he had stored in his barn. He was aware that unless he could hide his few remaining valuables, his household would starve. So he desperately sought a secure hiding place.

Late one evening Fyodor aired these concerns to Sonechka. Taken aback that he should unburden his fears to her of all people, she set about finding a hiding place. She prayed for a place where the Cheka would be unlikely to search. Miraculously, her mind cleared and she saw that the answer lay right before them, in the kitchen. Pointing to the large cast-iron stove she exclaimed, 'I've got it! If we remove the bricks from one side of the stove we can dig a hole large enough to store the valuables and dispose of the soil in the cesspit.'

Though sceptical, and knowing they would be shot if the Cheka discovered their hiding place, Fyodor conceded that it was probably their only chance of survival. Glasha and Frosya agreed. Loathe to soil her hands, Liza did little. With their lives at stake, they toiled furiously throughout the next two nights. Having removed the bricks on one side of the range, they then dug a hole underneath it. The family marvelled how my mother, a mere slip of a girl, had provided them with this unexpected lifeline.

CHAPTER FIVE

The next week, as Sonechka made her way to school, a revolver-wielding militiaman, dressed in a Tolstoy-type peasant blouse under his unbuttoned black leather coat, confronted her. He wore an ill-fitting cap bearing a red star. Screaming in broken, heavily accented Russian, he accused her of carrying a weapon. When he found nothing, she assumed he would let her go. Instead, he thrust the revolver into the small of her back and forced her to walk ahead of him. Terrified, she imagined being raped, tortured and killed by this young savage.

After they had walked a short distance, he shrieked at her to stop in front of an impressive two-storeyed house on the outskirts of the city. He unlocked the front door and ordered her into a spacious marble foyer and along a wide, panelled corridor to the right of the staircase, all the while jabbing the revolver into the small of her back. He then knocked on a door, marked 'Commissar', and shouted in a language she did not understand. A similarly dressed, rugged-looking man opened the door and growled at her to come in. No longer conscious of the pressure of the revolver, she glanced back and saw that the militiaman had gone.

Sonechka stood petrified in the middle of the room, with the commissar glowering at her. Her mind raced, trying to imagine what he wanted from her. Suddenly, he bellowed, 'The White vermin and their filthy supporters have fled. I am the commissar of this area's All-Russian Extraordinary Commission for Combating Counter-Revolution and Sabotage.' His verbose job title confused her. He proceeded to berate her for not knowing the official title of the Cheka, accusing her of being a hated bourgeois. Smirking, he said, 'Don't look so worried, I'm not going to kill you, at least not yet. You're going to work for me. I need a pretty young assistant. Comrade Stalin, the Party's Commissar for Nationalities, insists that we record everything we do. You'll start here tomorrow morning, sharp at 7 o'clock.'

When she tried to explain that she had not done this sort of work before, and that she was still at school, he sniggered and retorted, 'You've had a good education, I bet. That's just what I need, someone who can read and type and do addition.' Then, grabbing her hand, he exclaimed, 'Ah, just as I thought! The smooth skin proves that you've never toiled long and hard on the land or in a factory. People like you deserve to die! Mark my word, you'll learn quickly enough what you have to do.'

Mortified, she raced back home to tell Glasha and Frosya what had happened. Though they consoled her as best they could she could not sleep that night, haunted by nightmares of the commissar trying to kill her. Spurred on by the commissar's dire threat should she fail to measure up to his expectations, Sonechka quickly became a proficient typist. She was helped by Frosya, who had taught herself to type when Fyodor's secretary disappeared during the Civil War. It was a forlorn attempt to keep his business going.

On Sonechka's first morning the commissar dictated several short reports. She then filed a large pile of death certificates into their respective folders. In the afternoon he had her report for work in the courtyard. She was sickened by the sight that confronted her – several vehicles were piled high with dead bodies collected daily from the streets. Many, often whole families, had starved to death. Mixed with these were the bodies of those executed by the Cheka.

The driver ordered Sonechka to get into the vehicle beside him. As she sat down he leered at her and said, 'I can see that my pretty girl fancies a joyride.' The smell of his filthy clothes and foul breath made her want to vomit. He then started the vehicle, and once they were out on the road, he placed his hand on her thigh. Disgusted, she slid across the seat to the far side of the cab. She thought of jumping out of the vehicle, but knew that even if she did manage to get back to Fyodor's, they would hunt her down. Travelling to the outskirts of Simferopol and through the adjacent countryside, she saw cadaverous adults and children clothed in rags, wandering in search of food. Revulsion and pity consumed her.

Eventually, they stopped at the edge of a forest, where two men flung the bodies from the vehicle into a large shallow pit. She was commanded to count the numbers buried. Mechanically, she marked them down. By recording the thump of each new body as it was cast into the pit, she could keep count without having to watch too closely. This sound haunted her for evermore.

Later she learned that the Cheka forced prisoners to dig their own graves before shooting them. It was rumoured that some victims were not buried properly. Those that did not die dragged themselves out of their graves. Survivors joined partisan groups such as the Greens. She could see no end to this spiral of death and destruction. It was a never-ending nightmare.

From the description Sonechka gave Fyodor of her Cheka tormentors, he thought they were poorly educated peasants whom the Bolsheviks had recruited from the ethnic minorities who had suffered under Tsarist rule. Consequently, the Cheka had to rely on literate and numerate women such as Sonechka to collate and record what they did. She now knew that Lenin meant to destroy everything Imperial Russia had stood for.

By chance, Sonechka overheard a conversation at the Cheka headquarters that sent a chill down her spine. She hurried home that evening to warn Fyodor that the Cheka would soon be searching their area.

Late one night the next week, five burly Chekists stormed into their house and, without saying a word, began to search it from top to bottom. Petrified, they watched as the Chekists tore up the floorboards, tore out wall panels and smashed furniture. The Chekists were livid that they had not found any valuables or substantial quantities of food hidden in this bourgeois merchant's property.

To the family's enormous relief, the Chekists did not look under the rug that covered the kitchen floor near the stove. Nor did they notice the two sacks of flour that Frosya had put near the door. The hole beside the stove was not large enough to hide them. Undeterred, Frosya had covered the two sacks with a cloth on which she placed a wooden board with a large container of fresh water and several mugs. Before the Chekists left she offered them a mug of water. One of them accepted. This 'watering hole' remained in place for some time.

The next morning the commissar, scowling, said to Sonechka, 'I understand that my men found nothing at your relatives' home last night.'

Taking a sudden interest in the report she had before her, Sonechka tried to ignore his comment. It was soon apparent that this was a prelude to a deeper line of questioning. Instead of going into his office, he turned and walked back in her direction. She pretended to concentrate on her work, but knew he was standing just in front of her. She carried on reading the report, but was forced to look up when he took hold of her hand. He turned his inquisitor's gaze on her. He showed no sign of emotion. Her heart pounded, she wanted to pull away but knew it to be futile. She felt his steely grip tighten. Then he began bending her ring finger backwards. 'Where have they hidden it?' he sneered. She gasped as pain shot up her arm. Through gritted teeth he grunted and hissed, 'We know that a bourgeois merchant like him must have valuables and food hidden away somewhere!'

As he leaned over her, his putrid breath filled the air. She felt sick. In a quavering voice, she blurted out, 'I don't know. I really don't know. I'm here most of the time.'

The commissar, infuriated by now, bent another of her fingers backwards. As he did so, he snarled, 'Don't take me for a fool, girl!'

Screaming and writhing in pain, she grabbed hold of the desk with her free hand to prevent herself falling to the floor.

'We'll find what you've hidden, if we have to search the house a hundred times!' he bellowed. 'And you know what will happen to you then. It would be far better for you to tell me what I want to know now!'

She kept on repeating, 'I don't know. I really don't know anything.'

'Have it your way then,' the commissar said, releasing her finger. He sneered and his face became hideously contorted.

Instinctively, in a bid to relieve the pain, she clasped her swollen hand to her chest.

'If you're lying I'll shoot you myself,' he muttered, before turning his back on her and storming back into his office.

Secretarial duties in the mornings and recording the burials in the afternoons became her daily work pattern. Night after night, bodies writhing in pits, pitiful cries for help and the mutilated bodies of her brothers, Sasha and Mishka, filled her *koshmary* (nightmares). Frequently, she woke up screaming.

Liza complained of being disturbed during the night so Sonechka moved into Glasha's room at the back of the house. The treasured family icons which Glasha had brought with them and managed to hide from the Chekists were a great solace to Sonechka as was Glasha's soothing presence.

The commissar taunted her like a cat playing with a cornered mouse.

One morning, he leered at her and said, 'I've decided that it would be a good idea for you to be my mistress. I want to get to know the bourgeoisie better. After all, you're by far our best customers.'

Sonechka was stunned.

'You know what I mean you bourgeois bitch,' the commissar screamed, his face flushed red with rage.

'You walk in here every day, you with your fine manners and speech, such a proper young lady, and then every night, out you walk again. There are plenty of your kind who come here and never leave. It's my decision whether you get to leave each night or remain here as an enemy of the people. You can't deny me.'

Terrified, she could not stop thinking of the Cheka interrogator she had heard screaming at a prisoner, 'We're judge, jury and executioner, and everything is ours!'

Though the commissar's rage passed quickly, his lecherous advances sickened her. She vowed to thwart him, but how?

The next day, as Sonechka sat typing, there was a commotion outside her window. An overly plump woman brandishing a revolver was striding towards the entrance. She shouted in a raucous voice, 'Don't tell me what to do, you scumbag! Get out of my way.'

A Chekist burst into the office. He grabbed Sonechka and pushed her through the back door. He whispered in her ear, 'Shut up if you know what's good for you'.

As they crouched in the bushes under the commissar's window, Sonechka could hear the woman berating her husband.

'Where have you hidden her? My spies tell me she's a fresh little piece you've found to amuse yourself with. I know you've been with her the last two nights. I warn you, if I find her I'll shoot her.'

A shot rang out. Petrified, Sonechka realised that this foul-mouthed woman was speaking about her as if she were the commissar's mistress.

That evening Sonechka worked a later shift than usual. At 10 pm she was allowed home for an hour. While walking back to the Cheka headquarters, she stopped for several minutes to admire the star-studded heavens adorned by a beautiful crescent moon. Placing her hand on her gold christening cross under her blouse, she beseeched God and his Blessed Mother to save her from this hell on earth. Suddenly, on nearing her destination, she saw that the headquarters were in uproar. Several people were being dragged out of the building and bundled into two large vehicles whose lights shone directly at her. From inside came shouts and screams as more people were being dragged out. Frozen on the spot, she watched as a young man broke free from the bedlam and raced in her direction. As he came near, she recognised him as one of the Chekists. He opened his mouth, but before he could say anything, a shot rang out and he fell down at her feet, his lifeless eyes transfixing her. Praying she had not been seen, she threw herself behind a bush, out of the glare of the headlights. It was all over in a few more minutes. The vehicles sped off in the opposite direction, and all was silent again.

Uncertain whether any of the raiders had remained in the headquarters, Sonechka waited for what seemed an eternity before getting out from behind the bush. Then, once she had summed up the courage, she crept into the headquarters. Chaos confronted her. Office equipment, furniture, folders and papers were strewn everywhere. In the cellar the guns and ammunition were gone and the prison cell doors stood wide open. In the courtyard she came across three bodies, two more Chekists and a man she did not recognise. Devastated, she slumped down into a chair and cried bitter tears of fear and revulsion. She shuddered to think what might have happened to her, for she knew that whoever these raiders were, had she not stopped to gaze at the night sky, she could have been raped, tortured and killed. In the eerie silence that followed, she whispered a prayer of thanks for her amazing deliverance.

The next day the Cheka headquarters remained abandoned.

Soon afterwards Liza and Pavel were married. Fyodor, Frosya, Glasha and Sonechka attended the brief civil ceremony. Standing in the ornately decorated hall with portraits of Marx and Lenin staring down at them, my mother could not help thinking about how much more beautiful and meaningful it would have been to have this ceremony held in their church in Alushta. A profound feeling of sadness overwhelmed her. Tears welled up in her eyes as she thought about how different all this would have been had her parents been alive. No doubt, Anastasia would have insisted on at least a priest blessing their union.

CHAPTER SIX

Reports of murders and attacks on property increased in Simferopol, as did stories of abductions and disappearances. Because she had worked for the Cheka, the family was concerned for Sonechka's safety, since they felt she must be on their wanted list after what had happened at their headquarters. So they decided to send her to Fyodor's sister, Vera, who lived in Bakhchysarai, a town between Simferopol and Sevastopol, not far from Pavel's property. So, when Pavel next visited them, Fyodor asked him to take Sonechka to his sister's. Though heartbroken to be parted from Glasha, Sonechka realised that, for the time being, there was no alternative. Glasha was like a mother to her, comforting her in times of stress and soothing her tears of sadness. Who would she turn to now?

Fyodor's sister, Vera Nikolayevna, and Alexander Petrovich, her husband, had a secluded dwelling on the outskirts of Bakhchysarai. Vera, a charming and sprightly elderly lady, made light of having to look after Alexander, who suffered from severe rheumatism. Since he was virtually confined to a wheelchair they occupied the ground floor of their dilapidated manor house, which had once been the principal residence of a substantial landowner. It stood like a majestic relic in a large overgrown garden, the estate having been sold off bit by bit over the years by Alexander's uncle, who had bequeathed it to him.

Alexander looked forward, personally, to restoring this dwelling. However, his illness, inflation and the Bolsheviks' decrees quashed this cherished dream.

Vera and Alexander were married in the 1880s in the aftermath of the Crimean and Turkish Wars. They saw the French and the British as being the old enemies, with Russia's defeat in the Crimean War a disaster. Sonechka knew more about her country's successes fighting the Turks than its defeat at the hands of the French and British. Like her family, she was proud of how their soldiers had distinguished themselves against the Turks. Alexander's view, however, was less glorious. He had fought the Turks, and although

Russia was victorious, he maintained that it had been a struggle between two once great imperial powers in decline.

The early years of Vera's marriage had been a time of great change for Russia. However, like much of the intelligentsia, by the early 1900s the couple could look back on that period as an example of a missed opportunity for Russia, especially after the emancipation of the serfs by Tsar Alexander II in 1861. This enlightened measure, which liberated tens of millions from serfdom, was wasted, since few peasants had either sufficient capital or expertise to farm profitably. As they saw it, the peasants had gained their freedom but were no better off.

Until they inherited their ramshackle remnant, Alexander and Vera had not appreciated the extent of the gulf that existed between many estate owners and the peasantry, the overwhelming majority of the population. They deplored how the estate owners had neglected their properties; often the dissolute nobles gambled and womanised in St Petersburg, Moscow and Europe. The extravagance of Alexander's uncle had driven his German estate manager to suicide.

At the time of the March 1917 revolution, the agricultural methods in large parts of Imperial Russia had more in common with the Middle Ages than those in modern Europe. Alexander also regretted that the voice of the enlightened nobility was not heard. Prince Lvov, the former Provisional Government prime minister, had modernised his estate, significantly improving the lot of his tenant farmers. Lvov's voice was drowned out by reactionary nobles who held sway at court and in government circles.

For Sonechka, life in this tranquil setting was a far cry from her Simferopol existence. Her formal education ceased, since the nearest *gimnasia* was too far away to attend. However, she found that Alexander's library and stimulating discussions with Vera and Alexander on a wide range of subjects more than compensated for the lack of formal schooling. She tended the former kitchen garden with Vera, who taught her how to milk the cow and feed the hens. The plentiful nutritious food meant that she rapidly regained her health. However, after her Cheka ordeal she could not bring herself to kill a chicken. Before long, her hands were hardened and unless scrubbed vigorously, discoloured. She chopped wood for the kitchen stove and for the fireplace in the library, where they spent the winter evenings. She mused that the Cheka commissar might even have considered her a proletarian.

Vera explained how, early on in the revolution, their good friends had fled to France and that she had wanted to go with them. In the end, it had been

Alexander's decision to stay. He reasoned that they could always join them later if things got difficult. Now, of course, it was too late.

It surprised Sonechka to learn that Pavel had long been a socialist. Both Alexander and Vera thought he must be hand in glove with the revolutionaries, and perhaps even the Bolsheviks, to remain in charge of his estate and to travel about so readily. Sonechka recalled how Lev, her papa, abhorred how privileged people like Pavel could be so supportive of socialism. Therefore, though fond of Pavel, who treated her kindly, she thought it unlikely that Lev would have approved of him as a son-in-law. On the other hand, she knew that Lev's disapproval would not have mattered, since Liza had a mind of her own.

Pavel kept them informed of what was happening in the country with his regular visits. By April 1920 a semblance of law and order was restored when the White Army gained control of the area where they lived. In the summer evenings Vera sat with Sonechka on the veranda reminiscing while Alexander dozed. Sonechka was reminded of her carefree childhood in Alushta and how her father would sit on the veranda, during the long balmy evenings, entertaining guests and friends with his wonderful stories. For the first time since leaving her home, Sonechka felt at ease. She told Vera, who became her confidante, what the Cheka had forced her to do.

Vera refused to be worried by the Civil War being waged in the Crimea. Besides, considering it pointless to be concerned with things that could not be changed, she maintained that no one would want to raid such a broken-down property as theirs. However, Vera's chickens began to disappear, as did vegetables from the garden. Sonechka lived in constant fear of the home being raided by people desperate for food and valuables for bartering.

Towards the end of December, Sonechka was awoken by a terrible series of crashing bangs at the door. No one brought good news at this time of night. Struggling to come to her senses, Sonechka rushed out of bed and hurried to see who was there. As she neared the door, two burly Chekists burst their way in. Brushing her aside they proceeded to rampage through the home, watched in horror by Vera and Alexander who by then had joined her.

Upstairs, above their heads, the Chekists thumped and crashed about making a tremendous noise. Suddenly, one of them came hurtling down the rickety stairs screaming and waving something in his hand, 'Whose is this?' With eyes bulging he confronted them, brandishing a rusty old pistol in their faces.

In his calm, matter of fact way Alexander tried to explain that it was a Turkish pistol, a souvenir of the war in which he had fought. For several minutes, as if possessed, both Chekists shrieked and hurled abuse at Alexander, accusing him of being bourgeois and a 'White Guard', intent on using the pistol to kill them. When Vera pointed out that it was a useless old relic, one of them spun round and hit her in the face with his revolver. She fell to the floor.

'How dare you!' Alexander shouted. Gathering all his strength, he made a massive effort to get up out of his chair. He pulled himself up to his full height. Without warning, the Chekist who had struck Vera shot Alexander dead.

The Chekists left without saying a word, their pockets bulging and clutching hold of the goods they had taken. It was as if Alexander's death had sated their bloodlust.

In the deathly silence that followed, Sonechka tried to console Vera. It was some time before Vera could fully comprehend what had happened.

'How could they? An old cripple who couldn't hurt anyone even if he wanted to,' she sobbed repeatedly, her voice choking with emotion. Throughout that night Vera sat cradling Alexander's body. The next morning Sonechka persuaded her that they should wash and dress him in his best suit. While carrying out this sombre duty, Vera reminisced about her happy marriage. 'Alexander and I had so many contented years. I only hope you find someone as good as him.'

Meanwhile, my mother prayed that Pavel, who was expected any day, would come.

On New Year's Eve, Pavel arrived with gifts of food. Welcoming him with open arms, Vera poured out her heart. Horrified, he quickly took control of the situation. With great tact, he explained that an Orthodox burial service would be out of the question: the local church had been closed and the priests had fled.

The next day Pavel returned, as promised, bringing a man with him to help bury Alexander. As he was laid to rest, Vera read out several prayers. They then all sang *Vechnaya Pamyat*. Sonechka found it difficult to believe that Pavel, who participated actively throughout this solemn religious ceremony, could be a radical secular socialist.

Concerned for their safety, Pavel tried to persuade Vera to go and stay with her brother, Fyodor, in Simferopol. Sonechka was to come and live with Liza and him. But Vera refused to be parted from her property. It invoked cherished memories of her happy marriage. Remaining there meant she could tend the grave of her beloved Alexander. Neither did Sonechka accept Pavel's proposal. She felt that Vera, who had been so good to her, could not be left to fend for herself. Though Pavel grudgingly agreed with their decision, he promised to keep as close a watch on them as his commitments allowed.

As winter set in they spent most of the day inside, either in the kitchen, library or dining room. Vera liked to reminisce about her long life with Alexander, whom she described as being a loveable and learned gentleman.

Though they lived in constant fear of the Cheka returning to raid their home and attacks from gangs of one sort or another, the winter and spring passed uneventfully.

One spring morning in 1921, Pavel came with a letter that the family had received from Sasha, sent from Shanghai three months earlier. He was working as a chauffeur for a Mr Kerr, an English businessman. Sasha hoped to save enough money for a visa and go to America. He wanted the family, especially Sonechka, to join him.

He explained that Mr Kerr would be glad to help them once they got to Shanghai.

Pavel dismissed out of hand the idea of leaving Russia. He berated Sonechka for even considering it. The family in Simferopol agreed.

However, Sonechka thought otherwise. She knew her destiny lay in America and come what may she would go to Shanghai to get there. She shared this secret with Vera who, at first, thought it a preposterous fantasy. Even so, Sonechka decided to write to Sasha, explaining that though she would love to join him, the rest of the family were much against this proposal. For Sonechka it was the fulfilment of what Sasha had promised their mother before she died – he would always take care of her.

Realising that Sonechka could not be deterred from joining Sasha in Shanghai, Vera suggested that she beseech the Almighty for his help in this matter, for only He could protect her on such a perilous journey. She advised her to make a pilgrimage to the Assumption Monastery, one of the holiest places in the Crimea. It was about two days walk away.

Pilgrims from afar visited this spiritual retreat to pray for loved ones and to beseech God for help in every facet of their daily lives. The monastery contained many holy relics of saints, including a miraculous icon of the Mother of God, believed to be centuries old.

Despite Lenin's well-publicised edict to destroy the Russian Orthodox Church, pilgrims continued to visit the Assumption Monastery, which, as yet, had not been targeted by militant atheist Bolsheviks. Holy men, who came from all over Russia to find their peace with God, had built it in the eighth and ninth centuries. They dug out their dwellings, known as a *kelya* (cell), in the hillside limestone rock, where they spent the rest of their lives fasting and in prayer. Monasticism, having been attacked by Peter the Great and his successors in the eighteenth century, flourished during the next century. During this period, before Lenin seized power, hundreds of monasteries and convents were built throughout Russia. Many people, from every sector of society, went on pilgrimages to these holy places.

Sustained by her faith in God, Sonechka set off on foot early one autumn morning. Dressed simply with a large shawl covering her head and *valenki* (thick felt boots), she walked all day, staying overnight with a friend of Vera's. The next evening, as she climbed a hill, she caught sight of the monastery about 2 kilometres away. As she neared the entry gate towers, she saw many pilgrims walking barefoot and others shuffling forwards on their knees in an act of penance.

On arrival the pilgrims were welcomed and fed simple fare consisting of a filling vegetable soup and *kasha* (buckwheat). They were accommodated in single-sex dormitories. For two days Sonechka attended various services throughout the day; the first began at 5am.

The solemnity of these services, held in this tranquil monastic setting, strengthened Sonechka's resolve to fulfil her God-given destiny.

On her return, Sonechka set about improving her mind in preparation for her 'departure'. She so wanted Sasha to be proud of her. She spent many hours reading books on China and the Orient, which she discovered in Alexander's extensive library. Intent on understanding America, besides rereading Mark Twain's works, her favourites, she read Jack London's *The Call of the Wild*.

Though the grand piano badly needed retuning, it did not stop her spending hours on end practising her scales and limited classical repertoire. Impressed by Sonechka's application, Vera, who was an accomplished pianist, encouraged her in this endeavour. In due course they played duets together that filled the house with the pleasing sound of long forgotten music. Pavel, who particularly enjoyed their piano recitals, commented on how much he enjoyed visiting such a harmonious home. Vera thanked God for having sent her this young companion who, although she could never replace her beloved Alexander, had made her life worthwhile. For Sonechka, her time spent with Vera would hold cherished memories as her destiny unfolded.

CHAPTER SEVEN

Towards the end of June 1921 Pavel visited, bringing various bits of news to Vera and Sonechka. The sad news was that Glasha had died two weeks earlier. Pavel consoled Sonechka by saying that Glasha had not suffered. For Pavel, the joyous news was that Liza was pregnant, with the baby due in December.

Soon it would be the busiest time of the year on the estate and he desperately needed reliable kitchen staff to feed the large number of seasonal workers. In view of his staffing problem, he asked Sonechka if she would be prepared to help him out.

Taken aback at the thought of leaving Vera, Sonechka did not know what to say. Since her father's death, Pavel had been there for her when she needed him. Now he needed her. While she mulled over her response, Vera said she could easily manage on her own. She felt Sonechka should accept the offer, since it would be safer for her living on the estate. Reluctantly, Sonechka agreed with Vera, knowing she had her best interests at heart.

For Sonechka, heart-rending partings seemed to have no end.

On their journey to Alma, his estate, Pavel explained to Sonechka that she would be employed as an ordinary worker and not as one of the family. She would be sharing a room with Katya, a young woman who came from a neighbouring village. For Sonechka's safety he had prepared the necessary papers to change her surname. Pavel maintained that if she retained her real name someone could find out that she was Liza's sister, and despise her for being one of the hated bourgeoisie. Sonechka knew that many people changed their names, sometimes several times.

When she saw Alma, Sonechka understood why Pavel was so proud of his estate. To one side of the road there were row upon row of apple and pear trees and, on the other side, grapevines extending along the hillside. At a bend in the road, she caught sight of a large courtyard enveloped in wisteria and grapevines, with the ground floor of the house covered in greenery. Pavel, who had inherited the estate in 1910, had managed Alma profitably before the revolution. It was named after the river Alma, which ran at the back of the property.

Since Sonechka had last seen Liza they had both changed. Liza had become the wife of a *pomeshchik* (landlord of an estate). Despite Pavel being forced to relinquish the ownership of his property, Liza continued to play the role of the lady of the manor. Bolshevik political activists, known as commissars, resided in their home, with visiting commissars regularly 'inspecting' the estate. They all had to be accommodated. It seemed that life had changed little for Liza since the days when her parents had run the pension in Alushta.

When they first met, Liza hardly recognised her younger sister. The awkward, malnourished child had blossomed into a rosy-cheeked young woman. Liza had come into the kitchen to give instructions to the staff. As the two sisters gazed intently at each other, neither betrayed any sign of recognition. This charade continued for some time.

Katya proved to be a chatty roommate. On their first evening after work they sat on the veranda steps behind the kitchen. Katya spoke with pride about how her family had worked and lived near the estate for generations. Suddenly, with eyes gleaming, her agreeable manner was transformed. This young Bolshevik firebrand proceeded to thunder out a string of Marxist-Leninist revolutionary phrases such as: 'Down with the bourgeoisie', 'The bourgeoisie exploit the workers' and 'Death to them all!' It both astounded and reassured Sonechka that Katya did not consider Pavel a member of the bourgeoisie.

Sonechka's kitchen duties proved to be tiring, with long hours and heavy work, including cleaning vegetables, preparing meals, baking and washing up. They cooked for between forty and fifty people daily. One day she overheard one of the middle-aged cooks, Tanya, grumbling about the amount of work she was expected to do. She said that it had been much better in the 'good old days'. She resented having to work like 'some machine'.

Tanya never turned up for work again. Sonechka soon realised that not only did one have to keep one's thoughts to oneself, but few people, if any, could be trusted. Until now she had been sheltered from such behaviour. How prudent Pavel had been to change her name. Later Sonechka learned that Tanya was punished for criticising the present regime. Her fate was unknown.

Early on Katya asked Sonechka where she came from. Sonechka, without hesitation, said that she lived in Simferopol, the capital of the Crimea. Sonechka felt that her identity as a city dweller would be a safe disguise for now.

With yet another staff shortage in the kitchen, the workload increased considerably but the two girls managed to cope and soon became friends. It was the first time since her friendship with the Jewish girl Rachel that Sonechka enjoyed the company of someone her own age. Katya, who was two years older than Sonechka, liked to gossip. Having grown up near the estate, she had many stories to tell, especially about the youths who worked there. Most of them, like Katya, came from the neighbouring *selo* (village). She was not surprised to hear that Sonechka had fled from the city as she had heard about the fate of homeless children, and how families had starved to death. Also there were robberies and murders. She sympathetically asked if Sonechka was an orphan, to which Sonechka could, at least, answer yes, truthfully.

In the evenings Sonechka and Katya liked to stroll down the paths of ripening fruit trees along the riverbank. Often other girls and youths joined them to sing popular melodies.

On her first Sunday morning at Alma, Sonechka attended a compulsory lecture on Bolshevism, given by a visiting commissar. The estate workers duly gathered in the courtyard, where a number of people, including Liza and Pavel, sat on a podium placed in an elevated position facing the assembly. Standing near the front, Sonechka caught Pavel's eye. He gave her a fleeting half-nod whereas Liza gazed above and beyond her.

When one of the men on the podium stood up and spoke, Sonechka's heart missed a beat. Although it was a warm day, the speaker wore a black leather coat identical to that worn by the Cheka. Could he be the commissar who had terrorised her, or was he just a look-alike? Sonechka hoped and prayed that the two years that had passed since she worked for the Cheka would have changed her appearance. Once the commissar began to speak she realised he was not the ogre who still haunted her.

In a torrent of vitriolic abuse that had Sonechka imagining he was addressing her alone, this commissar attacked the murdered Tsar, the aristocracy, gentry, bourgeoisie and religion. He proclaimed with zeal how 'they', the Bolsheviks, would create the ideal Soviet socialist citizen together with radical social and economic policies. Glancing at both Pavel and her sister, Sonechka thought they appeared entranced. Could it be that Pavel was a communist sympathiser together with her sister?

Sonechka recalled how Alexander had condemned Pavel for being a socialist radical and that he would do anything to save his precious estate. Though her mind wandered, sickened by the commissar's fanatical tirade, she could recall most of what he said. Parents should discount their offspring and consider them as being accidents of birth and the responsibility of the State. Families were to be abolished and replaced by communal living with everything shared – not just kitchens, bathrooms and possessions but one's husband, wife and children. Freudian psychoanalysis would replace formal teaching and pupils, not teachers, would be dominant in the classroom. He produced facts and figures about industrial conditions and production in Germany, France and Britain, which were meaningless to Sonechka. He carried on in this vein for an hour or so.

Marxism-Leninism was heralded as the equivalent of the vigorous regenerative growth that follows the devastation of a forest by fire, a new beginning cleansed of the detested bourgeoisie. The commissar left no doubt in Sonechka's mind that these zealots would not rest until everything Imperial Russia stood for, including God himself, was destroyed. His parting words were that the tenets of the Marxist-Leninist gospel should be learnt by heart by every man, woman and child. At the end he turned to Pavel, whispered something in his ear, shook his hand and departed.

At the end of the harvest season most workers, including Katya, were sent elsewhere. Sonechka had enjoyed her boisterous manner and her snippets of gossip. On the other hand she appreciated having their room to herself. With fewer mouths to feed, the head cook and her helper, Svetlana, also left. Sonechka and another young woman, Lyuba, who had little to say, shared the kitchen duties.

As the autumn days shortened, Sonechka's treasured evenings on the verandas ceased. How she had enjoyed those nights with the scent of roses wafting from the garden accompanied by the sound of countless cicadas. Now that the flora had lost its magical allure and the paths became muddy, she was reluctant to venture beyond the rain-soaked courtyard.

As Liza's pregnancy progressed, she spent most evenings knitting for the forthcoming arrival, in the presence of the resident commissars. On several occasions Pavel spent long periods away from the estate. Sonechka later learned that these trips took him to Moscow. Having proved her usefulness as a kitchen hand, she was made not only head cook but put in charge of the upkeep of the household. When it became known that she was Liza's sister, this did not seem to worry the resident commissars. In Pavel's absence, Liza encouraged one of them, Shura Ryzhkov, to flirt with her. This sickened Sonechka.

As time passed, Sonechka began to appreciate Pavel's precarious position. Though the Bolsheviks had forced him to relinquish the ownership of his orchard estate the workers insisted that he remain in charge of them. In their estimation, he was a good employer who had done a great deal for them since long before the revolution. Reluctantly, the resident commissars tolerated Pavel's managerial role, provided he followed their directives.

In October, articles appeared in the local Bolshevik press slandering Pavel for remaining on his estate. He was 'enjoying his bourgeois lifestyle at the expense of the people.' A few days later the same paper published a scurrilous satire about Liza's soon to be born baby. 'Weren't they (the Bolsheviks) trying to rid the country of the bourgeoisie instead of letting them reproduce? Why hadn't the commissars done their duty properly?'

That same month there was a brief letter from Sasha, addressed to Sonechka. Having just received his visa he was able to leave for America at the end of October. His employer, Mr Kerr, had helped pay for his ticket. Sasha was thrilled that Sonechka was so keen to join him in America. He would write again when he got there.

Sonechka had mixed feelings. She didn't know whether she should be happy or sad. On the one hand, Sasha had his wish and was going to America. On the other hand, she was still in Russia. When and how could she leave? Who would pay for her passage? While Sasha had been in Shanghai there was hope that she would join him there and then the two of them would travel to America. Now the family would never let her go. *Bozhe moi* (dear God), was she destined never to go to America?

Listlessness overtook Sonechka. As the winter set in her heart grew heavy like the dreary days beyond her window. Most of all, she missed having someone to confide in. She and Liza had never been close. Now she was at her beck and call. Most of all, Sonechka missed Vera's company. It was during this lonely period that she decided to record her thoughts in a notebook. It became her sole friend. It would never abandon her and she could confide in it.

She wondered why the people she loved most were torn from her. Her mama had died, followed three years later by her papa. She had found a trusted friend in Vera with whom she had shared moments of joy and great sadness. Now all her cherished hopes of ever leaving Russia and joining Sasha seemed to have evaporated.

CHAPTER EIGHT

Sonechka felt ashamed to be wallowing in self-pity. Hadn't Pavel come and saved her and Glasha when everything seemed so bleak? Here she was being cared for and well-fed when millions of Russians were starving and untold numbers had perished. She knew from her job with the Cheka in Simferopol that thousands had died from starvation. Bands of orphaned children scouring for food and valuables roamed the streets. Thousands like her friend, Rachel, and her family had been killed.

There had been rumours of a massive famine in the Volga region. What had gone wrong with 'the ideal world' that the Bolsheviks claimed to be creating? These and many other questions were on everyone's lips. Would private trading again be allowed? Why had millions died for a cause that seemed doomed?

Desperate to save his regime, Lenin announced a new policy, the New Economic Policy, or NEP. He proclaimed that it would stimulate commerce to get the country back on its feet, despite Bolshevik zealots claiming that NEP stood for 'The New Exploitation of the Proletariat'.

Did this mean that Pavel would regain the ownership of his estate?

Pavel had brought some books from Moscow, mainly Marxist-Leninist propaganda. Sonechka thought she should read these works to better understand what drove these Bolshevik believers.

One night at dinner the commissars, Stepanov and Ryzhkov, vehemently condemned the White Army and their supporters, describing them as vermin who had betrayed Russia. According to them these deserters should have stayed to help create 'a socialist utopia'. They sneered that the 'White traitors' would soon be returning from the West, pleading to be allowed to live in the paradise they were making.

With the approach of Christmas, a festive feeling filled the air. Sonechka, who had driven into town with Pavel, was amazed to see so much merrymaking. People rushed about and many of the previously boarded up shops did a brisk trade. There were stalls everywhere. With NEP in full swing, everyone was determined to cash in, fearful that private trading could be prohibited at any moment.

Pavel gave Sonechka a few coins to do some gift shopping. Having money to buy gifts was a novelty for her. Her eyes darted from one stall to the other with one particular stall holding her attention. It displayed an eclectic selection of goods – colourful shawls, shoes, candied fruit, cups and saucers along with a bizarre assortment of paintings. As she made a purchase an accordion struck up a well-known tune. Suddenly the young gypsy girl serving her began to dance. Others joined in and before long everyone seemed to be singing and dancing. There was more merrymaking in several of the *traktir* (bars.) She was shocked to see women with heavily painted faces lurching out of these bars arm in arm with drunken men. One lecherous lad beckoned her to join them. As she tried to evade him he clutched hold of her saying, 'Come with me, my pretty one. I'll show you a good time.'

To her enormous relief Pavel appeared as if from nowhere. The youth slunk off. Although she had enjoyed her outing she was happy to return home. This incident caused her to reflect on what might happen to her travelling alone all the way to America.

Since their church was one of the few in the area that had not been closed, Sonechka and Liza were able to attend the Christmas Day liturgy. They disguised themselves by wearing peasant clothing and thick woollen shawls. The many worshippers were overwhelmingly old women. Outside the church a group of militant Bolshevik demonstrators hurled abuse at the churchgoers, ensuring that only devout and mainly elderly worshippers dared to attend the service.

Pavel had been a generous *pomeshchik* long before the revolution and saw no reason to discontinue the Russian tradition of 'open house' on Christmas Day. He had managed to get a good selection of food and decorations that day in town, enabling the dining table to take on a festive look. The previous two days Sonechka and Lyuba had been busy preparing food. They baked many large *pirogi* (savoury and sweet pies), with fillings of cabbage, mushrooms, potato and soft fruits. Many guests came, including Pavel's relations, workers and retired workers. Children ran about everywhere. By nightfall Sonechka was exhausted. Liza, ensconced in an armchair, supervised the goings-on.

Given a gift of a pen and a bottle of ink by Pavel and Liza, Sonechka sat huddled on her bed that night writing in her notebook. Until then she had used an old pencil. This gift was precious to her. She would use it only sparingly since she wanted the ink to last her until she left for America.

Two days later Liza, after a prolonged, agonising labour, gave birth to a little girl. At the last minute, Pavel decided to get his doctor friend to attend the delivery. It was just as well since the local midwife felt she could not have coped on her own with such a difficult birth. The next morning when Sonechka held the tiny bundle of joy, she was amazed how the baby's fingers instinctively grabbed hold of hers. Here in her arms lay a precious new life. She vowed that come what may she was going to love and help care for it.

That winter Sonechka was content to stay indoors, enjoying her new responsibilities. Unable to decide on the name for the baby, Pavel suggested they call her Sofia, after his deceased mother.

While together in the kitchen one spring morning, Liza astonished Sonechka when she announced that she wanted her to be Sofia's godmother. She also wanted Sonechka to get a priest to perform Sofia's baptism at their house on the day that Pavel and the commissar Stepanov would be in Simferopol. Sonechka hugged Liza, whispering that mama and papa would have been thrilled.

On the day that Pavel and Stepanov were away, Liza came into the kitchen with Shura Ryzhkov and an elderly retired priest. Sonechka, who was heating some water to be used for the baptism, looked up in astonishment. Not only did this commissar participate in the ceremony, but he was also Sofia's godfather. Throughout the service, Sonechka wondered why this commissar standing beside her, holding the baby, was renouncing the devil and proclaiming his allegiance to God. Later, when she questioned Liza about Shura's godfather role, she was told to mind her own business.

That Easter Sonechka surreptitiously slipped out of the house to attend the midnight *Paskha* liturgy service in their village. To her amazement, Shura was there. Was he a genuine believer or simply fulfilling his role as a commissar and keeping an eye on who was there and what they did? In the early days of their rule the Bolsheviks allowed some churches to remain open. However, few places of worship escaped being stripped of their gold and silver to fund Lenin's frenetic industrialisation policy. Grateful worshippers had been donating treasures to the churches for hundreds of years.

During the service Sonechka regained her inner strength. A calm feeling overtook her as she prayed, gazing with reverence at the familiar faces of the icons. She beseeched the Mother of God to help her, somehow, to join Sasha in America. They had not heard from him for several months. Had he reached America safely?

The next day being Easter, Pavel and Liza opened their doors to their family, friends and the villagers. My mother and Lyuba, along with a new cook, had been busy for days preparing the traditional *Paskha* fare.

Some of the youths who Sonechka had met during her evening walks that summer with Katya came to pay their respects with the traditional Easter greeting of *Khristos Voskrese* together with the customary three kisses on the cheeks. By now, most knew she was their *pomeshchik's* sister-in-law. They jokingly addressed her formally as Sofia Lvovna. Volodya, a lad her age, remained at her side throughout the evening. He complimented her on everything from the delicious *kulichi* that she helped bake to her bewitchingly blue eyes. By the end of the evening he had professed his undying love for her. These effusive compliments were a novel experience for Sonechka.

That night Sonechka gazed intently into the cracked mirror hanging behind her door. Was she really that pretty? Did her eyes sparkle like a million stars? Feelings stirred inside her that she had never felt before. On parting, when Volodya held her hand to his lips, he murmured, 'I'll dream of you for evermore.'

CHAPTER NINE

With the advent of summer in 1922, Sonechka's kitchen duties increased considerably. She and Lyuba did their best to cope with the long hours and demanding schedule. In July, to their great relief, the cook who had helped at Easter returned, with an assistant.

Besides her kitchen and household duties, Sonechka occasionally looked after Sofia. The placid infant presented few problems.

Liza found motherhood an onerous challenge that she could well do without. At night she ignored Sofia's cries and Pavel attended to his daughter's demands.

In the evenings that summer, Sonechka enjoyed promenading with villagers along the banks of the Alma. Arm in arm, they sang their favourite ballads. They liked playing hide-and-seek among the fruit trees and vines. One could hide and never be found among the dense vines. Sonechka enjoyed sitting with friends in the moonlight, on the veranda at the back of the house, drinking *kvas* (homemade ale) and singing songs to the accompaniment of balalaikas and guitars. Some recited well known poems and others their own verses.

Sonechka's admirer, Volodya, proved to be the most prolific poetry writer. She received many verses from him that summer. These always flattered her. She enjoyed his company but knew in her heart that he would be just a friend and nothing more. In the evenings Liza and Pavel entertained their neighbours and friends.

Alone at night Sonechka would sit by her window gazing at the stars, pondering her future. Why was it that she alone, out of all the people she knew, wished to leave Russia?

Volodya had said to her, 'Sonechka, you are a strange girl. You say that you love Russia, yet you long to leave it and live in a far away country that you have romanticised reading those Mark Twain stories.'

Yes, perhaps he was right, for she really did love her Motherland. Then why was she dreaming of abandoning it? Had not life improved in the last year? The terrible famine that had gripped the country was over. However, she found it disturbing when Pavel told her about the role the American aid workers played during the height of famine in 1921. Lenin had gone to great lengths to discredit them, despite the way they had given enormous quantities of food and medicine to Russia, saving the lives of millions. He ensured that Comintern[4] (Communist International) propaganda had the world believe the Soviet Union alone had given famine relief and the Americans were called spies and *agents provocateurs* who masqueraded as aid workers.

Pavel also heard that many of the tens of thousands of Russians who had helped the American aid workers were imprisoned by Lenin. The last thing Lenin wanted the world to know was that capitalist America had saved the lives of so many Soviet citizens.

Later that summer a long letter from Sasha arrived. Liza read it aloud after the evening meal. He wrote how his ship to America, which he boarded in Shanghai, had stopped in Japan. On board he had met other White Russians seeking refuge in America, the 'promised land'. They had fled from all over Russia to China, during the Civil War.

Sasha's first impressions of America were mixed. On the whole he found Americans to be a friendly people. However, few knew anything about the world beyond their borders. The Russian Revolution meant nothing to them. He was grateful though that the American government was assisting young immigrants, like himself, to gain technical and university qualifications. He had applied for a scholarship to study geology. In the interim he was working as a house painter. When he had saved enough money for Sonechka's boat fare to America he would send it to her. He stressed that as soon as she got it she should go to Shanghai.

At this point Liza glared at Sonechka, who wished she could disappear beneath the floorboards. Sonechka confessed to having written Sasha several letters. Liza admonished her for being deceitful and ungrateful, saying, 'Hasn't Pavel given you a home and treated you kindly?'

Pavel interjected, saying that her wanderlust was just a young girl's whim. Shura countered that travel broadened the mind and how much he had enjoyed travelling throughout Europe with his family.

Stepanov, the other commissar, retorted that he was duty-bound to report Shura for speaking enthusiastically about his privileged family before the revolution.

Pavel broke the stunned silence by speaking in defence of Sonechka's 'fantasy of going to America'.

Alone in her room that night Sonechka tried to console herself by writing in her notebook. So much had happened that evening. Her destiny hung in the balance. Perhaps it was God's will for her to remain in Russia. Tears blurred her vision, as she wrote. She felt so alone and helpless, if only there was someone she could trust.

The next morning Liza ignored her. Sonechka's mood did not improve when she heard that Pavel had left for Moscow on urgent business.

Sonechka was in a quandary. Every night she prayed that by some miracle she would still be able to go to America. If she failed to reply to Sasha's letter, he could conclude that she had changed her mind. Only Shura seemed to be her ally. And what would happen to him after Stepanov's caustic comment?

It was during this time that Shura suggested they form a theatrical group with some of the summer workers and stage a play. All the participants in this project thought it a wonderful idea. Nevertheless, Sonechka sensed that the decision to stage a play celebrating Bolshevism did not meet with universal approval. Not that anyone voiced their objections.

Shura directed the play. Liza was one of the producers. Sonechka had the role of a young revolutionary woman who worked in a munitions factory in Petrograd during World War I and the revolution. As a Soviet group leader, she proclaimed the Bolshevik gospel.

Although Sonechka would have much preferred a role in a Chekhov play, she was surprised how quickly she learned her lines. Her fellow actors and several others, including Liza, showered her with praise, describing her as a born actress.

The night before the first performance Pavel returned from Moscow together with Nikolai Zhukov, the new commissar who replaced Stepanov. Pavel had done well in Moscow with the sale of his produce, permitted under the NEP. He brought back several presents for Liza: a silk dress, a coat to match and a pair of high-heeled shoes. Sonechka had not seen such luxury since before the revolution. This finery reminded her of what their parents' guests had worn in Alushta. It heartened Sonechka that this largesse lifted Liza's spirits.

CHAPTER TEN

Nikolai, the handsome new commissar with his clean-shaven face, made a striking figure in his well cut uniform. He was much younger than Stepanov, his predecessor. In 1915, aged eighteen, Nikolai had enlisted in the army to fight the Germans and Austrians. Early on in the Civil War, like tens of thousands of other soldiers, including many officers, he defected from the ranks of the former imperial army to join Trotsky's newly created Red Army. After the defeat of the White Army in European Russia in 1920, he joined the Cheka. Recently made a commissar, he was sent to Bakhchysarai, his first posting outside Moscow.

From the moment that the curtain went up and Sonechka stepped onto the stage she felt at ease. Though she disagreed with her character's Bolshevik beliefs, the actress in her blotted out the propaganda she endorsed so enthusiastically. Her young Bolshevik zealot role had her proclaim the ideals of the failed French Revolution, 'liberty, fraternity and equality' that were supposedly about to be fulfilled by the glorious Russian Revolution. No sacrifice, including death, was too great to achieve this goal, with the path being blazed by the Bolsheviks the envy of the world. Towards the end of the play, before her tragic heroic death, as she proclaimed her undying love for her Motherland, the audience, in a wild frenzy, rose from their seats to applaud her.

At the end of the play, as Sonechka stood on the makeshift stage accepting her accolades, she knew in her heart that she wanted to be an actress. The play proved such a success that Nikolai, the new commissar, asked the new-found Alma Workers' Solidarity Theatre Group to repeat the performance in Bakhchysarai's town hall.

Subsequently, their theatre group performed several plays in town, with Sonechka acknowledged as a talented young actress. Though delighted to be acting, it disturbed her how much of what she mouthed was outrageous. Sonechka deplored how the Bolsheviks played on the age-old Russian belief that true salvation could be attained only through suffering and self-sacrifice.

Liza and Pavel hoped that this new interest would put paid to Sonechka's American dream.

With NEP in full swing, Pavel was pleased to have Liza help in the estate office. After years of turmoil, goods were abundant in the market stalls. Pavel was permitted not only to sell some of his produce, but was also allowed to keep the money he made.

As a treat that October, Liza accompanied Pavel to Moscow, leaving Sonechka to care for Sofia. They attended the opera, ballet and saw several plays. Moscow's nouveau riche surprised Liza, especially at the opera. Many women were dressed in the latest Parisian fashions. They wore opulent jewellery and had their hair cropped in the latest style, which Liza adopted. Pavel and Liza stayed at a Party boarding house near the Kremlin. It was the former sumptuous residence of a wealthy Moscow merchant. For Liza, each day proved to be an exciting new adventure.

Pavel brought back a Singer sewing machine from Moscow for Sonechka's birthday, which delighted her.

In late November they received another letter from Sasha. He had started his university geology course and had a budding romance with a young American woman. He continued to work part-time as a house painter. Soon he would be sending Sonechka one hundred dollars for her fare to America. Yet again, the family dismissed her hopes of joining Sasha as a childish fantasy. It shocked Nikolai that Sonechka wanted to leave Russia. Infuriated, he accused her of being no different from the 'White traitors' who had fled during the revolution and Civil War.

Later that evening Pavel took Sonechka aside and said, 'My child, for all our sakes, I beg you not to mention your brother or your American fantasy.'

That winter, although not a resident at Pavel's estate, Nikolai joined them for dinner most evenings. Afterwards they usually played cards or lotto. Pavel would play on his guitar while the others sang or hummed along. One evening, on hearing Sonechka singing a popular romantic ballad called 'Chrysanthemums' Nikolai joined in with his melodic baritone voice complementing her soprano. They made a charming couple. From there on, life followed this agreeable pattern.

At night alone in her room Sonechka poured her heart out into her notebook. After Pavel's warning about her American dream she thought it prudent to find a hiding place for her 'precious friend'. Noticing a few loose floorboards under her bed, she decided that this would be a good hiding place.

She found a small empty trunk, which she filled with some old clothes and placed on top of the loose floorboards. Memories of her tormented time in Simferopol at the hands of the Cheka flooded back.

Intuition made Sonechka wary of the increasing attention Nikolai paid her. His gaze pursued her everywhere, making her flustered and confused. His crafty courtship was flattering, yet unsettling, for the inexperienced Sonechka. Despite her reservations, in her innocence she succumbed to his charm. With feelings previously unknown to her she began to bloom like a budding rose.

As their friendship progressed, Nikolai recommended literature for her to read. With his guidance, and to please him, she began to read in earnest. Most of these books dealt with Lenin's utopian dream: the Bolshevik Russia that he and his zealous followers were creating. This propaganda included figures and statistics and targets to be met, by all for the good of all. On reading these figures Sonechka was reminded of the lecture when she first arrived on the estate.

During this period Liza's watchful eye missed little. One morning she confronted Sonechka for shamelessly flirting with Nikolai. Having made her feel guilty, Liza then added that perhaps the relationship could be advantageous to them all. 'After all,' Liza said, 'who could resist Nikolai's charming manner and his good looks. Besides, who knew what the future held for such an ambitious man?'

In the weeks that followed Sonechka pondered her future. She was falling in love with Nikolai. But what were his feelings? Having read many romantic novels she tried to compare her feelings with those of her favourite heroines. Often the heroes were bold and powerful men with strong convictions. In her daydreams she pictured Nikolai as one of these heroes, rescuing heroines in distress. She knew that loving him would mean remaining in Russia. What should she do?

One evening Nikolai casually mentioned that he had read her Cheka file. A cold sweat ran through Sonechka's body as he calmly proceeded to interrogate her about the raid on the Cheka headquarters on that fateful night. Clasping her sweating hands on her lap she tried to compose herself. Gazing innocently into his eyes, Sonechka answered all his questions. Satisfied with what she had to say, Nikolai terminated the interrogation by telling her that two of the guards at the Cheka headquarters had been under suspicion for some time. One had been killed the night of the raid. The other was captured and executed.

Putting his arm affectionately around her shoulder, he complimented her for having worked for the party at such a young age. For my mother, what had begun as a pleasant evening became an ordeal. That night she slept little, trying to make sense of her feelings for Nikolai. How could she possibly love a dedicated commissar of the dreaded Cheka?

That Christmas Liza strongly advised Sonechka not to attend any of the church services. She had heard that the Cheka had issued a decree targeting the churches in their area, with anti-Christian propaganda marches planned during the Christmas vigil and liturgy. Liza also heard that the *Komsomol*, the Bolshevik youth organisation, had been ordered to picket the church. They were to record the names of people attending the services. Sonechka's heart sank on hearing this news. How could her Nikolai be a militant atheist determined to destroy the very essence of the Russian soul, its Christian faith?

That year the Christmas celebrations at Pavel's home were replaced by a secular New Year's Day celebration.

Though her heart ached for Nikolai, his fervent Bolshevik beliefs filled her with apprehension. Yet his very presence aroused her innermost feelings. When alone together he would hold her hand, but make no other advance. How she longed for him to take her in his arms and kiss her. If he had any feelings for her why did he keep his emotions so under control? Was she just an amusement for him?

She thought of confiding her feelings to Liza but felt embarrassed to do so. Liza had already decided that Nikolai was a suitable suitor. In her emotional turmoil Sonechka had no one to turn to.

Her bewilderment, together with her family opposing her leaving Russia, began to take its toll. She became despondent. Her rosy cheeks took on a lacklustre appearance. Liza, noting that Sonechka's appetite had decreased, accused her of trying to diet. They had a bitter argument, with Liza maintaining that should she lose any more weight no decent man would look at her.

Sonechka felt ashamed that she had forsaken the once familiar prayers her mother had taught her, replacing them with romantic daydreams. She decided, once again, to place her trust in God, knowing that He would guide her towards the right path.

CHAPTER ELEVEN

Arriving unexpectedly during dinner one evening in May, Nikolai asked Sonechka if he could speak to her in private. From his intense expression she sensed her future was at stake. All eyes were fixed on them as they went into the adjoining room, with Liza's gaze increasing her apprehension.

Having closed the door, Nikolai took Sonechka's hands in his. He explained that he had been recalled to Moscow, and would have to leave the next morning. He proudly proclaimed that it was a promotion. He had no doubt that his future in the Party was assured, making Sonechka feel she was privileged to be in love with him.

All her doubts about him disappeared as he embraced her. Overwhelmed, her body trembled uncontrollably as she passionately responded to his advances. Her whole being wished this moment would never end. She was prepared to do whatever he wanted, even go to the end of the world if need be.

The sound of the door opening behind them startled the lovers. Liza stood in the doorway silhouetted by the bright light behind her. Returning to the dining room, Nikolai announced his imminent departure for Moscow. Clinging to his arm, Sonechka accompanied Nikolai to his chauffeur-driven car in the courtyard. As they embraced for the last time, he whispered that he would do everything in his power to get her to Moscow as soon as possible.

That night Sonechka sat on the veranda outside her room alone, with only the stars to share her newfound joy. Hugging her knees to her chest she recalled all that had happened that evening. With eyes closed she savoured Nikolai's passionate kisses. Never before had she felt such ecstasy. Unlike Pushkin's tragic Tatyana and her thwarted love for Onegin, Sonechka was convinced Nikolai loved her.

Within a short while, everyone noted the difference in Sonechka's demeanour. Her gaunt appearance had gone, to be replaced by a blissful radiance. The next week, Leonid Ivanov, the new commissar, arrived. Their lives were never to be the same again.

Leonid had long been a fervent Bolshevik believer. Pavel got to know him when they were both students in St Petersburg. The city was a hotbed of revolution at the turn of the century. Together they had marched with hundreds of others to present a petition to the Tsar on that fateful afternoon in January 1905 that became known as 'Bloody Sunday'. They both escaped unscathed from the gunfire and the flashing Cossack sabres. However, they were arrested soon after and imprisoned in the Peter and Paul Fortress for several days.

Whereas Pavel had believed in a constitutional monarchy, Leonid was a radical socialist. Leonid's political allegiance was repaid. After the Bolsheviks seized power, he was invited to join the Cheka.

On completion of his studies in St Petersburg, Pavel returned to the Crimea, where his family had been landowners for many generations. Pavel, like several of his brothers, had his own substantial orchard and vineyard estate. When the Bolsheviks took charge of the Crimea in November 1920, they considered Pavel a supporter of their regime by virtue of his imprisonment in the Peter and Paul Fortress.

Leonid and Pavel greeted one another warmly and proceeded to recall their youthful student years together. During dinner they drank many toasts as they relived that eventful period.

Sonechka and Liza might just as well not have been present. At the end of the meal they left the men in the smoked-filled atmosphere.

The next morning Liza joined Sonechka and Sofia for a walk by the river. Sonechka was shocked to learn that before Nikolai had left for Moscow he had ordered the closure of their church. The priest and deacon were arrested and taken to God knows where. Pavel understood that all the churches in their area had suffered a similar fate. Some were extensively damaged.

Knowing that this news would be a shock to Sonechka, Liza comforted her by putting her arm around her shoulders. Sonechka welcomed Liza's affectionate embrace. Tears filled her eyes. Between sobs she kept murmuring, 'How could Nikolai do such a terrible thing?' As the heart-rending revelation sank in she asked Liza how could she possibly love, let alone marry, a man who forbade her attending church. She was devastated. She beseeched God to show Nikolai the error of his ways.

Liza tried to console Sonechka. Though she could hear Liza's voice it made no sense in her trance-like state. She kept on asking herself, 'How could she love someone who so defiled God?'

Later on the two sisters stood arm in arm on the riverbank deep in thought.

They recalled poignant memories of their home and how Christian beliefs governed their parents' lives.

Unlike Nikolai, Leonid, the new commissar, visited them rarely. However, Pavel often met him in Bakhchysarai, usually staying for dinner and returning home late. Sometimes he was drunk.

Last summer's carefree evenings of song and harmless games became a distant memory. In June, when Shura Ryzhkov was transferred to Kiev, Sonechka noticed a difference in Liza. Her sister's wistful sighs whenever Shura's name was mentioned made Sonechka question whether their relationship was more than a friendship.

With Pavel's frequent absences, Sonechka and Liza spent the evenings reading *War and Peace* and other classics aloud to each other. They reflected on the characters' lives and aspirations, drawing comparisons with their own. Sonechka encouraged her sister to reminisce about their family life in Alushta. They liked recalling the winter evenings by the fire when their father read to the family. They visualised their mother sitting at the dining table, mending or sewing. They admired how her faith in God sustained her during her dying days. Anastasia had accepted her fate and did not forsake God. Sonechka and Liza pondered on the meaning of life. Liza's provocative musings, such as her belief that everything in life was predestined, surprised Sonechka. She thanked God for her new-found friendship with her sister.

As the summer progressed Pavel became aware of increasing unrest among his workers. Igor, yet another commissar, was appointed to oversee him. It did not take Pavel long to realise that Igor was an agitator who spent a great deal of time inciting the workers. Concerned by this, before Pavel left for Moscow, he warned Liza and Sonechka to be on their guard.

Sonechka and Liza heard that the previous Sunday morning Igor had held a large meeting outside their abandoned church. Liza's hands shook as she read out the report of this meeting in their local paper: *Tovarishi!* (Comrades!) We are all workers. Here you are, working for your old *burzhui pomeshchik* (bourgeois landlord). Wake up and look at yourselves! What were you fighting for in our glorious revolution? Where are the ideals that Lenin preaches? Take up the red flag and let it fly high. Why are you letting this *pomeshchik* sit on his property and rake in all the profits?'

Her worst fears realised, Liza ceased reading.

CHAPTER TWELVE

On his return from Moscow, Pavel read the newspaper article that had so upset Liza and Sonechka. Since he had long suspected that their days were numbered, it did not surprise him. He then mentioned that he had two letters, one from Sasha and the other from Nikolai. My mother was lost in thought as she fondled Nikolai's letter. Her reverie was broken by Liza, demanding that she read Sasha's letter first.

Sasha assumed that Sonechka had received the hundred dollars, sent some time ago, to Uncle Fyodor. He urged them all to join him in America since the government was proposing legislation to severely restrict immigration from Eastern Europe and the Soviet Union. Though they would find it very different from Russia, he felt the American way of life would appeal to them. For Sasha, America was truly a land of opportunity and freedom.

Stunned, they tried to digest what Sasha had written. Sonechka could not understand why Fyodor had said nothing to Pavel about this money. However, Pavel had no doubt what had happened. He maintained that since the Bolsheviks controlled the country's banks, someone must have either pocketed it or placed it in the Bolshevik coffers.

Deep in thought, Sonechka sought solitude in the most secluded part of the garden, all the while pressing Nikolai's cherished letter to her heart. Oh, how she had dreamt of this moment. Why then was she hesitating to read it? What was holding her back? Finally, she tore open the envelope and devoured its contents.

Sonechka,

Please forgive me for not writing to you sooner. My duties here in Moscow have kept me very busy. When I saw Pavel we formulated a plan to get you here. He will explain it to you. Please give my best wishes to Liza.

I remain as always your Nikolai.

Sonechka sat re-reading Nikolai's short note, which puzzled and dismayed her. How could he not mention loving and missing her? Uncontrollable tears tumbled down her cheeks. For months she had imagined the love letters she would receive from him. Now this long-awaited moment had arrived. After all, it was her first-ever letter from him. She kept comparing it to the letters that the heroines depicted in the great romantic Russian novels had received.

During supper that evening Liza, concerned by Sonechka's subdued mood, gently broached the subject of Nikolai's letter. Before Sonechka could reply, Pavel announced that Nikolai and he had devised a plan to get Sonechka to Moscow. The more he thought about it the more it appealed to him. Lowering his voice, he repeated that their days on the estate were numbered. Belatedly, he had become aware that the new commissar, Igor, was not only spying on them, he was also agitating the workers to take control of the estate and have them evicted. It dismayed Pavel how his once-loyal workers had succumbed to the blandishments of Bolshevik propaganda and turned against him. Bitterly, Pavel related how Leonid frequently joked that had it not been for their long-standing friendship, he would have been evicted long ago.

Liza and Sonechka reflected in silence on Pavel's revelations. Liza was appalled that they could be thrown out with nowhere to go. At that point, Igor burst into the room. While wondering just how much he had heard, Sonechka was amazed when Pavel amiably beckoned to their intruder to join them. She felt uncomfortable listening to Pavel's polite conversation with Igor. How could he be so pleasant to Igor knowing him to be his enemy? Sonechka was relieved when Liza excused herself, explaining that she needed to attend to Sofia, enabling both of them to leave.

Liza suggested that they sit on the veranda outside Sonechka's room. It was a beautiful August moonlit night. They listened enchanted to the chirping sounds of the cicadas while watching the mist slowly envelop the outer corners of the garden. Liza then asked about Nikolai's letter. Having memorised the brief contents, Sonechka related it word-for-word. Once again, she was glad to share her feelings and fears with Liza.

Liza listened sympathetically to her sister's heartbreaking concerns, agreeing that Nikolai's letter was far from one written by an ardent suitor. Pausing, giving Sonechka a conspiratorial look, she proceeded to tell her what Pavel was about to say when Igor burst into the room.

Both Liza and Pavel had been so impressed with her acting that they felt she should pursue a career on the stage. After all, at nineteen, she should be thinking of her future. While in Moscow, Pavel had been surprised by

Nikolai's knowledge of the theatre. Furthermore, Nikolai had promised that he would help Sonechka meet a reputable theatre director. That Nikolai was to help her thrilled Sonechka, partly dispelling her previous doubts about his love for her.

Returning to Sasha's letter, Liza astounded Sonechka by saying that perhaps they should all join Sasha in America, adding that nobody knew what was going to happen to them in this 'godforsaken country'. At first, Sonechka could not believe what Liza had said. Then, on reflection, she realised that fleeing Russia could well be their salvation too.

That night Sonechka tossed and turned in bed, mulling over their predicament. Pavel's situation saddened her. Here he was, about to lose the highly successful estate he had done so much to create after giving well-paid congenial employment to his workforce. As for his marriage, Sonechka did not know what to think. She knew that Liza married him out of necessity, almost on a whim, when life became intolerable for her. Did he deserve to be compromised by Liza's liaison with Shura? Sonechka knew about love triangles only from novels. The risk that Pavel could be hurt and Liza disgraced distressed her.

With sweet lingering thoughts of Nikolai, Sonechka finally fell asleep.

Waking the next morning, as the dawn's pale pink rays of the sun caressed her face, she heard a rustling sound at the bedside. It was Sofia playing on the floor. Looking up at the icon corner of her bedroom, Sonechka made the sign of the cross, thanking God for His blessings. She could not understand how anyone could live without believing in God. Recently their desecrated church had been converted to a recreation centre where on Sundays Party officials instructed the villagers, including the children, in the tenets of Marxism-Leninism.

The previous night's conversation played on Sonechka's mind, especially their imminent eviction. Though delighted that Nikolai promised to help her, his atheism disturbed her. She recalled the agony of not knowing his feelings for her, then the ecstasy when he finally kissed her.

Imagining herself as a famous actress in Moscow she hoped that Sasha would understand why she had decided to remain in Russia.

That afternoon Sonechka wrote Sasha a long letter. She told him about their forthcoming departure for Moscow and how she planned to join Nikolai there. She felt he would understand her newfound happiness, having fallen in love himself. She believed that she could always go to America later.

Along with a further spate of vindictive articles in the local newspaper castigating Pavel and Liza, Igor, the commissar, stepped up his surveillance, including dining with them most evenings.

To discuss anything important Sonechka and Liza would sit on the veranda outside Sonechka's room, away from eavesdroppers. One evening, Liza suggested they go for a walk. As they climbed the hill overlooking the estate the magical stillness of the night took Sonechka's breath away. On reaching the summit they could see the outline of the house partly hidden by a profusion of beautiful flora. Sonechka marvelled at the view across the river where the moonlight illuminated the village and the church cupola, sadly no longer adorned by a gold cross. Liza proceeded to outline Pavel's plan. He was leaving for Moscow in three days to exhibit his fruit at the First Agricultural and Craft Show in Moscow. He hoped that this exhibition meant the regime's acceptance of at least a limited form of private enterprise. He felt he might even win a prize since he had had a bumper harvest. What was more, the Bolsheviks allowed substantial sums of money to be awarded to the winners. Should he win a lot of money he would not return to his estate. Meantime, Liza, Sonechka and Sofia were to stay with their uncle and aunt in Simferopol. Later, they too, were to join Pavel in Moscow.

Liza and Sonechka surreptitiously prepared for their departure. Pavel had asked Leonid a personal favour – to help Liza with transport to Simferopol. He told Leonid that Fyodor's family had yet to meet the two-year-old Sofia and that he would collect them from Simferopol on his return from Moscow.

Whereas Sonechka looked forward to embarking on her new life in Moscow, Liza felt a profound sense of foreboding.

CHAPTER THIRTEEN

Once they got to Simferopol, Sonechka and Liza were both struck by how their aunt and uncle had aged. Whereas Frosya was overjoyed to see them, Fyodor remained as reserved as ever. Furthermore, he had no wish to be involved in Pavel's plan. Therefore he had made arrangements for Sonechka, Liza and Sofia to stay at a friend's house in the city centre. His hard-hearted precaution proved a godsend for them both – a week later the Cheka came to his house, demanding the whereabouts of his nieces.

Fyodor's friend hid them in the attic of his home in the town centre. They spent three weeks in this hideaway before Pavel sent word to Fyodor for them to join him in Moscow. They were to travel to Moscow via Kiev, where Shura Ryzhkov would meet them. It delighted Sonechka and Liza to read in the local newspaper that Pavel was one of the winners at the Moscow Agricultural Show.

For fear of being apprehended by the Cheka, Pavel advised Liza and Sofia to travel together, with Sonechka departing two days later. Fyodor's friend duly accompanied Liza and Sofia to the railway station. On entering the station they mingled with the multitude. Many were laden down by their possessions.

The day before leaving Simferopol, Sonechka paid a fleeting visit to her aunt and uncle. As they sat around the kitchen table, Frosya produced a dainty little box which Vera had bequeathed to Sonechka. On opening it Sonechka gasped in astonishment. There before her lay a beautiful emerald and diamond ring. Sonechka was overwhelmed by Vera's generosity. Fyodor thought the ring should remain with them for safekeeping. Frosya, however, insisted that Sonechka keep it. For Vera had told her that she wanted Sonechka to have it as a memento of their friendship. Also, should her survival be at stake, the ring could be bartered. Frosya advised Sonechka not to wear the ring but, instead, to hide it well on her person.

Drifting off to sleep that night, Sonechka recalled the kindness and friendship that Vera had shown her. Knowing that Vera and Alexander's marriage had been such a happy one she wondered what they would have thought of Nikolai. Would they have advised her to follow her heart and stay in Russia or to go to America? Her last thoughts before drifting off to sleep were of Nikolai. She longed to see him again. She imagined his lips pressing gently on hers and his melodious voice whispering how much he loved her.

Sonechka had never travelled on a train before, let alone by herself. She was grateful that she had only a small amount of luggage. On entering the crowded carriage a sea of glum faces looked up. 'Do you mind if I sit here?' she asked a shabbily dressed man with an ill-kept beard. She concluded he had not heard her question, when he grunted and nodded his approval. She squeezed into a space just large enough to accommodate her slight frame, wedging herself between him and another equally bedraggled man. There was barely room to breathe, let alone move. She assumed that, like many others on the train, these two men were 'Nepmen'.

'Wouldn't you agree that this is quite a spectacle?' the burlier of the two men she was sitting between said to her in a booming voice. She did not reply. The last thing she wanted was to be the centre of attention in a carriage crammed full of strangers.

With a sly grin he added, 'I don't imagine such a pretty young thing as you is used to being thrown together with people like us.' Sonechka was not sure if he was mocking her. He proceeded to harangue the carriage at large.

'Look at us! Ordinary people burdened with goods we've either bought or hope to sell to survive, yet Bolshevik propaganda labels us as vile speculators despite Lenin's directives to the contrary.'

The carriage fell silent. Undeterred, he carried on.

'We're living in a fool's paradise. Remember how the 'bagmen' were at first tolerated and then hunted down like animals? Mark my words, that will also be our fate. We're pawns in the hands of the Bolsheviks.'

With informers everywhere it did not surprise Sonechka that no one said a word or gave any indication of approval. During the terrible famine of 1921 to 1922, while at Pavel's estate, she recalled hearing how the 'bagmen' came in their droves from the towns, desperate for food, which they exchanged for clothes and other valuables. They got their name from the large bags they carried. At one stage their numbers were said to have become so great that the rail system nearly ground to a halt.

A short while later, the man seated on the other side of her gave his opinion. Speaking in a whisper he agreed that the Nepmen's days were numbered.

He had once been a bagman and was now a Nepman. He deplored the blatant profiteering and ostentation of many of the Nepmen since they provided the Bolsheviks, vehement opponents of private traders, with such easy propaganda targets. With their expensive foreign cars, costly attire, gaudy jewellery and appalling taste he preferred the old pre-revolutionary imperial order. Though he decried the aloofness and exploitation of the old order at least its leaders were mainly cultured, mild-mannered and less self-righteous. He felt sorry for the Jews since the Bolsheviks maintained they were all rootless cosmopolitan speculators. That explained why so many of them had changed their names and renounced their religion, he said. He cited a number of prominent Bolshevik personalities in this category. Leon Trotsky, formerly Bronstein, was the most prominent.

Each time the train stopped peddlars descended, as if from nowhere, to ply the travellers with every imaginable ware for sale. Every time the Cheka entered her carriage Sonechka prayed she would not be arrested. She was greatly relieved her ticket and papers proved to be in order.

As the journey progressed the two Nepmen grew weary and spent most of the remaining time dozing, all the while keeping a tight hold of their belongings. The train thundered through hundreds of kilometres of endless steppes, wasteland and villages. The latter, once populated and prosperous, were now mostly in ruins, burnt down and desolate. The smell of unwashed humanity, dirty clothing and stale food sickened Sonechka. Her only wish was to get to her destination as soon as possible.

Shura, whom she immediately recognised, was waiting for her on the platform. They swiftly made their exit. Walking through the streets of Kiev was an exhilarating experience for Sonechka as she admired the impressive architecture interspersed with the many beautiful churches. However, that several churches had clearly been desecrated sickened her.

They stopped at a tall tenement building in a narrow street. They climbed several flights of stairs before Liza opened a door to welcome them. Thrilled to be reunited, the two sisters fell into each other's arms. Sonechka noticed how Liza glowed whenever she and Shura exchanged glances, something she had not observed when they were living at Alma.

A week later Pavel sent word that he had found an apartment for him, Liza, Sonechka and Sofia. He had a temporary job at the local market selling fresh produce. Meanwhile, Shura was being transferred to Petrograd to work in one of the Cheka departments.

The train to Moscow was packed with a similar mix of travellers to that

Sonechka had encountered on her previous journey. Thankfully, their carriage was in a better condition. As a consequence of the Civil War many carriages had broken windows and stoves that did not work. Some had great holes in the floor where the stoves had been ripped out. They were fortunate to get seats opposite one another. As they sped towards Moscow it began to snow, transforming the countryside into a magical fairytale wonderland. As Sonechka dozed on and off to the sound made by the train's wheels, she kept thinking about her long-awaited reunion with Nikolai.

Nikolai and Pavel met them at the station. On seeing Nikolai, Sonechka's heart skipped a beat. She wanted to rush to him, but instinctively held back. As their eyes met she was reassured by Nikolai's captivating smile. How handsome he looked in his uniform. She felt proud to be by his side. Nikolai's driver helped her into a waiting car.

Pavel had managed, with Nikolai's help, to find them accommodation: two stark rooms in what had once been a merchant's mansion in Beli Gorod near the Kremlin. None of the furnishings remained of what must once have been a gracious home, judging by the marble entry hall, elegant staircase, ornate ceiling and panelled walls. Their two rooms had the bare essentials: beds, a table, chairs and a couple of stools. A large ceramic *pechka* took up half of the wall of the larger room, which they used both for cooking and heating. The fuel they were allocated was barely enough to cook with, let alone keep them warm. Sonechka and Sofia shared the smaller room, which had an enormous curtain-less window overlooking a busy street. Some fifteen other families lived in this mansion.

Pavel and Nikolai joined forces to make Liza and Sonechka's first evening in Moscow a memorable one. Nikolai's position in the Cheka allowed him to shop in their specially designated stores, ensuring they had all the food they needed. In this stark setting they recalled fond memories of those balmy summer evenings spent at Alma together with their exuberant toasts. Sonechka's apprehension disappeared. Gazing into Nikolai's eyes a feeling of peace enveloped her as his reassuring arm caressed her. At last they were reunited in Moscow, the centre of her universe.

Before Nikolai departed, Pavel and Liza tactfully retired to the other room, leaving the lovers on their own. As Nikolai took her tenderly in his arms and passionately kissed her. Sonechka knew that there was nowhere else on earth that she would rather be.

Nikolai promised to return the next day to show her the wonders of the capital.

CHAPTER FOURTEEN

The noise in the city centre was deafening. Tramcars clattered past and motorcars hooted their horns. It was such a contrast to provincial Simferopol.

Walking arm in arm, Nikolai pointed out to Sonechka the colourful facades of the impressive buildings where a number of Russia's distinguished families had once lived. They included the Sheremetyevs, Golitzyns and Trubetskois. It dismayed Sonechka how pleased Nikolai was that these buildings were 'now in the rightful hands of the representatives of the proletariat' – government offices and the residences of the Bolshevik rulers. He agreed with Lenin's decision to liquidate all the country's many foreign businesses and close the stock exchange without compensation. For Nikolai, the expulsion of foreign enterprises was long overdue. He deplored how the British, for example, owned Moscow's most prosperous shopping centre, Muir and Mirrielees, a household name throughout Russia. Also, how the English Club, in the estimation of Russia's imperial elite, had been the city's most exclusive establishment. He was equally critical of the 'bourgeois golf club' the British had created on the outskirts of Moscow. As for the French, Nikolai thought that the million-and-a-half stock market investors deserved to lose their money for propping up 'rotten Imperial Russia'. They were 'evil bourgeois capitalists exploiting the downtrodden Russian people'.

On the Moskva River embankment they stopped by the mighty Kremlin fortress with its numerous towers and golden church cupolas encompassed by a formidable wall. Sonechka wistfully wished that she could visit these ancient churches where the Tsars had been crowned and buried. However, the rigid security did not allow it. There was so much else to see. It would take her weeks to explore the many parts of this ancient city. Nikolai had planned a wonderful day for them.

After walking for several hours, they entered the multi-coloured marble-mosaic foyer of an elegant hotel. Conscious of Nikolai's commanding presence, a uniformed hotel attendant rushed forward, bowed low and ushered them to a corner table for two in the gracious dining room. The potted palms reflected in the mirrored walls created a romantic *fin de siecle* ambience.

Taking her hands in his, Nikolai kissed one then the other. A Muscovite, he wanted to know her first impressions of his city. It pleased him that Moscow was once again the country's capital. He deplored how Russia had suffered for three hundred years under the yoke of westernised Russians and foreigners who had ruled and administrated the country from St Petersburg.

He had wanted to take her to a play directed by the renowned Konstantin Stanislavsky. Unfortunately, his Moscow Art Theatre troupe was abroad on an extended European and American tour. But Nikolai thought Sonechka would enjoy the contemporary play that he had chosen. Furthermore, he had arranged for her to meet the director of this theatre company.

Sonechka wanted to pinch herself. Was she really here in Moscow sitting next to Nikolai? Or was it all a dream? After weeks of uncertainty, Nikolai's privileged world beckoned her.

As he playfully twisted then kissed each of her fingers she wished this moment to last forever. She was oblivious to the world beyond. Nikolai broke her reverie, exclaiming that if they didn't hurry they would miss the first act. Rushing out into the now darkened half-lit street they hurried along the freshly snow-dusted pavements to the nearby theatre.

Once seated, the lights dimmed. With a swish of the stage curtains parting, my mother saw the upturned faces, all around her, waiting to be transported into another world. Compared to the theatre in Bakhchysarai this stage was vast, towering above them with the middle section jutting out into the audience. As the play unfolded, Sonechka felt she was participating in it. It intrigued her how the director's experimental presentation encouraged the audience to take part in the final crowd scene.

At the end of the play Nikolai led Sonechka on to the stage to meet the director, who greeted them both warmly. As it happened, it was the director's fiftieth birthday. They were invited to join the festivities. In no time, tables laden with food and drink filled the stage. Sonechka and Nikolai sat near the director. The many toasts made that night even included one for Sonechka. Relaxed, she chattered away amiably. On leaving the gathering, the director arranged to give her an audition the next afternoon.

Walking home in the snow with Nikolai, Sonechka felt she was about to enter an exciting new world. She could not be happier. Nikolai loved her and there was the prospect of an acting career.

The next morning, in preparation for the audition, Sonechka rehearsed several excerpts from Chekhov's play *The Cherry Orchard*. The audition went well. Although the director praised her diction and portrayal of Anya, unfortunately, she was two months too late to apply for the trainee actor intake. However, should someone drop out he would consider her. When he learned that she could sew he offered her the post of wardrobe assistant. Though disappointed, Sonechka decided to take this position when he explained that it would allow her to watch some of the rehearsals.

Most days Sonechka's sewing duties commenced in the late mornings, not ending until well after the evening performance.

The legendary bitter Moscow winter was setting in fast. Sonechka had never experienced such cold. Brought up in the Crimea, with its mild climate, she found Moscow an ordeal. Pavel would stoke up their *pechka* before leaving for the market, opening the door between the two rooms. As the day progressed the chill took over, since they had so little fuel to burn. Sonechka and Liza took turns to queue for food in the early hours of the morning. Despite fur-lined boots and being well wrapped up, the icy winds that dropped to minus 20 degrees and below cut through her body. It was a nightmare. She soon lost her rosy cheeks and healthy appearance, which had early on drawn angry stares from the half-starved Muscovites. She yearned for the warmth of the Crimean sun to caress her skin and the scent of the orchard blossoms. It amazed Sonechka how Sofia withstood the cold better than any of them. She spent hours, lightly clad, gazing out of the large window, transfixed by the people and traffic passing below.

Sonechka was thankful that she had learned to use the sewing machine. One of her first tasks was to hem costume skirts. Valentina, the head wardrobe mistress, complimented her on her work. Quite often they sat together hand-sewing near the stage, allowing Sonechka to watch the rehearsals. Valentina, who had been with the company for several years, seemed to know everyone in the theatrical world. Sonechka learned that her predecessor had left to join Stanislavsky's theatrical company. Valentina suspected that the real reason was because the company would be touring America, where this woman longed to live. Sonechka wondered whether Valentina sympathised with this woman's decision.

Valentina was curious why Sonechka had left the warmth of the Crimea, the wonderful fruit bowl of Russia, musing that, 'Ah, when one is young and trusting one will do anything for love.' Spending so much of their time together Sonechka sensed that Valentina had certain reservations about Nikolai, not that she condemned him outright. However, much as Sonechka enjoyed their tête-à-têtes she did not feel she knew Valentina well enough to reveal her inner feelings.

On New Year's Eve, Shura Ryzhkov arrived unexpectedly from Petrograd. Though he was not due to attend an important meeting in Moscow until the next week, he decided to surprise them by coming earlier to celebrate the New Year. Nikolai, aware that Shura was coming, had ordered special food from the Cheka delicatessen to be delivered to Liza and Pavel's *kvartira* (an apartment of one to several rooms). It was a joyous reunion. With the vodka and champagne flowing, they reminisced about the happy carefree days on Pavel's estate. The next day, Shura told Liza and Pavel that there was a shortage of qualified stenographers in Petrograd. He felt Liza was well suited to fill one of these vacancies. Furthermore, with Nikolai's help he thought that Pavel could also be found a job in the department distributing food in Petrograd.

On returning home from the theatre one evening, Nikolai took Sonechka into his arms. Standing under the soft light of an ornate lamppost he kissed her passionately. In his mellifluous voice he again told her how he longed for her to be his, adding that he had come to a most important decision. Trembling, through half-closed eyes, she waited for those long-awaited words: Will you marry me?

Nikolai was sure that with both his and Shura's assistance, Liza and Pavel would soon be working in Petrograd. He pointed out that she could not remain in the *kvartira*, since another family would be allocated it. Therefore, he thought it logical for Sonechka to come and live with him. After all, he reasoned, they loved each other and had he not respected her innocence? He knew Pavel and Liza would agree. Nikolai saw marriage as being a ridiculous bourgeois tradition that no one believed in any longer. People had a right to live with whomever they chose, when and where.

Sonechka felt numb. Her head spun trying to make sense of what Nikolai had said. His voice became indistinct. Why did it echo so? He seemed to be speaking to her from afar. She had so hoped that tonight he would, at last, ask her to marry him. She had long dreamed how they would vow to commit their lives to one another in the sacred Russian Orthodox marriage ceremony. Why was marriage so abhorrent to him? What if they were to have children? 'Oh, dear God what am I to do? Please help me.'

When she opened her eyes, Liza was anxiously bending over her. Where was Nikolai? Apparently, she had fainted. Liza gently stroked her forehead saying that she had probably fainted through lack of food. Finally, Sonechka's gaze fell on the impassive Nikolai, standing at the foot of her bed. She tried to recall his exact last words to her. She was certain, though, that he had made no mention of marriage, only of living together.

CHAPTER FIFTEEN

On January 21, 1924, Lenin died.

The populace was stunned. Bands of students, wearing red jackets, paraded the streets bearing banners with such inscriptions as: 'Lenin is dead, but Lenin lives, and Lenin will live!' Day and night the sobbing crowds filled the streets, whispering and wondering who would be the next Chosen One. Would it be Trotsky, Kamenev, Zinoviev, Bukharin, Dzerzhinsky or Radek?

Members of the Committee of the Soviet Congress would be bringing the coffin with the body of Lenin back to Moscow from his country estate in Gorky (formerly Nizhny Novgorod). His body was to lie in state in the *Kolonny Zal* (Hall of Columns) of the newly renamed House of Unions. A nobleman formerly owned this mansion. Firemen draped the massive columns in mourning shrouds with a large portrait of Lenin dominating one of the walls. Workmen toiled around the clock removing the snow and digging the ground where Lenin was to be buried, beside the Kremlin wall facing Red Square.

Rumours about Lenin's poor health had been circulating in Moscow for some time. Even so, the news of his death came as a great shock to the bewildered populace. Despite the freezing temperature falling to below minus 30 degrees, hundreds of thousands of people queued during four days to pay their respects to the man who had changed their lives forever. His regime was hailed as The Great Experiment, 'The Dictatorship of the Proletariat'.

The grief-stricken city came to a virtual standstill, with offices, schools, theatres and places of amusements closed that week. During this time, Sonechka did not see Nikolai. She assumed that being one of Dzerzhinsky's commissars, he was fully occupied.

Pavel and Liza felt duty-bound to view Lenin's body lying in state and suggested Sonechka should do likewise. Infuriated, she told them that she had only contempt for Lenin, since he had stolen her youth. He was the last person she wanted to see.

Unmoved, Pavel pointed out that she would enhance her Bolshevik credentials by viewing his body. Being seen as a Bolshevik believer could well help her theatre career and might even facilitate her leaving Russia.

Sonechka felt confused since none of this made sense. Surely the Bolsheviks needed all the help they could get here in Russia without letting their supporters leave the country.

Pavel went on to explain that Bolshevism was an international revolutionary movement and how Lenin used propaganda generated by the Comintern to promote his crusade for a worldwide workers' revolution. Pavel maintained that the Comintern funded Communist political parties in many countries. For Lenin was determined to let the world know his regime was about to create a socialist paradise in Russia, a beacon to every nation. According to Pavel, Lenin wanted people like Sonechka to project a favourable image of their country abroad.

Sonechka now realised why she had had to endure those boring lectures at Alma by Bolshevik activists about countries that meant nothing to her.

Liza and Pavel confessed that they had felt the same about those lectures. Pavel joked that the socio-economic theories were such make-believe that the lecturers might just as well have been pantomime performers.

Bundled up beyond recognition, Sonechka duly went to the presentation of Lenin's body to the public. She queued for five hours in the unbearable subzero cold. She was surprised to see so many grief-stricken people around her. Though Red Army soldiers kept campfires burning along the length of the queue, this seemed to make little difference.

On entering the *Kolonny Zal*, Sonechka was struck by the solemnity of the mourners listening to the orchestra playing Chopin's Funeral March. How macabre, she thought, for a man responsible for the deaths of millions, that Chopin's Funeral March was one of his favourite pieces.

The massive columns were festooned with red and black ribbons intermingled with greenery. A red-draped open coffin dominated the centre of the *Kolonny Zal*, beside which stood, practically motionless, Lenin's widow, Nadezhda Krupskaya, and her sister. Behind them Sonechka recognised the familiar faces of Bukharin, Zinoviev, Kamenev, Dzerzhinsky and, standing slightly apart, Josef Stalin. Nearby, a sculptor was working intently on a bust of Lenin. Subsequently, replicas of this bust were sent throughout the Soviet Union and to the Bolshevik faithful abroad.

After Lenin's funeral, speculation continued concerning his successor. No one seemed to know who would lead them. Would life improve or get worse? What would happen to NEP?

Sonechka had her own emotional turmoil to face. Perhaps she should heed Sasha's advice about applying for entry to America before it was too late. What would she do when Liza and Pavel went to Leningrad (Petrograd/St Petersburg was renamed Leningrad in honour of Lenin shortly after he died). Everything in her upbringing told her that she should not live in sin with Nikolai. She beseeched God to give her the strength to forsake him.

CHAPTER SIXTEEN

Feeling ashamed, Sonechka told no one about Nikolai's proposal that they should live together. When he announced that he was being sent urgently to help quell unrest in Kiev she was relieved. It meant she had time to think on her own. Eventually, one morning she told Liza why she fainted that evening. After pondering awhile, Liza asked if Sonechka would be prepared to forsake her Christian beliefs in marriage and live with Nikolai in sin. Since Liza had encouraged her relationship with Nikolai, Sonechka assumed that she would want her to agree to his proposal. It therefore pleased her when Liza, embracing her warmly, said that she understood her dilemma and would agree with whatever she decided to do.

When Nikolai returned to Moscow for two days, Sonechka saw him only once, briefly. He told her that at times such as this, law and order must be maintained. She hardly recognised the man she thought she knew and loved. He thought he would be stationed in Kiev for some time, since the Ukrainians, who exasperated him, were proving troublesome. Once settled there he expected her to join him. He was confident that she would find a suitable position in one of the city's theatrical companies. Crestfallen, Sonechka realised that in the aftermath of Lenin's death, the well-being of the Party was Nikolai's all-consuming concern.

She recalled her conversation with Pavel the day she queued to see Lenin lying in state. She had no doubt that he had long ago lost his revolutionary fervour. However, for his family's sake, she knew he must remain a Bolshevik supporter, since their very survival depended on this pretence.

Speculation continued as to who would succeed Lenin. Standing in the early morning food queues she heard that though most wanted Trotsky to lead them, quite a few supported Kamenev and Zinoviev.

It startled Sonechka when someone yelled out, 'There are too many *Zhidi* (Yids) in power already! They are literally crawling all over the place! Why can't we have a Russian rule us?' He then went on to say, 'Two or three *Zhidi* are like yeast, but en masse they are compost.' Several people in the queue chuckled, the others, like Sonechka, ignored these racist remarks. She found it difficult to believe that people could be so critical of the Jews whom she had mixed with so freely in the Crimea.

During the next week Sonechka tried to imagine what her life with Nikolai would be like. Sadly she realised that he would always be first and foremost a dedicated Bolshevik for whom, no matter what, the Party would be paramount. How could she live with such a zealot? How could he have professed to be so much in love with her? She missed those romantic moments, when he took her in his arms, proclaiming his love and passionately kissing her.

However, what Valentina revealed shattered any hope she might have had of rekindling her love for him.

She and Sonechka were sitting near the window sewing, catching the last rays of the winter sun, when Valentina made a devastating disclosure about Nikolai. She maintained that he had had an affair with an actress who was now abroad with the Stanislavsky troupe. Furthermore, they had a child. Besides, he was well known in the theatrical world as a ladies' man, revelling in his conquests. Looking sheepishly at Sonechka, Valentina confessed that she should have told her this sooner.

Feeling she could now trust Valentina, Sonechka opened her heart out to her. Valentina sympathised with her dashed hopes of a church wedding, pointing out that a dedicated Chekist such as Nikolai would be fanatical in his determination to abolish religion and its traditions. She warned Sonechka not to profess her Christian beliefs, since spies and eavesdroppers were everywhere. In a hushed voice she told Sonechka that the Lubyanka, where Nikolai worked as an interrogator, was full of people whom, she alleged, had unwittingly criticised the regime.

That Nikolai could descend to such depths as imprisoning and interrogating innocent people devastated Sonechka. She recalled her first encounter with the Cheka while living in Simferopol with Fyodor and Frosya. Eva, Froysa's much younger sister, Sonechka's other aunt, had been imprisoned for no apparent reason. Knowing that Eva would starve unless helped, Sonechka was sent to queue daily at the prison with food and essentials. The pretty young Sonechka was sometimes able to charm one of the Chekists to deliver her parcel to Eva. The family later learned that while in prison the women were humiliated and many were raped. Eva became pregnant and gave birth to a stillborn child. When released from prison Eva was so ashamed that she went to live with relations in a distant village.

The next day Liza's job in Leningrad was confirmed and Sonechka made a momentous decision: she must leave Russia and with God's help get to America.

CHAPTER SEVENTEEN

When Sonechka told Liza and Pavel of her decision to leave Russia she was overjoyed that they were so supportive. Pavel offered to help her. She knew that that meant bribing bureaucrats to get the necessary papers. His generosity astounded her. She would never forget it.

Pavel admitted that if he had won more money at the Agricultural Show he would be applying for all four of them to leave the country. In despair, he described how he once had had high hopes for Russia becoming a constitutional monarchy like England. He thought it a tragedy that the Bolsheviks had hijacked the revolution. Their dishonesty knew no bounds. Their promise of peace, bread and land was a cynical charade. In no time they had plunged the country into a barbaric civil war to destroy all opposition to their ruthless rule.

Since Liza was due to start her job in Leningrad in early March, Pavel had limited time to help Sonechka with fulfilling the requirements for her exit visa. He warned her that due to bureaucratic inefficiency and corruption and even with substantial bribes, it could take some time before she could leave Russia.

Just before their departure for Leningrad, Shura wrote that there was a job for Pavel in the city's central food distribution department. He had also found them accommodation.

Knowing that she would be unable to continue living in the *kvartira*, Sonechka asked Valentina where she could find temporary accommodation. Valentina kindly had her stay with her on the understanding that Sonechka would soon be going to Kiev.

Sonechka was obliged to go to the Lubyanka several times to be interrogated during the next month. On each occasion the officials would ask her to fill out more documents. Sometimes these were identical to the ones she had previously completed. Compared to how the passport officials treated some applicants, Sonechka felt fortunate. Judging by their dignified bearing and refined speech, these unfortunates had been privileged before the revolution.

Made to wait hours, they were shouted at and humiliated before the other applicants. Some were threatened with prison and execution for trying to leave the country. Sonechka dressed shabbily and spoke in a rural Crimean accent. This saved her from being subjected to the same verbal abuse. The officials addressed everyone as *Tovarish*, using this term in virtually every sentence they spoke. My mother felt she was again working for the Cheka. It came as no surprise, therefore, when she discovered that the foreign passport department was under the diabolical secret police.

She thanked God for Pavel's advice on several matters, in particular, on how to discreetly bribe the officials. During this time she wrote a long letter to Sasha hoping that the American government would still allow her to enter their country. She was thankful that besides Mr Kerr's address in Shanghai, Sasha had given her the name and address of a lady to stay with in Harbin.

Spending so much time with Valentina, Sonechka did not feel it wise to divulge her plans to leave Russia. She feared the older woman might, inadvertently, let this information slip. The consequences could be dire for Sonechka and possibly also for Valentina. Accordingly, Sonechka continued to have Valentina believe that she would soon be going to Kiev to live with Nikolai. Valentina could not understand how she could do this. It soured, but fortunately did not end, their friendship.

Sonechka was thrilled when Liza wrote and suggested she come to Leningrad at the end of April. Liza thought that it would be a pity for her not to see this beautiful city. In addition, it would give the sisters precious time together.

Two days before Easter, Sonechka boarded the train for Leningrad at the *Leningradsky Vokzal*[5] (Leningrad Railway Station).

CHAPTER EIGHTEEN

Sonechka was pleased to be alone with her thoughts, mulling over the tempestuous last few weeks. She recalled how, as a rosy-cheeked provincial, she had set out by train imbued with the expectation of a wonderful life with her beloved in Moscow. Was it only three months ago? She wondered how, despite Nikolai's character flaws and ideological fanaticism, she could still be in love with him. She had once read that one's first love remained forever imprinted in one's memory, come what may. Sadly, she realised that only in a romantic novel could the heroine change someone such as Nikolai.

Sonechka now had no doubt that her destiny lay in America. She thanked God for Pavel's unexpected largesse. She thought it ironic since the prize money he had won, sanctioned by the Bolsheviks, was enabling her to flee their socialist paradise to a country that their propaganda vilified.

Unable to endure the pretence of remaining in Russia and going to live with Nikolai in Kiev, Sonechka decided to reveal her true intentions to Valentina. She wholeheartedly agreed that Sonechka should go to America and promised to help her. Had she been younger, she too would have left Russia. For her safety, Valentina advised Sonechka to leave the theatre job and to stay in hiding with one of her friends across the other side of Moscow.

Pavel met Sonechka at Leningrad's Moscow station. Being a beautiful spring day, he suggested they walk to the *kvartira* on the Fontanka (Fountain Canal). From the *vokzal* they crossed the Liteiny Bridge and walked down Nevsky Prospekt, the city's principal thoroughfare. Pavel explained how, before the revolution, the broad, 5-km-long Nevsky was one of Europe's most fashionable streets, bustling with elegantly-dressed people. Despite the revolution and the Civil War, most of the city's magnificent palaces and buildings had not been destroyed. However, many of their treasures had been either stolen or damaged.

Sonechka tried to imagine what it was once like in this city, long renowned as the Venice of the North. Images of magnificently uniformed cavalry officers cantering on their Arabian mounts, and the skirts of elegant ladies dressed in silk swishing on the cobblestones flooded her mind. As they neared the canal she could hear dear old aunt Olya narrating her youthful escapades of dashing sleigh rides on the icy Moika canal whisking her to parties and palace balls. Pavel brought her back to reality by warning her not to call it Petrograd or St Petersburg but, instead, Leningrad. The names Petrograd and St Petersburg were blasphemy to the Bolsheviks.

They entered a gracious foyer with a sweeping staircase. Looking about her, Sonechka was dismayed by the crude makeshift lamps on the peeling walls that replaced the once beautiful chandelier that had hung from the ceiling. As they neared the *kvartira* the door burst open and Sofia rushed into her outstretched arms, closely followed by Liza. It amazed Sonechka how their stark two-room dwelling in Moscow had been replaced by a comfortably furnished six-room Leningrad *kvartira*.

The next day Liza took Sonechka to see some of Leningrad's famous buildings. At the *Zimny Dvoretz* (Winter Palace), they crossed Palace Square with its impressive archway and government offices. Liza explained that the city's great architects had nearly all been foreigners, with the Italians Rastrelli and Karlo Rossi arguably the most famous. Rastrelli built the beautiful Rococo-styled Winter Palace. Karlo Rossi, a hundred years later, designed many memorable buildings, including the magnificent ensemble commemorating Napoleon's defeat that encompassed three sides of the square facing the Winter Palace.

The story of the unveiling of the Triumphal Arch, the centre-piece of this ensemble, intrigued Sonechka. Not long before it was completed everyone thought the 16-tonne weight of the six bronze horses, chariot and charioteers would cause the arch to collapse once the scaffolding was removed. Rossi duly climbed to the top of his masterpiece while the scaffolding was being dismantled, and declared, 'If it shall fall, I will fall with it!' It has stood ever since.

On entering the Winter Palace, Sonechka was awestruck by the majestic marble staircase. She felt a cold shudder run through her body imagining how the raging revolutionaries, brandishing their red flags, had surged up these very same stairs, about to defile and destroy all before them in a crazed fury. It saddened her to see the once beautifully furnished reception halls laid bare.

Liza explained how the regime wanted to encourage as many people as possible to visit the palaces, art galleries, museums and cultural centres, where entry for the masses, prior to the revolution, had been very restricted. Her provocative interpretation of this ruling was that though Leningrad's Bolsheviks might be monsters, they were not cultural barbarians. It sickened Sonechka that the vast main hall was plastered with the photographs and portraits of Bolshevik revolutionary heroes and heroines. Liza whispered that viewing this exhibition was an obligatory Bolshevik pilgrimage. Hence, one should show due respect. Only with difficulty could Sonechka hide her revulsion.

Liza and Sonechka decided to take a risk on the Saturday night by slipping out of the house dressed as two old babushkas. They walked to a church on the Vasilyevsky Ostrov, where Liza had heard that several priests were gathering to celebrate the traditional *Paskha* midnight service in the church's crypt. It was packed with elderly worshippers. Fortunately, this shortened service, which impressed both Liza and Sonechka by its solemnity, passed without any unwelcome intrusions. They walked home through the darkened streets in silence, pondering the profound spiritual experience of the service, a memory for Sonechka that lingered for many years.

The next day being *Paskha*, Liza and Pavel invited a handful of their trusted friends to join them for the celebration. Liza, with Shura's help, provided a fine selection of festive fare. Seated next to Yevgenia Alexandrovna (known as Zhenya, a diminutive of Yevgenia), Sonechka felt an instant rapport with this raven-haired young woman, whose drab, ill-fitting clothes did little to lessen the beauty of her dazzling green eyes. Before long they were engrossed in conversation. Zhenya nostalgically recalled the idyllic summer of 1914 when everything had seemed so perfect, particularly the hospitality of Sonechka's parent's pension and the delights of the Tauride coastline. She reflected how no one could have imagined that the outbreak of war, a few weeks later, would lead within a little over three years to Lenin's seizure of power and the collapse of their world.

She told Sonechka that after the Bolsheviks killed her father, she and her mother were left to fend for themselves. Knowing how wealthy they were, and her father having been a prominent court official, the Cheka did everything to make their lives as ghastly as possible. On the slightest pretext they struck them with their rifle butts. Everyone they knew suffered similarly. People were shot dead before their very eyes, often for no obvious reason. They were forced to sweep the streets and clean the public toilets on their hands and knees. Their tormentors revelled in humiliating them. Not content with that, the Cheka repeatedly ransacked their mansion for valuables and forced them to live in just one of its rooms. The food they got was mostly inedible: rotten fish, unthawed potatoes and bread made mainly from sawdust. When a horse fell dead in the street it was stripped of flesh within minutes. Cats or dogs were nowhere to be seen.

Towards the end of the third winter (1920), they nearly froze to death, since their furniture, which they had been using for firewood, ran out. Had Zhenya not become a bagman they would probably have starved to death, as so many of their friends and acquaintances did. She was by no means the only female bagman. These were desperate times. Starvation was widespread, not just among Zhenya's class of people, but afflicting everyone except the Bolshevik elite. Desperate to survive, some succumbed to cannibalism. Dead bodies lay about everywhere. One had to be careful not to stumble over them on the footpaths and streets.

Recalling her Cheka ordeal, Sonechka admired how Zhenya had outwitted them too. Besides using other peoples' permits and forging documents so she could travel by train, she hid valuables, such as silver and gold to barter for food, in a tub of icy water and soaking soiled clothes. She correctly assumed that the Chekists would not want to place their hands in it.

Finding a train to go out into the countryside to barter for food was daunting for Zhenya. She waited hours and sometimes days to catch one. She then had to fight her way on board. Besides avoiding being crushed, in some of the carriages she had to be careful not to fall through the hole in the floor where the stoves had been ripped out. When she finally got to her destination, she had to walk for half an hour or so through forests to get to a village where she knew she could exchange her valuables for food. There was always the risk of attack on the way from packs of hungry wolves. On several occasions Bolshevik militia threatened her. Once, one drew a pistol and pointed it at her head. It astounded Sonechka to hear how Zhenya calmly turned around and slowly walked away without looking back. With her heart pounding furiously, she fully expected a shot to ring out at any moment. She assumed that her apparent sang-froid persuaded him not to shoot.

Though Sonechka had not endured such terrible and protracted hunger and cold as had Zhenya, she felt that their respective encounters with the Cheka created a bond between them.

Zhenya was forced to give violin lessons to those Bolsheviks wanting their offspring to acquire some of the trappings of the regime they had overthrown. Zhenya's mother, a brilliant pianist, had to give piano lessons to the same people. However, her mother defiantly refused to perform in public, since she did not want to be seen endorsing the regime. This was a bizarre twist of fate since before the revolution she had very much wanted to be a concert pianist, but the nobility had then been forbidden to perform in public.

Zhenya had thought they would starve when the peasants in the only village where she knew she could barter for food, refused to trade with her. An uncle, her mother's brother, proved to be their saviour. In a peasant village school, at the turn of the century, the uncle had taught one of the commissars who were now overseeing them. In his gratitude, this commissar ensured they got enough food to survive.

Her uncle had sacrificed a promising career when, like many of the privileged class, he 'went to the people'. An idealist, he believed his villagers to be wonderful people who could do no wrong and would appreciate his self-sacrifice. Tragically, early on in the revolution, they accused him of being a Tsarist spy and shot him. This reminded Sonechka of the peasant workers on Pavel's estate. She thought their ignorance of events beyond their immediate world explained why so many had succumbed so eagerly to the Bolsheviks' evil but beguiling propaganda.

Sonechka found it equally revealing that many of Zhenya's friends before the revolution had been starry-eyed idealists. They had welcomed the revolution, with many taking active parts. But once the Bolsheviks gained power it did not take long for most to realise the disastrous forces their revolutionary fervour had unleashed.

Mulling over Zhenya's incredible story of survival, bravery and resourcefulness, Sonechka had no doubts about fleeing the Soviets.

That evening Shura, taking Sonechka aside, told her that Nikolai had telegraphed him asking where she was. Shura tactfully answered his query by explaining that Sonechka had, on the spur of the moment, accepted Liza's invitation to visit them in Leningrad before going to Kiev.

The relationship between Shura, Liza and Pavel continued to baffle her. Perhaps it was not a love triangle after all. Shura's gentlemanly behaviour and that he was Sofia's godfather contrasted strikingly with Nikolai's beliefs. Yet, Shura was a Chekist.

Throughout that night she had *koshmary* (nightmares) of Nikolai hounding her through the damp, dark bowels of the Lubyanka, brandishing her documents. It horrified her that in her nightmare she longed to be caught and possessed by him.

Sonechka was thrilled when Zhenya, beaming with pride, offered to show her more of St Petersburg – as, like many other inhabitants, she insisted on calling it. She felt it belonged to her.

With Liza and Pavel working, and Sofia at a day nursery, Sonechka explored more of the city with Zhenya. The two young women became inseparable.

Before long Sonechka told Zhenya about her tormented love for Nikolai. Zhenya agreed with Sonechka's decision to leave Russia, seeing it as her sole salvation. Zhenya's only sister and her husband had escaped just after the revolution and were living in New York. They had tried to persuade Zhenya and her mother to join them. Unfortunately, their father had just been murdered and her mother was too distraught to make this decision. In no time it became impossible to even dream about fleeing. Perhaps, God willing, one day they might also be able to leave. Trying to make light of her situation she added that, on the other hand, how could she ever leave her beloved St Petersburg?

For several days they walked along the embankment of the Neva River and throughout the city centre. Zhenya explained how Peter the Great had opened a window to the West in creating St Petersburg. He abhorred how Russia had been set back hundreds of years by the uncreative and barbaric Mongol Tartar horde that had dominated and devastated the country for so long. Astonishingly, Peter began building St Petersburg, on a foetid and mosquito-infested marshland, while still fighting the Swedes from whom he had just wrested the territory. Determined to modernise Russia, Peter forcibly introduced western culture and science and a Germanised bureaucracy to St Petersburg. He had St Petersburg replace Moscow as Russia's royal residence and administrative capital. Peter made Russia powerful and feared by her enemies. However, in so doing, he created an unbridgeable gulf between the westernised Russians and foreigners, who ruled and administered the country from St Petersburg, and the overwhelming bulk of the populace, the peasantry and most of the merchants, for whom Moscow remained their cultural, spiritual and national capital.

Sonechka explored the collection of canals and numerous small islands connected by countless bridges that had led to St Petersburg being compared with Venice.

Approaching the famous Falconet statue of Peter the Great, the friends recited in unison a verse from Pushkin's famous poem, *The Bronze Horseman* (1833):

I love you, Peter's creation,
I love your stern and comely face,
The broad, Neva's majestic current,
Her embankment's granite carapace,
The patterns laced by iron railings,
And your meditative might

97

The lucent dusk, the moonless paling;
When in my room I read and write …

In this poem Pushkin describes the great flood of 1824 when the floodwaters in the city reached over four metres. It was believed by many that another such catastrophe was long overdue (There was a disastrous flood just a few months after Sonechka left Leningrad). No wonder the city was so prone to flooding, since it was built only just above the level of the Neva and the high tides in the autumn and spring blocked the outflow of the Neva into the Gulf of Finland.

At the Smolny Institute, where she had been a pupil, Zhenya became irate. She still could not believe that Lenin had proclaimed the Bolsheviks' victory from her school and that it was from the school that at first he governed the country. It was little consolation to her that Lenin and his Bolshevik lackeys did not remain for long in Peter's city. It was said that they much preferred Moscow to St Petersburg, with its European atmosphere.

She mused that if Dostoevsky were alive he would think Lenin had stepped into the shoes of his fictional character, Pyotr Verkhovensky, the fanatical and ruthless revolutionary in his great work, *The Possessed*.

Trying to sympathise with Zhenya, Sonechka asked her what life had been like before the revolution.

Closing her eyes and speaking as if in a trance, Zhenya described how wonderful it had been. She took for granted the tight-knit little world that governed and administered Russia's enormous land-contiguous empire. All the people she knew had some connection with the palace or government. What is more, they all lived near Nevsky Prospekt, the Moika and Fontanka canals. Before the revolution she did not realise just how small a part of the city they occupied. They attended the same elite schools and academies. They went to the same balls and banquets. The men were members of the same exclusive clubs.

Sonechka apologised for having apparently upset Zhenya by getting her to reminisce. However, far from being upset, Zhenya said that it had given her great pleasure to show Sonechka her magnificent city, since it helped her to forget the reality of her situation.

Sonechka did not know what to say. Whereas she could look forward to the future with a degree of confidence, Zhenya had nothing to hope for beyond surviving as best she could.

CHAPTER NINETEEN

Towards the end of May, Sonechka was summoned to collect her documents and exit visa papers from the Lubyanka. During the month she had spent with Liza and Pavel she received several letters from Nikolai demanding to know when she would join him in Kiev. His latest letter said he would be returning to work at the Lubyanka in two weeks. Though he didn't know how long he would be there, he assumed that she would return to Moscow to live with him.

That evening Shura came to dinner. His sympathetic understanding of her predicament reassured Sonechka. He advised her to leave immediately for Moscow. By acting quickly, Shura was confident Sonechka would be on her way to China before Nikolai got back to Moscow. Being able to stay with Valentina's friend was fortunate; Nikolai was unlikely to know her whereabouts. He told her that as soon as she collected her papers from the Lubyanka, she was to buy her ticket for Chita, in the Far East. As Chita was in a buffer zone Sonechka would need two permits. One from the Chita Soviet authorities would allow her to leave the buffer zone, the other from the Chinese diplomatic mission to let her enter Manchuria. At Chita she was to buy a ticket to Harbin.

Only Pavel and Liza, Zhenya and Shura were present at her farewell party. Beneath the veneer of joviality and bonhomie, Sonechka sensed real apprehension and fear. When, if ever, would they be together again? Afraid that an emotional farewell would attract undue attention, Shura would be the only one to accompany Sonechka to the *vokzal*.

As was the custom before setting out on a long journey, they all sat down as Liza said a prayer. She made several signs of the cross over Sonechka's bowed head and gave her a small metallic icon of St Nicholas, the patron saint of travel. The two sisters embraced, joined a moment later by Pavel. For some time they clung to one another. Sonechka wept tears of gratitude for all Pavel and Liza had done for her.

As Sonechka boarded the train, Shura gave her a farewell kiss and whispered in her ear. Before she could reply he gently pushed her up the steps into the carriage. When she turned around, he was nowhere to be seen.

Shura told her that within a week he would be in Berlin working for the Comintern. Sonechka wondered if Liza and Pavel were aware of his imminent departure. Perhaps he would help them to escape too. Shura puzzled her. Only the elite worked for the Comintern. Their ambassadors promoted their doctrines to the West. His fluent German – the Comintern's language – and his French and English made Shura an ideal candidate. He knew Europe well as he had holidayed there with his family before the revolution.

On her arrival in Moscow, Sonechka went directly to Valentina's friend.

Shura had warned her that it could take several days for the formalities to be completed at the Lubyanka. For four consecutive days she was interrogated by several impassive Chekists, who all asked her much the same questions. Why did she want to leave the Soviet Union? How could she go to America, one of their country's greatest enemies? Sonechka made out that once she got to America she would do her utmost to convince the Americans that they should do everything possible to help the Soviet Union in its quest to create a wonderful country.

Each morning she was terrified as she entered the grim building. Her constant worry was that she might meet Nikolai, and that he would interrogate her. No matter where she went in Moscow, Chekists were there. She lost count of the number of times she was stopped on the street and forced to show her papers and searched for weapons. Their sinister large black vehicles, nicknamed Black Ravens, terrified her. This was especially so when they sped on their way, sirens sounding, to the Lubyanka where their victims, who peered desperately through the vehicle's small window grates, were interrogated.

On May 31, having just received her precious documents, she had a nasty shock as she walked past a half-open office door in the Lubyanka. She caught sight of the Chekist commissar for whom she had worked in the Crimea. Her mind began to race. She did not think he had noticed her. Walking slowly, so as not to attract attention, Sonechka left calmly.

Taking Shura's advice she went directly to the *vokzal* and bought her ticket for Chita. She hoped that Sasha had, by now, received her letters telling him of her decision to leave Russia and join him in America.

Above: Sonechka's photograph superimposed on the first page of her memoir, written in Shanghai, 1924.

CHAPTER TWENTY

On the night of June 2, 1924, Sonechka boarded the Trans-Siberian Railway, bound for Chita. The journey would take just under two weeks.

When she arrived at the station she was relieved to find it crowded. There were only a few Chekists. Then, just as she was about to sit down in the carriage, she saw two of them running towards her carriage. Instinctively, she jumped off the train and mingled with the crowd. After what seemed ages, the two men emerged from the nearby carriage and walked back towards the exit.

With an overwhelming sense of relief, she returned to her carriage. She then realised that, in her haste to leave the train, she had dropped her small bag containing food and a few personal effects. It was nowhere to be seen. Distraught, she collapsed onto the seat, oblivious of all else.

Regaining her composure, Sonechka looked round, wondering whom she was travelling with. Opposite her sat a distinguished looking middle-aged man who gave her a wide smile, as did the dark-haired woman sitting beside him. There was no reaction from the three young women who occupied the adjacent seats. The man shook her hand and introduced himself as David. His wife was called Esther and their three daughters Miriam, Sara and Rachel.

David pointed to the rack above Sonechka's seat. He had picked up the bag she had dropped. David explained that he had caught a fleeting glimpse of her when she identified her seat. He asked if the Chekists, who had checked his family's documents, had been looking for her.

Sonechka assured him that was not the case. She said that she had forgotten to tell her sister something important. Sonechka felt that this incident had created a bond between them. Throughout the long journey David and Esther made her feel part of their family, insisting that she share their food. In return Sonechka purchased fresh produce for them all from the hordes of traders who plied the train at every station.

Sonechka learned that her companions were going to America to join David's brother, who was living in the southern part of California. He worked in the motion picture industry, which David called 'the movies'. When Sonechka mentioned she wanted to be an actress they thought that with her good looks she should try for a career on the screen.

During the day the girls kept themselves occupied by reading, doing embroidery work or hand-sewing. Knowing the journey ahead of them to be tedious, Esther had ensured they had the essentials to do these activities.

Sonechka was grateful to be included in this loving Jewish family that had befriended her. She learned from David that they had originally planned to go to a new Jewish settlement in Palestine, but decided that like Europe, the Middle East was burdened by history. For him America was the Promised Land. Sonechka told them about the experiences of her brother, Sasha, and how she hoped to join him.

In the evenings, Sonechka, and the three girls, joined others in their carriage singing traditional Russian ballads and gypsy melodies to the accompaniment of balalaikas or accordions.

The behaviour of the carriage's commissar, Ivan, who was under the influence of vodka most evenings, did not suggest that Sonechka was under surveillance. But Sonechka's heart pounded and she came out in a cold sweat whenever a Bolshevik official approached.

Often their train stopped for long periods due to repair work on cuttings and bridges damaged during the Civil War (known as the Railway War). In many villages and settlements on the way, Sonechka saw destroyed buildings and dwellings, including, much to her consternation, defiled churches with their shattered cupolas and dangling crosses.

The further east they went, the more Asiatic the people became. They besieged the train, trying to sell an extraordinary variety of food and goods. For hours on end Sonechka gazed in wonderment at the Siberian landscape. The endless forests of pine, birch and spruce, the vast plains and deserts, the mountain ranges, the innumerable lakes and rivers amazed her. The trees were so high often their tops were invisible. The size of their tree trunks was breathtaking. It was summer and the profusion of flora astonished Sonechka, as did the knowledge that everything was covered in snow for at least eight months of the year.

As they approached Lake Baikal, the world's largest freshwater lake, Sonechka marvelled how the railway track, skirting its southern shoreline, ran right by the water's edge as it darted in and out of numerous tunnels. She likened the adjacent cliffs to the teeth in a gigantic shark's mouth.

David shared his knowledge on the building of the Trans-Siberian railroad.

The financially strapped imperial government could afford only a quarter of the money required for a modern rail system. So, it was built mainly with convict labour. They had the most primitive equipment. For each day's work on the railway, a day was deducted from a prisoner's sentence. The food was better than in prison, but the work was dangerous. Without power tools, the tunnels had to be dug with light picks and wooden shovels. Dynamite was too expensive, so gunpowder was used for blasting. Very few volunteers worked on the project. Even the army refused to be conscripted. In desperation, fifteen thousand Chinese were enlisted. The slightly built Chinese displayed incredible stamina, enduring the terrible cold.

Contrary to Liza's forebodings, the vastness of Siberia fascinated rather than frightened Sonechka. Mankind seemed irrelevant in this gigantic natural wonderland.

At night, trying to get off to sleep, Sonechka reflected on the last few days before her departure. The further she travelled the more of what had happened receded, becoming a blurred memory. Each night she thanked God for granting her the opportunity to leave Russia. She would never forget Pavel's selflessness. She knew that the substantial bribes he had paid had enabled her to leave. This meant it would be all the more difficult for Pavel to find sufficient money for him and his family to follow.

On the last evening before they arrived in Chita, Sonechka joined the others to celebrate the end of their journey. Though her fellow passengers did not say as much, Sonechka assumed that most of them had lost everything and were, like her, fleeing the Bolsheviks.

Ivan, the commissar, smiled slyly at her. In a drunken slur he blurted out a warning: anyone on the run from the Cheka should disappear before the next station. Stumbling over the base of her seat he bent down and mumbled, 'The Cheka are coming on board to check all documents.'

Sonechka was petrified. Had this drunken commissar known all along that she was a fugitive or had Nikolai tracked down her whereabouts? It was said that to be a commissar you needed the sixth sense of a dog. She recalled how, during one of their romantic walks home from the theatre, Nikolai told her that if she ever tried to leave Russia he would find her. Passionately, grabbing her, he added that he would perhaps even kill her because he despised America and everything it stood for. At the time she had been flattered by his determination to have her at any cost.

On returning to their carriage, David took charge, saying that the warning Ivan had just given should be taken seriously. Sonechka was a fugitive and for whatever reason their commissar seemed to have a humane streak in his crooked Bolshevik body. Somehow she would have to leave the train before the Cheka came aboard. Perhaps she could jump off before the train stopped. But would the land alongside the railway tracks offer her a safe hiding place? Sonechka prayed that having got this far, God would not abandon her.

Esther gave Sonechka a small rucksack for her essentials. Her documents and the money Pavel had given her were strapped around her waist. The family would take the rest of her belongings to their boarding house in Chita.

As soon as they felt the train starting to lose speed Sonechka and David hurried down the darkened corridors. Approaching the end carriage they could feel the train coming to a gentle grinding halt. Lurching forward they came face to face with Ivan. With a sly smile, he asked, 'Where do you think you're going?'

David, in an unruffled voice answered. 'What is your price?'

'Well, that depends. What are you prepared to pay?'

Revulsion gripped Sonechka. Quickly bending down she pulled at the threads of the hem of her skirt. Vera's image flashed before her. Triumphantly, she pulled the diamond and emerald ring out of its hiding place. Both men stared at it in disbelief. 'Here, will this do?' she asked.

They could hear voices approaching the train. Grabbing Sonechka quickly, Ivan pushed her into the empty compartment and, pulling up the bench seat, shoved her in. Turning to David, Ivan assured him that since this was his compartment Sonechka would be safe in there.

Lying in her stinking hiding place for what seemed ages Sonechka wondered what Ivan's intentions were now that she was his prisoner. Would he rape her and then turn her in? Did Ivan do this regularly, she pondered – preying on persons like herself? When the train stopped she imagined the passengers leaving it. But her fate lay in Ivan's hands.

Eventually, Ivan returned and released Sonechka from the suffocating darkness. He handed the terrified Sonechka a bundle of workers' clothing to wear. As she tied a sooty kerchief around her head, he lifted her chin and smeared some soot on her face. On the platform he pointed to a metal box which she picked up. For a short distance they joined a group of cleaners. She then followed him into a side-office where he scrawled his signature on a piece of paper attached to a board hanging on the wall. Turning to her, he whispered, 'Well, girl, you're free now. Go quickly.'

Stunned, the speechless Sonechka calmly made her way towards the *vokzal* exit.

CHAPTER TWENTY-ONE

Chita was a no-man's-land between Russia and China. Here the Bolsheviks were constrained by the presence of Chinese railway officials. At this point the railway forked. One line went to the Pacific Ocean port of Vladivostok and the other to Harbin in China.

On leaving the station Sonechka wondered whom she would ask for directions to the boarding house where David and his family were staying. Looking furtively around, she saw David standing in a doorway across the street. With a barely perceptible nod in her direction, he turned and started walking. Sonechka followed him at a discreet distance. On passing a synagogue, he turned into a side street with market stalls and a variety of shops doing a brisk trade. This surprised her. She remembered standing in long queues for food in Moscow. Eventually, they came to a substantial three-storey boarding house where David and his family were staying.

Esther and the girls welcomed her with tea and refreshments in the dining room. The smell of the freshly baked bagels was inviting. After Sonechka recounted how nearly she had fallen into the clutches of the Cheka, David said, 'I am sure Chita is seething with Soviet agents who could be on your trail. Therefore, I think it would be best for me to go and buy your ticket for Harbin.'

Sonechka stayed that night with them and left the next evening. Having been together for nearly a fortnight, it was sad to bid farewell to people who had been so good to her.

Sonechka appreciated David accompanying her to the *vokzal*, where she was due to board the 11pm train to Harbin. A teeming mass of Asians and a sprinkling of Russians were sprawled out on the platform. Nobody seemed to know when the train would arrive. All around her people with mask-like faces babbled away, surrounded by a sea of bags, bedding and caged birds. She found it difficult to imagine how she would possibly find a seat on the train amid this bedlam.

At midnight a whistle sounded, and everyone scrambled across the railway tracks to the opposite platform, where the train to Harbin pulled in. Sonechka joined the heaving throng scurrying into the empty carriages. Miraculously, she managed to find a seat. She threw her big bag, containing all her worldly goods, onto the string rack above her.

Sonechka sat squeezed between an elderly toothless Chinese man with a long white beard and a young mother whose infant never ceased crying. Apprehension overwhelmed her, trying to imagine what lay ahead tomorrow at the dreaded Junction 86, the border town of Manzhouli. It was the Bolsheviks' last chance to search and interrogate the passengers.

She shuddered as she thought what might lie ahead, especially if Nikolai, or the commissar she had worked for in Simferopol, had discovered her whereabouts. All the while, she drifted in and out of an exhausted and nightmarish sleep.

Several hours later the train came to an abrupt halt. Everyone was ordered off and divided into males and females. A pockmarked, expressionless female screamed at Sonechka, 'Citizen, get undressed. I'm going to search you thoroughly!'

Every part of her body was examined. She had never been so humiliated. Having found nothing, the official barked at Sonechka to get dressed. Later, she heard that they were looking for opium and other drugs concealed on passengers' bodies. Fearfully, she joined the queue for the final document inspection. She could not believe that her papers were hardly looked at, allowing her to return to the waiting train.

CHAPTER TWENTY-TWO

Approaching Harbin, Sonechka was struck by the well–tended, fields. It was such a contrast with civil war-ravaged Russia. The sight of the St Nicholas icon dominating the station concourse lifted her spirits. Noticing people praying, including several Chinese, she too stopped, lit a candle and thanked St Nicholas for her deliverance.

On hearing Russian spoken, Sonechka instinctively looked out for the Cheka. She soon realised that the only person in uniform was a Chinese man directing the traffic. The vitality around her was intoxicating. Before she knew it, she had stepped out onto the street, just avoiding a rickshaw. Shaken, she asked a man the way to the address of the boarding house Sasha had given her.

He replied: 'Young lady, I would suggest you take that rickshaw. That place is in the southern part of Novy Gorod (New Town). It's too far to walk with your big bag. I'll make sure the rickshaw boy knows where to go.' He then helped her into the rickshaw.

'I understand only too well. Five years ago, when I too was in your situation, fleeing from the Bolsheviks, I no longer thought it possible for people to be civil to one another. I hope I've restored your faith in humanity.'

He bowed, touched his hat and walked away.

Sonechka had seen photographs in Vera and Alexander's library of rickshaws pulled by human beings, but she was shocked to use one. The rickshaw puller's emaciated body reminded her of the starving people she had seen in Russia. How he managed to drag his laden rickshaw, while running many kilometres a day, amazed her.

The rickshaw boy wove his way through the Chinese squatting near the railway station eating rice and drinking tea from the same handle-less bowls. She felt how different China was from Russia. However, once she got beyond the station area she thought she was back in Russia. Russian-style town houses were fronted by birch and linden trees, cobbled streets bore Russian names and the golden cupola of a church shimmered in the setting sun. When they arrived at the address Sasha had written in his letter, it was a typical two-storeyed Russian dwelling.

The door was answered by the owner of the boarding house, Nina Borisovna, a slightly built, middle-aged Russian woman wearing a floral dress. Sonechka asked if there was a vacancy. She explained that her brother, Sasha, had stayed there several years ago.

'I'm afraid all my rooms are occupied.' Then she said, 'Would you mind sharing a room with Olya, a young Russian acrobat? It would mean having to pay only half the rent.'

Sonechka agreed immediately.

Nina showed Sonechka the small, spotlessly clean bedroom upstairs. Two beds filled most of the space. The lined curtains and the clean, sweet smelling sheets came as a shock to her. These were luxuries Sonechka had not known for some time.

In the boarding house dining room Sonechka caught sight of a beautiful icon of Our Lady of Kazan, illuminated by a *lampada*. Instinctively, she made the sign of the cross, bowing her head for a few moments. Then she burst into tears.

Nina's motherly arms reached out to comfort her.

'There, there, my child,' she said. 'I understand. No doubt the icons we display remind you of what you've suffered.'

Later, she explained that for several generations this icon had blessed each bride in Nina's family. It was her most treasured possession.

Nina had Sonechka join her for some refreshments. While Sonechka drank lemon tea and relished the homemade *povidlo* (plum jam) on the freshly made *bulochki* (yeast buns), Nina produced a large notebook and opened it.

'I thought I remembered him. So I checked my records and here he is,' she said, pointing to the entry, 'Alexander Lvovich Balk, White Army officer.'

Smiling, she continued, 'Such a pleasant young man. He was one of the few to survive unharmed the 'Ice March', a horrendous ordeal for the pathetic destitute remnants of the defeated White Army. They struggled for weeks, pursued by the Reds, as they crossed the frozen Lake Baikal in temperatures reaching minus 50 degrees. Nearly all of them suffered from frostbite, war wounds or typhus. Most were penniless. For months it was terrible seeing these wretched souls wandering the streets. In our church we helped as best we could, as did other Orthodox churches in Harbin and various voluntary organisations. Many died.'

Nina went on to relate how Sasha had saved the life of an English officer during the Civil War in Siberia. In gratitude, this English officer gave him a letter of introduction to his brother in Shanghai. This letter proved invaluable. Soon after arriving there, Sasha wrote to Nina saying that the Englishman's brother, a Mr Kerr, had employed him as his chauffeur.

That night, Sonechka mulled over Sasha's incredible story; no wonder Mr Kerr had been good to him. Yet, at the time, Sasha probably considered it unlikely that he would use this letter. For, as Nina explained, in early 1919 many Russians in Harbin were convinced that the White Army would win the Civil War. Admiral Kolchak's Siberian forces, with whom Sasha served, were advancing westward on all fronts and, in combination with General Denikin's army from the Volga region, appeared to be on the verge of victory as they swept towards Moscow. Furthermore, General Tchaikovsky's army in the north looked like taking St Petersburg. But it was not to be.

Sonechka's thoughts turned to her family in Leningrad. What if Nikolai knew that Pavel's winnings had enabled her to pay for the train ticket and bribes? A kaleidoscope of images flashed before her – her desperate escape from the Bolsheviks' clutches, the Cheka terror, summary executions, counting dead bodies, starving people and, saddest of all, the faces of those she had left behind.

The next day, Sonechka wrote a letter to her family in Leningrad, telling them of her safe arrival in China, and another to Mr Kerr, in Shanghai.

CHAPTER TWENTY-THREE

Late that night, Olya, a pretty, petite acrobat, returned to Nina's boarding house. She introduced herself to Sonechka and apologised for waking her.

'I'm afraid that this evening we were the last act,' she said. 'Nina's just told me that you too have fled from the Bolsheviks.'

Lying down on her bed, Olya continued, 'Nina is a good woman. We often stay here. Two years ago, I fled to Harbin with my brother and cousin. The final straw was when the Bolsheviks shot a friend acting as a clown for criticising the regime in one of his acts. To think he'd made many more critical jokes about the Tsar without getting into trouble with the authorities.

We realised we could suffer the same fate. So here we are. We travel on what I call our 'railway circuit' between Harbin, Beijing, Tianjin [formerly Tienjin] and Shanghai. Of course, we never come here during the winter. We'd risk becoming frozen exhibits at the city's annual ice festival!'

Olya had an American army boyfriend in Tianjin. Here in this treaty port he was part of a substantial American garrison that maintained law and order. Olya's face lit up when she added that her American boyfriend promised to take her to America one day.

While awaiting a reply from Mr Kerr, Nina made Sonechka feel part of her family. She learned that, during the Civil War, Nina's husband and brother were killed fighting the Bolsheviks. The family had been landowners in southern Russia.

Nina made light of her flight from the Bolsheviks, maintaining that others had experienced much worse, especially since she was fortunate to have had enough money from the sale of gold and silver jewellery to buy her boarding house in one of Harbin's better districts.

Sonechka admired the way Nina kept her family together. Besides caring for her ailing, elderly mother, she was bringing up Natasha, her twelve-year-old daughter and her deceased brother's twenty-three-year-old son, Grigory.

Her mother was a devout Russian Orthodox believer who longed for and dwelt in the past, whereas Nina looked to the future. She made sacrifices to ensure that Natasha and Grigory had a good education. Grigory was a graduate engineer. He got his degree from Harbin's prestigious Polytechnical Institute, run, since the early 1900s, by Russian émigrés and exiles.

On her first Saturday evening in Harbin, Sonechka went with the family to the *Vsenochnaya* (vigil) at the Church of Holy Wisdom of God (St Sofia's) on Harbin's main square. The choir's singing brought a lump to her throat. With trembling hands she lit several candles before a number of icons. She thanked God for His mercy in delivering her to safety and asked for His continued guidance in the journey ahead. As she stood praying a feeling of inner peace came over her.

At the end of the service, as they left the church, Nina smiled at a digni-fied gentleman talking to a large group of people listening attentively to him. Later, she explained to Sonechka, 'That gentleman you saw surrounded by all those people, as we left the church, was Mr Gibbes, an Englishman, the tutor for many years to the Tsar's children.'[6] Though he had lived in St Petersburg since the turn of the century, he remained a British subject. The Bolsheviks, fearful of antagonising the British government should he be killed, prevented him from accompanying the Tsar and his family to Yekaterinburg, their final and fatal destination. Devastated on hearing of their murders, Mr Gibbes fled to China, settling in Harbin.

The friendliness and courtesy shown by the family and others that Sonechka met contrasted with her life under the Bolsheviks. Within no time she felt as if a great weight had been lifted from her shoulders.

Nina's nephew, Grigory, offered to show her 'his' beautiful city. The tall, dark Grigory reminded Sonechka of Volodya, the lad who had worked at Alma, Pavel's estate, and who had written her love poems the summer before she fell in love with Nikolai.

They set off into the town one fine morning, visiting several of the city's twenty or so Russian Orthodox churches. One of them still being built was supposed to be the largest and most beautiful church southeast of Moscow.

Another day, Grigory escorted Sonechka to Harbin's luxury shops. He gave her plenty of time to view the beautiful clothes and jewellery on display in the *Pristan* (Pier) quarter of the city. It was located north of the railway station extending to the southern bank of the Songhua river. Like the railway, it was a vital trade link with the rest of China. She now understood why Nina maintained that Harbin's *haute couture* rivalled the best to be found in pre-revolutionary St Petersburg's Nevsky Prospekt and Moscow's Arbat.

Sonechka soon learnt that Harbin had a remarkable history. Only twenty-five years earlier Harbin had been a remote fishing village with an abandoned distillery and a minor portage facility for handling small riverboats. Fittingly, the name Harbin means 'a drying fishing net'. The construction of the Trans-Siberian Railroad at the turn of the century had transformed this hamlet, first into a railway town and then a large prosperous city.

Before the revolution about fifty thousand Russians lived there, outnumbering the Chinese by two to one. Now the Russian population had more than tripled. Initally all sorts of people had settled there, including Trans-Siberian Railroad workers building the Chinese Eastern Railway extension. Peasants and political dissidents seeking a better life also came. It became a multi-cultural city, which was obvious from its many impressive churches, synagogues and mosques.

At this time the Harbin-based White Russians controlled the Chinese Eastern Railway, but Grigory feared for their future as the Chinese were proposing selling their half share to the Soviet Union. Grigory, like many young Russian men, wanted to go to America, but only after he had worked several years for the Chinese Eastern Railway. He was paid in gold coins, which reflected the high regard in which jobs in the Chinese Eastern Railway were held.

Sonechka told Grigory of how she had wanted to go to America. 'It was from my reading, I've long yearned to see the great Mississippi River and travel on a riverboat. Now I want to become an actress in America's new moving picture industry.'

'That's interesting. It was Mark Twain's wonderful stories that got me first thinking about going to America. My dream now is to become an aeronautical engineer. Aircraft excite me and I've heard that in America there're lots of opportunities in this field. In the meantime, I must concentrate on my railway job and forgo any distractions.' Whereupon, slipping his arm around Sonechka, he whispered, 'You have the most beautiful and bewitching blue eyes.'

Struggling to keep her emotions under control, Sonechka made light of his amorous advances, saying, 'Who knows what destiny has in store for us? One day we might even meet again in America.'

The next morning Sonechka heard from Mr Duncan Kerr. His letter said a train ticket for Shanghai would be delivered to the boarding house within three days and that Larisa von Schneider would accompany her on the journey.

CHAPTER TWENTY-FOUR

A few days later, Sonechka boarded the train for Shanghai. The sumptuous carriages took her breath away. They belonged to a bygone age. Revelling in her newfound luxury, she was woken from her reverie by a commotion on the platform. Two rickshaws, one piled high with luggage, the other bearing a passenger, had screeched to a halt. Before she knew it, a lady wearing a stunning ankle-length coat trimmed with fur had swept into the compartment, exclaiming in mellifluous tones, 'My darling, you must be Sofia Lvovna Balk.'

Speechless, Sonechka sprang to her feet, whereupon this lady embraced her and said, 'I've heard so much about you. I'm Larisa Petrovna von Schneider, but please call me Lara.'

Sonechka could not help thinking how attractive Larisa Petrovna was: liquid green eyes, soft white skin and wavy hair streaked with gold. By now she had become conscious of a delightful fragrance pervading the compartment.

'I can see there is a resemblance. What's more you have Sasha's enchanting blue eyes,' she proclaimed.

'You know my brother Sasha?'

'But, of course,' Lara retorted, as she slipped out of her coat, placed it on a hanger and eased herself onto the plush upholstered seat. 'Didn't Duncan mention I was going to accompany you to Shanghai?'

'Yes, yes, Mr Kerr said so in his cable but …' At this point Sonechka was interrupted by a gentle tap on the door. A Chinese steward entered their compartment, bowed and addressing Lara said, 'Madame, the first sitting for luncheon is being served shortly.'

Lara nodded and turning to Sonechka said, 'Come, Sonechka! You'll feel a lot better after you've had something to eat. You can tell me all about yourself later.'

Entering the dining car, Sonechka marvelled at the magnificent silverware and sparkling crystal set out on pristine starched tablecloths. On each table stood an ornate lamp, its soft welcoming glow highlighting the vase of red roses.

As they sat down several heads turned in Lara's direction. No wonder she attracted their attention, Sonechka thought. She could not recall ever having been in the presence of someone so sophisticated. Everything about her seemed perfect, from her seductively angled cloche hat, elegant knee-length frock and gorgeous silk stockings to the stylish high-heeled shoes. Even her hand movements, enhanced by manicured nails, exquisite rings and a diamond-studded wristwatch, conveyed an air of elegance.

Sonechka felt out of place. Her hair was still braided and she was wearing a simple dress, cotton stockings and thick soled shoes.

Back in their compartment, Sonechka relaxed and recounted her life in Russia.

'I can't believe that one so young could have endured so much,' Lara murmured in admiration. 'I can now see how your faith in God and your goal of going to America helped sustain you. I must say that Sasha never doubted that you had the determination to leave Russia. I like him. He was the brother I never had. Before he left I promised him that if you came to Shanghai I'd look after you.'

'Lara, I'm overcome with gratitude. Words fail me.' Sonechka recalled how their mama had asked Sasha, all those years ago, to protect and care for her, come what may.

Lara told Sonechka about her life. 'I met and married Gustav in early 1914. We were living in Tallinn, Estonia's capital. At the time I was helping my mother in her *haute couture* salon. I suppose you could call it a whirlwind romance. He was thirty-four and I was nineteen. He worked in his family's international business based in both Tallinn and Hamburg. He had learned to speak Russian when he spent several years in the St Petersburg branch. Then his father suggested he go to the Shanghai branch. We arrived here just before war broke out in Europe. My mother, a widow, didn't like what was happening in Europe, so she decided to join us.

With Gustav's business commitments and frequent travel, I became bored. So my mother and I decided to open a *haute couture* salon on Nanking Road, in Shanghai's International Settlement. That's why I was in Harbin, visiting fur traders and other suppliers. You can't imagine the problems I've had. I hardly had time to breathe. In fact, I nearly missed the train.'

Sonechka explained how Nina had told her about Sasha's heroic deeds.

Lara said that he was one of the most modest men she knew, adding that both Duncan and his brother, Iain Kerr, whom Sasha had saved, spoke Russian.

Shocked that Sonechka wanted to be a movie actress in America, Lara exclaimed, 'An actress! Oh my dear, I wouldn't dare let anyone in Shanghai know that, especially Duncan.'

Sonechka explained how she had had several leading roles in local productions and how she had hoped to train at the Moscow Arts theatre. Though Lara saw nothing wrong with Sonechka joining a local amateur theatrical group in Shanghai, earning her living as an actress was out of the question. She might just as well be a prostitute.

Sonechka was stunned.

'But surely,' she muttered, 'it's not like that in America.'

'I don't know about America,' Lara replied. 'But don't worry,' she said, giving her an affectionate pat on the arm. 'We'll find you something worthwhile to do in Shanghai. Here we like to maintain appearances.' Having shattered Sonechka's acting aspirations, Lara made an even more devastating revelation – Sonechka might well have to remain in Shanghai for some time, years even. Lara had heard that the Americans proposed severely restricting immigration to their country.

Only moments ago, Sonechka had been marvelling at her incredibly good fortune. An English officer, whose life Sasha had saved, had a Russian-speaking brother in Shanghai. She hoped the brother and Lara would help her get to America.

But that dream was now in tatters.

Unable to control the tears welling up in her eyes, she looked forlornly at Lara and began crying. Lara, biting her lip, cried out, 'Oh, my dear Sonechka, I'm so terribly sorry. I should've been more tactful and at least waited until we got to Shanghai to tell you all this. Please forgive me.'

Lara spoke fondly of her mother who was at home with her six-year-old twins, Alexander and Peter. Since their birth her mother had not worked in the salon. She enjoyed being with the twins. Shanghai was too crowded and squalid for her mother's liking. Though Lara knew some people called Shanghai the 'Paris of the East', Lara thought some parts were more like Sodom and Gomorrah. In her estimation, with its some fifty different nationalities, Shanghai was unique, not just in China, but worldwide.

She went on to explain that the city's foreigners lived in either the French Concession or the International Settlement. The International Settlement was created in 1862 from the British and American concessions. Having the administration, public services and police within a single concession was thought to be more efficient.

The French had thought otherwise. They saw this proposal as an Anglo-

Saxon plot to dominate Shanghai. The French consul, supported by the French Foreign Office, opposed the idea. Though there were only a handful of French citizens living in the concession at that time, the consul built a sumptuous town hall. The French consul was an absolute monarch in all but name.

The International Settlement created impressive business buildings, such as those fronting the Bund, while the French Concession[7] built luxurious residences and pleasure complexes. This meant that the French Concession became a desirable place to live and the International Settlement was predominately a place of work.

Chinese outnumbered foreigners by more than fifty to one. The overwhelming majority of them lived outside the foreign concessions in abject poverty. The principal Chinese areas adjacent to the foreign concessions were Nantao, the squalid old city, to the south of the French Concession, and the equally seedy Zhabei at the northern aspect of the International Settlement.

It distressed Sonechka to learn that most of the Russians were struggling to survive. Many of the non-Chinese, especially the English, shunned them. Even though they were well educated, and had held prominent positions in Russia before the revolution, their accommodation was often appalling. Only a handful had well paid jobs. Others were lucky to have low paid jobs. They were in the lower ranks of the municipal police and caretakers and night watchmen. Others were nightclub 'bouncers', bodyguards and mercenaries in the Chinese warlords' armies. Poor unfortunate wretches begged on the streets alongside destitute Chinese.

Some Russian women were forced to become prostitutes. They were known as nightclub hostesses or 'taxi girls'. They danced with anyone prepared to buy them a drink. Often it was the only way they could feed their families.

Sonechka paid scant attention to the countryside, cities and towns they passed through. She was captivated by Lara's vivid account of her exotic life, and was enjoying the unexpected luxury.

They made the brief stops at Tianjin, Beijing and Nanking, but they saw little of them. Sonechka was not aware that parts of the stark, unpopulated countryside they travelled through were infested with marauding armed bands of Chinese. These fearsome gangsters had derailed several trains on the same route, taking passengers hostage and holding them to ransom.

Sonechka pondered what else China, this mysterious, frightening and fascinating country, had in store for her.

CHAPTER TWENTY-FIVE

As Duncan Kerr had just left for England, Lara decided that Sonechka should stay with her. Sonechka could not believe her good fortune.

Travelling to Shanghai, Sonechka was surprised that none of the Chinese officials had at any stage examined her papers. And it was an even greater surprise when Lara told her that you could reside in Shanghai without having to produce visas, passports or identification documents.

Yury, Lara's Cossack chauffeur, met Sonechka and Lara at Shanghai's North Station. He ushered them into the back seat of a large grey Packard. Sonechka admired how skilfully Yury managed to weave his enormous vehicle through the crowded streets without running anyone over. For parts of the journey, a sea of Chinese appeared to fill the streets.

Lara chuckled, 'I don't know how Yury manages this vehicle. At first I was terrified. Now I don't worry. He hasn't been involved in a serious accident since he started working for me four years ago. I'm sure he thinks the Packard is his horse.'

Later in the house she added: 'Yury's a man of few words. God alone knows what he has suffered and whether his deafness is due to a war wound. He fled to Harbin from Siberia, then he settled here. He comes from near Rostov-on-Don and served in a Cossack regiment. I don't even know where he learnt to drive. You'll find there are many Cossacks here in Shanghai; they are a tight-knit community.'

They drove from a Shanghai crowded with people into leafy suburbs reminiscent of Paris or London. In a broad avenue, the motor car slowed down, then stopped in front of a formidable black iron entry gate, topped with prominent spikes. As if by magic, the gate opened their vehicle entered a short gravel driveway, flanked on either side by colourful shrubs and flowerbeds. They were immediately surrounded by Chinese servants.

The twins, Alexander and Peter, rushed to greet their mother, then Lara introduced Sonechka to her mother, Maria Nikolayevna, an elderly, elegant lady who embraced her warmly.

Sonechka was shown to a vast bedroom which she thought was like a lavish stage set. An imposing four-poster bed, with a scalloped floral bedspread dominated the room. A handsome carved dressing table with everything she could possibly need filled a bay window. This overlooked part of the garden and tennis court. It was a startling contrast to what she had previously experienced.

That night lying in bed Sonechka worried about what she was going to do and how she would live if she could not get to America. She slept badly; the mosquito nets constricted her movement and the over-head ceiling fan whirled.

It was mid-morning before she appeared. Hearing voices coming from the lawn she went out into the sunlit garden to join Maria Nikolayevna, who sat under an umbrella on the edge in front of a small ornamental rock pool, full of the traditional carp.

While they watched the twins play Maria Nikolayevna told her that the Englishman who designed the garden was a botanist who had travelled widely in search of exotic flora. The house was of English design, known as mock Tudor. One afternoon, Sonechka had afternoon tea in Maria Nikolayevna's personal quarters. The sitting room reminded Sonechka of her parents' home in the Crimea. Cherished centuries-old icons hung in the corners and *objets d'art* were everywhere. She moved carefully, fearful of damaging these treasures, and listened to Maria Nikolayevna describe the history of some of the pieces: family photographs set in exquisite frames; beautiful papier-mâché; lacquered boxes and on the walls oil paintings and watercolours of rural Russia.

Sonechka was enchanted by Maria Nikolayevna's collection of miniature animals made from semi-precious stones, given to her by Peter Alexandrovich, her late husband. They included a carved agate Dalmatian and a humorous-looking nephrite elephant. Maria Nikolayevna's prized possession was a chain necklace on which hung a number of miniature Faberge Easter eggs. Each *Paskha*, Peter Alexandrovich had presented her with one of these. Some were encrusted with sapphires, rubies and diamonds. The life-like duckling hatching from a silver egg intrigued Sonechka.

Maria Nikolayevna apologised for the clutter, explaining that she found it difficult to part with any of her possessions. It saddened her that Gustav, her son-in-law, saw her as living in a bygone age amidst a 'musty old mess of memorabilia'.

Maria Nikolayevna had had a privileged upbringing in St Petersburg and knew little of the world beyond the imperial capital until she met her husband. When they decided to marry, her family opposed the match. They wanted her to marry a landed aristocrat, not a manufacturer from Estonia. Her marriage was her salvation. She dreaded to think what might have happened to her had she remained in St Petersburg. She said that in her youth she would never have thought she would leave Russia.

Sonechka helped Maria Nikolayevna teach the twins their Russian alphabet and she read Russian fairytales to them. She could not help comparing their life to the plight of her niece, Sofia. Then she found out the twins had their problems.

Gustav, their father, was determined his sons would preserve the family's German heritage. Next year they were to go to the German kindergarten at Shanghai's Kaiser Wilhelm School. Maria Nikolayevna believed that while she was alive they would continue with their Russian, but who knew what the future held. Looking at Sonechka she remarked disdainfully, 'You know what the Germans are like.'

Sonechka did not know what to say. She had never known any Germans before.

On her arrival in Shanghai, Sonechka had written to Sasha and to her family in Leningrad. On reflection, she regretted what she had written to Pavel and Liza. She felt guilty for describing her hosts' luxurious lifestyle, knowing that Pavel had lost his estate.

She started to have nightmares about those she had left behind. She could see Nikolai interrogating Liza and Pavel in the damp dungeons of the Lubyanka. These *koshmary* (nightmares) frightened her. She invariably awoke before finding out what happened to her sister and brother-in-law.

One night she woke sobbing. She had dreamt that the Cheka had taken Sofia away from her parents and placed her in an orphanage. Sonechka was convinced this was Nikolai's revenge. She began to dread going to sleep.

CHAPTER TWENTY-SIX

Not long after her arrival in Shanghai, Lara decided to smarten Sonechka up with new clothes and shoes. She thought a visit to Antoine's, the Parisian's coiffure, would get rid of Sonechka's ghastly braided hair. Excited at the prospect of being well groomed and dressed, Sonechka could not wait to see what she would look like.

First, Lara took her to see her business. It consisted of her own small office with a telephone, another similar room for fittings and a large extension to the rear, housing the workshop, where Chinese women worked on her designs. Then there was the salon, the showpiece where the customers were seen. She had put as much thought and flair into its décor as into any of her exquisite creations. A number of long mirrors stood about the edges of the salon and the floor was covered with a thick Chinese carpet. Several other Chinese items were displayed, including a pair of black and gold lacquer screens. However, the *piece de resistance* was the plush pale-blue velvet covering the gilt-wood chairs and the low settees. Lara, pointing to a pile of garments on a nearby table, asked Sonechka to try them on, adding that they were last year's samples and with her slim and well proportioned figure they should fit.

Each time she changed, Sonechka stood and looked at herself in one or other of the full-length mirrors. Both women laughed as she struck poses like the ones she had seen in the fashion magazines at Lara's home. She could have carried on like this for hours, but Lara was making snap decisions about each piece. She sat with a ruler, pointing with it to one of two piles, the acceptable and the unacceptable. Within a short while Sonechka had a day suit and several frocks, including a stunning cocktail dress. She also had a daring pair of white slacks to be worn with a navy-blue blazer. She could not believe the transformation. Lara, however, was not surprised, saying, 'I knew all along that I could transform you into a fashionable mademoiselle.'

'I'm amazed how little time it took you to decide whether an outfit was suitable,' Sonechka replied.

'But Sonechka, I've been immersed in this business for years. From the moment I saw you, I knew you would look sensational wearing the right clothes. You'd make a wonderful model. Would you be interested?'

'I'd love to, I'd love to. B-b-but, I wouldn't know what to do,' she stammered.

'You're a natural. Apart from your good looks, you move with such grace. Of course, Sasha is a good dancer. There is something about him, as the French say, *Je ne sais quoi.*

'Really?' Sonechka said.

Smiling, Lara said, 'Sonechka, don't get any ideas. Though I was very fond of your brother, I can assure you nothing happened between us. He was too much of a gentleman for that!'

Lara reminded Sonechka that Antoine, was expecting her the next day. Sonechka asked whether she would need to speak French. Lara told her that English was by far the most important foreign language. Her English was reasonable, but she preferred to speak Russian.

Mary, who worked for Lara, spoke fluent English and French. Lara communicated with the Chinese women in the workroom through her. 'As an infant Mary was abandoned by her Chinese mother, the mistress, I believe, of a Frenchman here in Shanghai,' Lara said. 'Had the Irish nuns not rescued her she would probably have died on the city streets like so many babies and young children. She might even have become a child prostitute, but I doubt whether she would have been suitable.'

'Why's that?'

'Chinese men have a foot fetish and Mary has large feet. The smaller a woman's feet the more sensual the sexual experience. That's one of the reasons why Chinese women, from an early age, had their feet bound to stop them growing. Although banned by the government early this century, I understand the practice is still widespread outside the cities. It's very painful. The feet smell horribly from the broken bones penetrating the skin and becoming infected.'

'How disgusting! ' Sonechka exclaimed.

'It must be said that for all our faults as westerners, the Christian missionaries have liberated countless Chinese women. Beforehand, a woman had only two choices in life – to be a wife or a whore. Women like Mary have been given a sense of personal worth, reinforced by learning to read and write not only in Chinese but, as in Mary's case, English and French as well. The nuns also taught her to sew and embroider.'

As she drifted off to sleep that night, Sonechka's thoughts were of Mary's extraordinary story.

CHAPTER TWENTY-SEVEN

Early next morning the sound of voices woke Sonechka. She got up and looked out of her bedroom window. Two men in white trousers and spotless white open-necked shirts were playing tennis on the court below. The one facing her was tall with light-brown hair. The other was short and thickset with dark wavy hair. Two servants, one at each end, scampered around the court collecting balls, returning them to the server. When the game ended, the men disappeared in the direction of the house.

At breakfast, when Sonechka remarked to Lara that she had just seen two men playing tennis, Lara said, 'That was Gustav and a neighbour of ours. Providing the grass is dry Gustav plays most mornings. Though the weather is good at the moment, autumn is often wet and miserable in Shanghai. Gustav returned late last night. He had to go off early this morning. You've just missed him, but it's just as well.'

Noticing Sonechka's puzzled look, Lara added, 'He has got a lot on his mind these days with business worries. You'll no doubt hear about his woes when you meet him this evening at dinner. I must warn you he is a stickler for punctuality. By the way, Yury will take you to Antoine's at eleven o'clock this morning. I can't come, not that it matters because nobody tells our Parisian what to do.'

On entering the salon, Sonechka admired the ornate mirrors that enveloped the foyer. The receptionist gave her a gown to wear and offered her a seat. As she sat down several women, who were chatting, stopped and starred at her. Conscious of her straggly long braid, Sonechka immersed herself in a French fashion magazine.

Within no time a dapper little man with sleek black hair and a distinctive moustache, swept into the foyer and proclaimed in a resounding, high-pitched voice, '*Bonjour, ma jolie Sonya. Je suis, Antoine le Parisien.*'

Casting an expert eye over Sonechka, he gesticulated with both hands and bid her to, '*tournez, tournez plusieurs fois!*' After mumbling something to himself, he clapped his hands together in glee and declared, '*Il faut coupez, coupez, coupez!*'

Antoine then bowed and ushered the bewildered Sonechka into his plush inner sanctum, where he helped her into a stylish thick-padded chair. Picking up a pair of scissors with a theatrical flourish, he began to perform like the conductor of an orchestra. Entranced by the ambience she did not realise what he was doing until he cried out in glee, '*C'est fini!*'

Distraught that Antoine had cut off a lot of hair, Sonechka felt close to tears, whereupon the Frenchman assured her that within the hour her bob would be the envy of all. True to his word, she could not believe that the elegant young woman with the chic bob, which complemented her high cheekbones and graceful neck contours, was her. As if by magic, she felt transformed from pauper to princess.

With her increased self-confidence Sonechka felt less apprehensive about meeting Gustav that evening. Piecing together what Lara and Maria Nikolayevna had said she could not expect him to welcome her with open arms.

Heeding Lara's advice, Sonechka was on time for dinner. Just as well, for Gustav entered the drawing room on the stroke of seven. He walked straight towards her. He was tall and dignified, although disfigured by a savage duelling scar on his right cheek. 'Sofia Lvovna, I'm pleased to meet you,' he said in a clipped voice, as he gazed at her with his piercing, blue-grey eyes, nodded and clicked his heels.

Sonechka thanked her host for his hospitality, thinking all the while how dour he seemed compared to the vivacious Lara. At that moment the dinner gong sounded and with Lara they processed into the dining room.

Gustav, positioned on her left at the head of the table, then leaned towards her and said how much he admired her brother Sasha and was sad he had left for America. They had had some interesting discussions. Now, he wanted to know all about the Soviet Union.

Throughout the meal Gustav bombarded Sonechka with questions. The longer he carried on, the more prominent the scar on his cheek became until it seemed to envelop his face. At times, she felt it might just as well be the Cheka commissar in the Crimea interrogating her.

Interrupting him, Lara said, 'Gustav, my dear, I think Sonechka has answered quite enough questions for one evening.'

Ignoring her plea, he struck the table with his clenched fist and proceeded to justify his merciless interrogation and monologue.

'These are extremely dangerous times. It is vital that I get as much information as I can on what is happening. Our future depends on it. What you have told me, Sonechka, and what others who have fled Russia have said, it is just as I feared. The Bolshevik regime is unlikely to be overthrown. What is more, it could well engulf Europe. Nor are we safe here in Shanghai. Did you know Sonechka that the Soviet government is supplying the Moscow-trained General Chiang Kai-shek and his Nationalist forces with arms, ammunition and advisers? Their leading adviser here is a Jew called Mikhail Borodin.'

Sonechka was surprised, 'I had no idea there were Bolshevik activists in China.'

Thrusting his chin forwards and glowering, Gustav thundered, 'Most of the foreigners are here for one reason, and one reason alone – to make as much money as quickly as possible. They have no principles. I am only here because I'm trapped.'

Suddenly he ceased his bombastic diatribe, stood bolt upright, and announced, 'I have some urgent correspondence to attend to. Please excuse me.'

'I must apologise for Gustav. I've never seen him so overwrought,' Lara said. 'I know he's a pessimist but recently he has got a lot worse. Besides the Communist threat, Shanghai's poverty, corruption and the exploitation of its people disgusts him. Germany's defeat and the way the Allies have treated it and taken its overseas territories haven't helped. His business here in Shanghai is all that remains of a once mighty international family enterprise. It has survived here only because it's registered in Estonia. His dire predictions do depress me. Anyway, what can I do?'

Having hardly spoken during the meal, Maria Nikolayevna said, 'Poor Gustav, the Germans see everything in black and white. They don't understand other peoples, especially our Russian mind and soul.'

'What then does Gustav think of us White Russians here in Shanghai?' Sonechka asked Maria Nikolayevna.

'Not much. Wouldn't you agree Lara?' the old woman answered.

The crestfallen Lara nodded in agreement.

Later Sonechka reflected on her meeting with Gustav. She could not imagine a more unsuited couple. She wondered what had attracted Lara to him. Was it love or his wealth and position in society? Gustav must have cut a handsome figure then, with his duelling scar adding a touch of glamour. In her eyes, Lara should have married someone much younger. She now understood Maria Nikolayevna's wistful sighs when she had asked her about Gustav. Sonechka felt Gustav's return disrupted the harmonious home she appreciated so much.

CHAPTER TWENTY-EIGHT

Later that week Lara took Sonechka to a charity luncheon fashion show held in the summer garden ballroom of the sumptuous Majestic Hotel. She had donated one of her stunning beaded evening creations to be modelled and raffled for charity. Sonechka watched spellbound as the glamorous and sophisticated world of *haute couture* unfolded before her. As the models moved among the tables where the guests sat eating their meals, Lara whispered to her, 'Now you can see what I meant when I said that with your grace and beauty you would easily fit this role.'

Sonechka felt she had entered another world. The subtle aroma of jasmine wafting in from the adjacent Japanese ornamental garden was a marked change from the putrid smell that pervaded the city's narrow, crowded streets. Often she found the smell unbearable even as she got used to the jostling crowds. Moscow had been bad enough but Shanghai, built on swamp land made foetid by the untreated sewerage used for growing produce and the noxious industrial waste, was much worse. No wonder French perfume sold so well.

On their way home from the Majestic Hotel, Lara said, 'Sonechka, you know how much I want you to model for me. What's more, if you agree, you'd be doing me a favour, since my principal model is leaving to have a baby.'

Sonechka thought how lucky she was to have Lara not only as a good friend but now offering her a job. 'Though I'm delighted, and flattered, to be asked to model for you, I'm still set on going to America,' she said.

On entering the drive of Lara's home, Sonechka commented, 'I can see why you live here. It's so beautiful and there are no beggars. Even in Russia I never saw so many with such grotesque deformities.'

'I'm sorry to disappoint you,' Lara said with a mischievous smile. 'We have several beggars here in front of our home. They live among the shrubs and bushes near the entrance. It's just that you have to look hard to see them.'

'Aren't you afraid? Couldn't they rob your home?'

Chuckling, Lara replied, 'Far from it. Each group has its own territory, and heaven help those beggars who encroach on their preserve. Our servants feed them the leftovers and, in return, they protect us from intruders and robbers.'

What a bizarre arrangement, thought Sonechka. It was so different from Russia.

Sonechka was worried about her first visit to the American embassy so Lara decided to go with her. Yury drove them along the bustling Bund and as they crossed the Garden Bridge, Sonechka noticed hundreds of multi-shaped junks jostling one another. They virtually blocked out the murky water below. As their motor car slowed down, Sonechka saw the Soviet consulate, a formidable building with the Soviet hammer and sickle flag flying high above it. The American consulate was close by and Sonechka felt that was unfortunate.

At the consulate Sonechka and Lara were ushered into a large reception room and were told to sit and wait. Eventually Sonechka's name was called and she was asked to come into an office alone. A nondescript, quietly spoken, bespectacled man questioned her in Russian. To Sonechka he didn't look Russian yet he spoke the language well. He asked why she wanted to go to America and what skills did she have to offer. Was she fluent in the English language?

'I want to join my brother in America. He fled there from the Soviet Union several years ago,' Sonechka replied. 'I might not be fluent in English, but I'm practising as much as I can.'

'Were you a Bolshevik revolutionary?' the official asked the startled Sonechka. Then, after glancing at her folder, he must have realised her age and quickly passed on to the next question. Sonechka answered his questions as best she could. Gradually it dawned on her that getting into America was going to be even more difficult than leaving Soviet Russia.

At the end of the interview she asked the official how long she should be expected to wait to get to America. Sighing and shaking his head, he replied, 'I am afraid, young lady, very few people from the former Imperial Russia are now granted entry to my country – a mere two thousand each year since the recent Johnson-Reed Immigration Act. Even those Russians with skills and fluent English find it difficult. I am so sorry, unless this act is rescinded, your chances are remote.'

Sonechka's mind reeled. Had all her dreams and struggles been for nothing? Sonechka recalled how Pavel jokingly said, on her last night in Leningrad, 'Sonechka, you might go as far as Chita and decide to return, daunted by the prospect of being all alone in a strange country.' No, she had nothing to go back to, everything she held dear had been destroyed. She would rather face the unknown in China than return to the Soviet Union.

Lara knew Sonechka was devastated by the news. She left her to spend the afternoon alone in her room. Sonechka's initial instinct was to burst into tears and bury her head in her pillow, but she realised that shedding tears would not help. With her American dream in tatters, she mulled over what she should do now.

That evening Sonechka put on a brave face. Gustav, hearing about her setback, expressed his regrets, but he sympathised with the Americans saying, 'For years they opened their arms to the world and now by rejecting the masses they can afford to be selective.' Nevertheless, he was sure that if you had enough money the American government would be only too pleased to have you.

Sonechka now realised that Lara's job offer was a godsend.

Above: Sonechka's elementary school class, Alushta, 1911.

Above: Anastasia, c. 1900.

Above: Sasha Balk, San Francisco, c. 1925.

Above: Sonechka, Shanghai, 1924.

Above: Sonechka in Lara's English garden, Shanghai, 1924.

Above: Sonechka and Lara presented with flowers after a charity fashion function, 1927.

Above: Sonechka at the wheel of Lara's car, summer resort north of Shanghai, c. 1927.

Above: Sonechka with her friend Nadia, 1928.

Above: Sonechka and Lara at the summer resort north of Shanghai.

Above: Sonechka on the beach at the resort north of Shanghai.

Above: Traditional Paskha (Easter) table setting in the Icon Corner, illuminated by the lampada.

Above: Sonechka (circled) at a ball at The Majestic Hotel in Shanghai, c. 1926.

Above: Sonechka with one of Lara's dogs.

Above: Sonechka in a kimono.

Above: Sonechka at the Masquerade Ball where she met Vladimir Rossi, 1929.

Above: Portrait of Vladimir Rossi in his Imperial Horse Guards uniform, painted by Father Nikodim.

Above: Karlo Rossi, one of
St Petersburg's greatest
architects and Vladimir's
illustrious forebear.

Above: Triumphal Arch facing the Winter Palace in
St Petersburg, by Karlo Rossi, completed 1824.

Above: Vladimir's father, General
Dr Emil Karlovich Rossi.

Above: Vladimir's mother, Sofia née
Rousseau, at the time of her marriage, 1890.

Above: Dora aged five and Vladimir aged three, dressed for a walk along the Neva embankment, St Petersburg.

Above: Vladimir aged five dressed as a Cossack, on his horse at the family estate, Merkuli, Finland.

Above: Playmates and cousins playing soldiers at Merkuli. From left: Dima, Vladimir, Vera, Vasya, Dora and Kolya, c. 1900.

Above: Sofia, seated, surrounded by family.
From left: Vasya, Vera, Dora and Kolya, with
Vladimir at his mother's feet, dressed in a
Chinese costume, c. 1899.

Above: Vladimir in uniform about to enter
the Imperial Corps of Pages military school,
photographed with his father, Emil, 1903.

Above: The Rossi family on their European tour, celebrating Dora's engagement to Andrei,
1909. Vladimir is standing in front of the wagon wearing a cream panama with Andrei and
Emil on his right. Sofia and Dora are seated in the carriage.

Above: Dora with Mademoiselle Louise, the Swiss-French governess, c. 1908.

Above: Dora and Andrei feeding the pigeons in St Mark's Square, Venice, 1909.

Above: Vladimir's Corps of Pages graduation, 1913.

Above from left: Their Imperial Highnesses the Grand Duchesses Anastasia, Tatyana (standing), Maria and Olga. During the Romamov tercentenary celebrations in 1913, Vladimir was one of the equerries to the Grand Duchess Tatyana.

Above: Vladimir with his fellow officers, third from right of those sitting on the ground, winter 1914, location unknown.

Above: Vladimir wearing a Cossack hat, taken in the Rossi's Yalta home during the Civil War.

Above: Vladimir, c. 1918.

Above: View of Rossi home adjacent to the Livadia Palace orchard in Yalta, Crimea, 1919.

Above: Vladimir, the cloth-capped limousine chauffeur/tourist guide in 1920s France.

Above: Sonechka, c. 1933.

Above: Vladimir, c. 1933.

Above: Margarita and Sonechka, c. 1933.

Above: Bishop John with his 'Lady Patronesses' of St Tikhon Zadonsk Orphanage, in Shanghai. Sonechka is standing behind Bishop John, third from the left, c. 1935.

Above: Sonechka, Vladimir and Margarita on holiday at the seaside resort of Dairen, 1936.

Above: The Amah, c. 1942.

Above: Group photograph of the Political Section of the Municipal Police, French Concession, 1934. Vladimir, dressed in a white linen suit, is standing in the front row, fourth from the right.

Above: The foreign Caucasian linguists and their secretaries in the 'supremely well informed' Political Section of the French Municipal Police, 1943. It was taken when the Japanese 'gave' the French Concession to their Chinese collaborators. Vladimir is standing second from the right. His friend Aprelev is standing in the centre, sixth from the right.

Right and below right: The front and back of Vladimir's honorary ticket to the Transbaikalian Cossack's Ball.

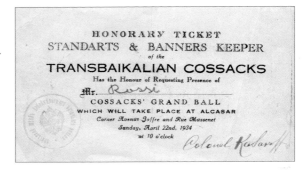

Above: Margarita, Vladimir and Sonechka, c. 1941.

Above: Vladimir and Margarita, aged twelve, 1942.

Right: Olga's christening, 19 December, 1942, at their apartment.

Above: Olga and Vladimir in the Georgia apartments garden, 1947.

Above left: Olga and her papochka, on her first birthday.

Left: The Rossi family at home in their apartment on Olga's 1st birthday, 16 October, 1943.

Above: Olga with her Amah, at the back of the Georgia apartment, summer 1947.

Above: Olga's 5th birthday party with friends, 1947. Olga is second from the left.

Above: Margarita's graduation ceremony at Sacred Heart Convent, June 24, 1947.

Right: Sonechka, Father Nikodim, Margarita and Olga, November 28, 1947, at Vladimir's grave side. Olga's smiling countenance caught on camera is a poignant reminder of how she was too young to appreciate the reality of her father's death.

Above: Margarita and Olga in front of the Georgia apartment, shortly before leaving Shanghai for America in 1948.

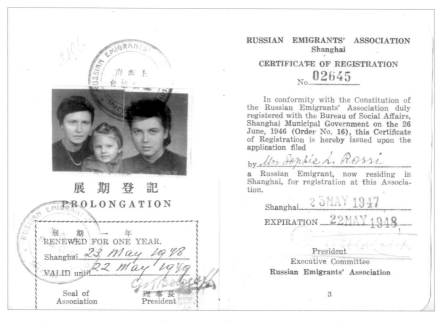

Above: Sonechka, Margarita and Olga's Russian Emigrants' Association Shanghai certificate of registration.

ERICA)

Before me,_____**Norman B. Hannah**_____, Vice Consul of
the United States of America in and for the consular district of Shanghai,
China, duly commissioned and qualified, personally appeared
Olga Rossi
who, being duly sworn, deposes and states:

    That ▓▓▓ (her) name is   **Olga Rossi**
       and ▓▓▓ (she) resides at   **3 Pershing Road,**
                                  Shanghai, China
    That ▓▓▓(she) was born at   **Shanghai, China**
       on   **October 16, 1942**
       ~~▓▓▓▓▓▓▓▓▓▓▓▓▓▓~~ _____, ~~▓▓▓▓▓▓▓▓~~
       ~~▓▓▓~~ _____ ▓▓▓▓_____

   ~~▓▓▓▓▓▓▓▓▓▓▓▓▓▓▓▓▓▓~~
    ~~▓▓▓~~

    That ▓▓▓ (she) is at present unable to obtain a valid passport or
       travel document issued by the Government to which ▓▓▓ (she)
       owes allegiance as ~~▓▓▓▓▓▓▓▓~~   ~~▓▓▓▓▓▓~~
       ~~▓▓~~
       she is stateless;

    That a signed photograph of the affiant partially impressed by
       the consular seal of the American Consulate General, Shanghai,
       China, is attached below;

    That ▓▓▓ (she) makes this affidavit to serve in lieu of a passport
       to proceed to the United States.

AND further deponent saith not.

                                        Olga Rossi by
                                    Sophie Rossi
Subscribed and sworn to before me this 2nd day of September 1948.

                                  Norman B. Hannah
                        Vice Consul of the United
Olga Rossi by Sophie   States of America at Shanghai, China
Rossi

                            DESCRIPTION OF AFFIANT

                            Height: **3'11"**
                            Color of hair: **blonde**
PHOTOGRAPH ATTACHED   Color of eyes: **blue**
AMERICAN   Distinguishing marks: **none**
CONSULAR SERVICE

FEE NO. 13838

                            Occupation: **none**

Above: The affidavit for Olga that served in lieu of a passport to gain entry to America, issued by the American Vice-Consul in Shanghai, September 2, 1948.

Right: The S.S. *General W.H. Gordon*, on which the family sailed to the USA.

S.S. GENERAL W.H. GORDON

Left: Margarita and Olga on board ship.

Left: A birthday party for one of the Russian children on board. Olga is wearing a pointed hat with Margarita on the right, wearing trousers.

Below: Sonechka, Olga and Margarita on their arrival in San Francisco on board the *General W.H. Gordon*, October 8, 1948, photographed with Sasha. After 30 years Sonechka is reunited with her brother, Sasha.

Above: Sonechka and Olga seated on the steps of Sasha's dacha at Russian River, c. 1950.

Right: Sonechka and Dora in Reading, England. Sonechka holding her granddaughter, Natasha, at her christening, June 1966.

Far right: Olga at Uncle Sasha's dacha in Russian River.

Above: Sonechka in England while living with Olga and John, c. 1966.

Left: Sonechka and Olga in Auckland, New Zealand Easter 1968.

Above: September 2006, Olga revisiting her child-hood home in Shanghai, 321 Hengshan Rd, formerly Avenue Petain in the former French Concession.

Right: This monument, commemorating the writer Pushkin, was erected by Shanghai's Russian community in 1937 – the centenary of the poet's death. Destroyed during the Cultural Revolution, it has been recently re-erected. Pushkin's original bust, hidden during the Cultural Revolution, is back in place.

SHANGHAI THE DOME
上海阿罗哈圆顶音乐餐厅
Restaurant / Tea house / Night club

Opening Hours :   m 1:00~Am02:00

Above: The former
Russian Orthodox
cathedral in the French
Concession, dedicated to
the Mother of God. It was
consecrated in 1934 and
desecrated during the
Cultural Revolution. Since
then it has had various uses
as shown by this sign (*left*).

Above: Sonechka, Olga, Dora and Margarita in Golden Gate Park, San Francisco, c 1951.

CHAPTER TWENTY-NINE

Mary taught Sonechka a great deal in Lara's workshop. In Soviet Russia, Sonechka had sewn out of necessity, using the most basic materials. The contrast with the fabrics used to create Lara's *haute couture* garments was immense. She learnt how to make fashionable clothes from the selection of the finest fabrics to the final fittings. She embroidered the intricate beadwork adorning so much of the evening wear. She came to appreciate what was involved in producing a masterpiece. Since everyone wanted their new outfit for the pre-Christmas and New Year party season, the salon staff were rushed off their feet.

Not long before Christmas, Sonechka received her first letter from Liza. The family were well. Sofia had started nursery school in September. She was an avid reader with a wonderful imagination. Liza and Pavel continued to work in the same jobs. She wrote that Shura had disappeared; they thought he was probably dead. Sonechka had the horrible premonition that she might be responsible for his death. She wondered if a fellow Chekist had assassinated him in Berlin. On the other hand, Shura had relatives there. Perhaps he had defected to the West?

Though Lara and her mother did not attend the Russian Orthodox Church regularly, they enjoyed the celebration of Christmas. According to the Russian Orthodox calendar it was on January 7.

On Christmas Eve, Sonechka, Lara, Maria Nikolayevna and the twins, attended the vigil service at the Russian Orthodox Church in the poverty-stricken Chinese district of Zhabei. The substantial brick church was built in the early 1900s, when Imperial Russia had a significant presence in Shanghai. It was one of a number of mission churches in China funded by the Tsar which served Russia's expatriate community before the revolution. Few foreigners lived in Zhabei, the Chinese district adjacent to Hongkou. Those who did were mainly impoverished White Russians.

As they drove along the streets in Hongkou and Zhabei, Sonechka was amazed to see many of the shop signs written in Russian. She could not help noticing the provocatively dressed Russian women loitering on the pavements. Nearing the church there were hordes of mainly Chinese beggars of all ages. They stretched out their hands, hoping to attract the attention of passers-by.

The Christmas star dominated the church entrance. Inside, fir tree branches adorned the iconostasis and columns. The church was ablaze with hundreds of candles lit by worshippers. They stood transfixed, reverently crossing themselves and each beseeching the Lord's mercy in his own way.

Conscious of the twins standing beside her, Sonechka's thoughts turned to her niece, Sofia, and to Liza. Where would they be spending this holy night? She thanked God for sending such a good family to look after her. She prayed that a way be found for her to join Sasha in San Francisco.

Recently, she had received two letters from Sasha. He was doing everything possible to have her join him in America. When he learned that because of his age, over thirty, he would find it difficult to get a job as a qualified geologist, he had abandoned his university course. Though disappointed, he felt fortunate to have plenty of work as a house painter.

For Sonechka the Christmas Eve festivities at Lara's brought back nostalgic memories of Christmas with her family in the Crimea. Lara and Gustav had invited Hans, a Russian-speaking Baltic German, and his Russian wife, Yelena, whom they had known since they first arrived in Shanghai. In the drawing room Lara and Sonechka, with the servants' help, had set up a splendid Christmas tree. Having lit the candles, on their return from church, Lara threw open the double doors to the drawing room as Maria Nikolayevna and Gustav, taking the twins by the hand, led them through. Overjoyed, the boys rushed forwards to open the presents lying, beautifully wrapped, at the foot of the tree. In a firm but kindly voice Gustav told the boys to sit down, as everybody had to wait their turn while he handed out the presents.

Sonechka was delighted with her present from Lara. It was an embroidered blue silk shawl fringed with long tassels. They then moved to the dining table, which was laden with Christmas fare surrounded by Christmas decorations.

Before long Gustav and Hans, speaking in Russian, were deep in conversation. Sonechka found what they had to say revealing. Gustav asserted that an Austrian, Adolf Hitler, could not only be Germany's but Europe's salvation as a bastion against Bolshevism. He regretted that a beer-hall *putsch* in Munich over a year earlier (1923), led by Hitler, had failed. Gustav believed that only someone with Hitler's courage could prevent the Bolsheviks taking control of Europe.

Hans disagreed. He considered Hitler a calculating, embittered little corporal whose ambition was to be a fascist dictator like Benito Mussolini. Gustav felt Hans maligned Hitler.

The men continued to argue. Gustav, who had been in Germany the previous year, thought that the once-prosperous middle class had been destroyed and its spirit broken by the hyperinflation. He was distressed by the number of Germans who had committed suicide.

Throughout the meal the ladies listened politely to the two expatriates' heated discussion, not daring to interrupt them.

Later the plump middle-aged Yelena asked Sonechka how she got to Shanghai. When Sonechka had finished telling her story, Lara told her that Yelena had helped many penniless fellow Russians settle in Shanghai. She and other well-established Russian ladies had organised many charity fund-raising functions, including the one at the Majestic Hotel that Sonechka had attended. Sonechka was upset to learn that a few well-to-do Russians were fearful their destitute compatriots would lower the standing of the white man in the eyes of the Asians. So they wanted nothing to do with them. This meant that few Russian refugees got good jobs. Most did degrading menial work for miserable wages.

Maria Nikolayevna added that it was not only Shanghai's foreign nationals who wanted nothing to do with stateless Russians, but the entire world. When the fate of hundreds of Russians who had fled Vladivostok hung in the balance the world turned its back on them. Sonechka heard how General Glebov had arrived in Shanghai with the remnants of a Cossack force. Knowing that no country would accept them, he had hoped they could settle in Shanghai. He was mistaken. Though they were allowed to come ashore during the day, at night they had to return to their vessel, anchored just off the Bund.

Some well-to-do Baltic Germans, resident for many years in Shanghai, advocated that these men return to the Soviet Union. When they made this proposal to Glebov's Cossacks, the Cossacks threatened to kill them.

So many of the White Russians were not only destitute and stateless, they were also subject to Chinese law. If convicted they served their sentence in the vile Chinese prisons.

In contrast, before the revolution, the Imperial Russian consulate offered Russian citizens the same protection which other foreign nationals took for granted. Now that the Soviets occupied the Russian consulate there was no question of Sonechka seeking its protection in the event of her falling foul of the Chinese authorities. Yelena told her that those White Russians who had considered storming the Soviet consulate realised it would be futile.

She now understood why some Russian women married foreign nationals, no matter how terrible or ugly they might be, just to get a foreign passport.

CHAPTER THIRTY

Early in the New Year Sonechka did her first modelling job for Lara. She wore several day frocks, suits and evening dresses for Francoise Dupont, who came to the salon with her mother. Francoise needed a trousseau for her September wedding in Paris. They were shown swatches of material and Francoise was measured for a toile. Sonechka was relieved that Lara liked the way she modelled her garments.

Since the mother of the bride and Francoise disagreed on what items to buy, they decided to return the next week. Francoise's lack of interest in her appearance baffled both Sonechka and Lara. Her elegant mother, a good client of Lara's, paid great attention to appearance. Lara had no doubt that, if it were not that she needed a trousseau, Francoise would never have come. She was marrying a distant cousin, a banker and they would live in Paris.

Francoise longed to be a scientist like Madame Curie, not the chic Parisian her mother wished her to be. Despite Francoise's rather large Gallic nose, Sonechka thought that with Lara's careful grooming and the correct wardrobe Francoise could be as elegant as her mother.

Since Francoise seemed to be so unenthusiastic about her forthcoming marriage, Sonechka wondered why she had become engaged. 'That's a good point,' Lara quipped. 'It baffled me too. Then I discovered that Francoise's fiancé, like the Duponts, comes from one of France's oldest Protestant banking families. So, the respective families decided the couple would make a suitable match. They met last year when the Duponts returned to France. Monsieur Dupont is head of the Shanghai branch of a French bank. They lost a great deal of money when the Bolsheviks closed down the Russian stock exchange and seized all foreign owned businesses without compensation. Her fiancé's family had not invested in Russia and remains very wealthy. That's reason enough for Francoise's parents wanting the couple to marry.'

It intrigued my mother that the republican French still arranged marriages. She understood they were a relic of such 'backward' countries as her

Imperial Russia. When Francoise next returned to the salon, Sonechka hardly recognised her. Antoine had stylishly bobbed her limpid locks and her hands were beautifully manicured. She wore a faint touch of lipstick. It reminded Sonechka of her own transformation from a dowdy duckling to an elegant swan only a few months earlier.

Francoise ordered a number of the outfits which Sonechka had modelled. Francoise had very definite ideas about the design of the wedding dress. She was delighted when Lara found a wedding dress material similar to the family's treasured heirloom, a Chantilly lace wedding veil.

The skill and patience that Mary demonstrated in making Francoise's wedding dress impressed Sonechka. Admiring Mary's masterpiece, Sonechka said she hoped one day to marry in a similar gorgeous creation. Mary said that she did not believe she would ever get married. As a Eurasian neither the white nor the Chinese men wanted her as a wife; they were equally despised by the Europeans and Chinese. She told Sonechka that though she had a Chinese boyfriend, his wealthy parents would never let him marry her. She appreciated the Irish nuns who had given her such a wonderful education. Furthermore, she was quite satisfied working for Lara. It enabled her to be independent.

Sonechka found it difficult to believe that Shanghai could treat such an attractive, pleasant and talented young woman like Mary so badly. Perhaps, Sonechka thought, Shanghai really was full of hard-hearted people exploiting one another. Compared to Mary's circumstances her situation was tolerable.

As the months passed Sonechka's life fell into a familiar pattern. She became accustomed to the heat and the stench of the summer months and the bitter winter cold winds that blew grimy grit into one's eyes.

She made regular inquiries at the American Consulate but to no avail. She was now resigned to staying in Shanghai, accepting that it was God's will. By no means could she describe herself as unhappy. After all, besides enjoying her work at the salon and meeting Lara's extensive clientele, she had made friends with several Russians at the church.

On several occasions Sonechka mentioned finding somewhere else to live. However, each time it upset Lara and Maria Nikolayevna that she should consider leaving them. She was now part of their family, with even Gustav's blessing. She was touched that the twins considered her to be their favourite 'aunt'.

Letters from Liza were infrequent and very brief, making Sonechka feel even more cut off from her loved ones.

CHAPTER THIRTY-ONE

One spring afternoon, Duncan Kerr telephoned Lara at the salon. He had just returned from England. Lara invited him for dinner the next evening. There would be just the three of them. Gustav was away on business and Maria Nikolayevna confined to bed with a chill. Sonechka looked forward to meeting the man who had been so kind to her and Sasha.

After completing his university engineering degree Duncan had, before the war, worked for his family's shipping business in St Petersburg. Russia held fond memories for him. It opened his eyes to a privileged world that he had no idea existed.

The next evening while waiting for Duncan to arrive, Lara suggested they celebrate the success of the salon's spring collection with champagne. Number one boy had just filled their champagne glasses when Duncan was ushered into the drawing room. He was a tall, handsome man, with wavy auburn hair, and light-blue eyes. He strode towards Lara and kissed her hand. Then, turning to Sonechka, he smiled and said how delighted he was to meet Sasha's sister.

In her carefully rehearsed hesitant English, Sonechka said, 'I can not thank you enough for what you have done for my brother and me. Words fail me.'

Replying in Russian, Duncan said, 'Think nothing of it. Any decent man would have done the same. After all, Sasha risked his life to save my brother, Iain.'

Sonechka replied, 'I look forward to meeting Iain, should he come to Shanghai.'

'Unfortunately, my brother keeps poor health and is therefore unlikely to travel outside England, but his son Angus is due in Shanghai soon.'

During dinner Duncan, in a gallant gesture, raised his glass to 'Russian beauty'. He spoke fondly of his family in England.

Sonechka saw how Duncan's face lit up when Lara asked if he had had a good hunting season.

Duncan spoke eloquently about the joys of hunting in England, where they chased a real quarry, the fox. It was a far cry from the swampy, undulating, smelly farmland where Shanghai's version of the foxhunt, the Paper Chase Hunt, was held. Even so, he believed that Sonechka would find this hunt an enjoyable outing. Much closer was the opening meet of the Shanghai Race Club and Duncan offered to escort both of them there. His ponies would be competing. To Sonechka, Duncan seemed the epitome of the English gentleman she had read about. The light conversation, pleasant food and wine made the meal pass quickly.

The next morning, two bouquets of flowers arrived, one for Lara and the other for Sonechka.

'Well, well. What an impression you've made on our Duncan. I've not seen him so animated for a long time,' Lara said. Sonechka admired the beautiful bouquet and read the card. She was touched beyond words. Nobody had ever sent her flowers before and to think they came from such a charming man.

Lara told her that Duncan had been separated from his wife for a number of years. She preferred living near her family in their manor house in rural England. Lara had never met her.

In Shanghai, Duncan was a popular host and escorted many society ladies, all of whom seemed to adore him. Provocatively, catching Sonechka's eye, Lara stated that now they would have competition from a young Russian beauty.

'Surely there are dozens of elegant young English ladies here in Shanghai who would be much more suitable than me.'

'Stop and think of the ones you've seen at the salon,' Lara retorted. 'Few are what one would call beautiful. Just ask any man here in Shanghai how English women compare with the Russians. Of course they consider us more attractive. Although according to the numerous articles and letters in the foreign newspapers and magazines, the women see us as evil, luring and trapping their husbands and fiancés. We're given all sorts of villainous descriptions including, "voluptuous vampires from Vladivostok".'

Sonechka was reminded of the Russian women she had seen walking the streets in Hongkou and Zhabei when she went there for the evening church service. She thought Duncan would be embarrassed to be seen in her company. Lara assured her that he was not typical of those who lived in Shanghai. They condemned Russian women, yet had them as their mistresses.

Sonechka was flattered that Duncan Kerr should not only be her benefactor but that Lara considered him a suitable escort.

On the opening day of the Shanghai Race Club's meet, Sonechka woke early in eager anticipation of her debut into what Lara described as *le beau monde* of Shanghai.

The last few days at the salon had been hectic. Everybody wanted to be seen wearing 'the outfit' at one of the highlights of Shanghai's social calendar. Sonechka tried on several dresses with matching coats, choosing the *eau de nil*, which she considered best suited her colouring.

Staying up late the night before, she had put the finishing touches to her stylish cloche hat, covering it with appliqué flowers. A pair of cream gloves and a clutch bag, lent to her by Lara, completed her ensemble. Lara chose a similar outfit in a dusty rose colour.

At 10.45am, Duncan arrived in his ink-black motor car with Vasily, his Russian chauffeur, at the wheel. Catching Sonechka's eye, he smiled, pursed his lips and nodded his approval.

Once seated in Duncan's box, Lara told Sonechka that before her was the prized playground that Duncan and his fellow Englishmen so enjoyed.

Taken aback, Duncan interjected, objecting to being described as English. He proudly proclaimed that he was Scottish. He gently admonished Lara, pointing out that the English were just one of four peoples who lived in the British Isles.

'Come on, Duncan, since you were born in India, by rights you should be an Indian,' Lara retorted. 'It mystifies me why you want to be identified with the likes of Jardine and Matheson, the Scots pirates, who made a fortune from smuggling opium.'

'Sonechka, this is a little game we like to play. Lara likes to provoke me. She knows how proud I am of my Scottish heritage'. It baffled Sonechka that Duncan was so determined to be identified as a Scotsman. To her he was so English.

Duncan explained that the races had been held from the time when the first British settlers arrived in Shanghai, nearly eighty years earlier. The racecourse and the extensive facilities for a wide range of sports and recreational activities occupied more than 25 hectares of prime real estate right in the heart of the city. For Lara this was confirmation that the English were obsessed with sport.

It amused Sonechka that Duncan's racing colours, of blue background with a white cross of St Andrew, were the same as his family's shipping line and that of the Scottish flag. When she mentioned this to Duncan, to her utmost surprise, he pointed out that when Peter the Great founded the Russian Imperial Navy it flew the cross of St Andrew as a flag. Most of the officers had been Scots, including the admiral of the fleet. They were representative of the numerous Scots who made their mark in Imperial Russia.

Sonechka and Duncan went to examine the ponies in the paddock. Descending the main stand's marble staircase, Sonechka became aware of Duncan's hand supporting her arm. As he guided her through the jostling crowds, conscious of his protective nearness, she felt serene. He introduced her to several of the passers-by, whose curious glances and nods in her direction were unsettling.

Before entering the paddock area, the two of them visited the Buddhist shrine where the Chinese lit red candles as they prayed for a win. Fascinated, Sonechka watched them place their offerings with reverence at the feet of the impassive Buddha statue. An intense fragrance filled the air. Though Sonechka did not light incense or a red candle, she made a wish that Duncan's ponies would triumph.

Approaching the paddock area Sonechka was taken aback; these ponies were so ugly with their short necks and stubby frames. Duncan explained that despite their appearance these Mongolian ponies were better suited to Shanghai than the English thoroughbred horses that raced in England. Sure-footed and with amazing stamina, they were ideal for the terrain on which the Shanghai Paper Chase Hunt was held. But being stubborn, they were difficult to break in and handle, such that the best of riders could be unseated.

Sonechka was struck by the many Chinese race-goers. Duncan told her that the Chinese were phenomenal gamblers and without them the club's finances would be shaky. Had the foreign die-hards got their way, and not allowed the Chinese to attend the meetings after World War I, their club would not have been able to maintain the racecourse, let alone run all the other sporting and recreational facilities. As it was, before World War I some wealthy Chinese, fed up with being excluded from the exclusive foreigners' racecourse, decided to build their own track on the outskirts of the city. Fortunately, Shanghai was more than capable of supporting both clubs.

One of Duncan's Russian stable hands presented Ruslan, the pony that was about to race, to Sonechka. She presumed that Duncan had named Ruslan after Pushkin's epic poem 'Ruslan and Lyudmila'. However, it transpired the Russians who traded in Mongolian ponies had already named it. Also many Russian exiles had jobs as trainers, jockeys, riding instructors, grooms, racecourse attendants and stable hands. Duncan's best jockey, a Cossack, was riding Ruslan. Duncan suggested that this Cossack could be a descendant of Genghis Khan's Golden Horde, who had ridden the very same breed.

Walking within the racecourse complex Sonechka saw many different Chinese street entertainers. The acrobats reminded her of Olya, the Russian acrobat with whom she had shared a room in Harbin.

Lara had chosen to remain in the box and watch the world go by. From this panoramic position she revelled in spotting the best-dressed women, several of whom were her clients. For Lara the fashion parade, not the horses, held her attention. As far as she was concerned a horse bit at one end and kicked at the other.

Ruslan duly won his race. Duncan unreservedly attributed the victory to Sonechka's presence. She was thrilled when Duncan invited her to be his partner at the Shanghai Race Club ball.

CHAPTER THIRTY-TWO

Throughout the ten days of the Shanghai Race Club spring festival the salon was busier than ever. On several occasions Mary deputised for Lara, allowing her to attend various business-related functions held during work hours.

One afternoon Sonechka asked Mary if she was upset by the rude way some clients treated her. With an air of resignation, Mary said that she had become used to this long ago, adding that it could be a lot worse. For, since she looked more European than Chinese and did not speak in the characteristic 'sing song' pidgin English of the Eurasians, most of Lara's clients did not take her for a Eurasian. They considered her as either English or Southern European, brought up in Shanghai. However, those who knew or suspected her of being a Eurasian could be rude and some even spoke to her in pidgin English. Laughing, Mary said that Lara mused that the rudeness of some could well be because they suspected their husbands of having a Eurasian mistress.

Though Sonechka used pidgin English speaking to the Chinese, she did not know its origin. Mary explained that it was a mixture of languages: Portuguese, Chinese, English and Indian. It had evolved over hundreds of years from the commercial contacts made by European traders with their Chinese counterparts. Virtually all foreigners spoke it, except for the handful who had learnt Cantonese, Shanghainese or Mandarin. Those Shanghailanders who spoke only pidgin never got to know the Chinese properly. They assumed they were stupid, since pidgin had a vocabulary of only a few hundred words. The well-educated Chinese found this humiliating.

Sonechka again pondered on how different China was from her Motherland. The more she learned about China, the more of an enigma it became. She marvelled how Mary could be so reconciled in accepting her lot in life. Was this the Asian fatalism she had read about?

Sonechka sensed that Mary found it difficult to believe that Duncan had invited her to accompany him to the prestigious Shanghai Race Club ball.

On the other hand, Mary enthusiastically helped her create a stunning gown to suit the occasion. Though thrilled to be going to the ball, Sonechka was worried that she did not know the latest dance craze, the Charleston.

'But Sonechka, judging by the way you model, you'll pick it up easily. Tai, my Chinese boyfriend, is coming here. I'm sure he can teach you in no time. I must warn you, though, he'll take offence if you don't treat him as an equal. He knows a great deal about the wider world, having studied at an American university and in France. Probably best not to discuss politics. He has very definite views on the subject.'

Tai, a dapper young Chinese man, wearing a well-cut western suit, arrived later that afternoon at the salon. As Mary had predicted, Sonechka quickly learned the steps to the Charleston.

After Sonechka had thanked Tai they sat down together with Mary for what Sonechka assumed would be a little light conversation. Instead, Tai's pleasant manner towards her altered abruptly. He sneered, wagged his finger at her, and bellowed in Russian, 'You, who lead such a pampered life, know nothing about the terrible suffering of my people.'

Flabbergasted, Sonechka stammered, 'B-b-b-but I do. I can see similarities here in China to the suffering in my country under the Bolsheviks.'

He ranted on, 'Your rotten Imperial Russia deserved to fall. China should do what the Bolsheviks did – free the proletariat, repressed by reactionaries like you. Wherever the white imperialists go, such as in my country, they create a hell on earth. Untold millions are exploited, starved, mutilated and murdered. Not content with that, the white man has tricked and kidnapped hundreds of thousands of my people. Those of us who work for you are called coolies. We do work you either refuse to do, or consider beneath you. Throughout much of the world we're slaves in all but name.'

While Tai carried on in this vein, Mary briefly left the room. On her return she gently reproached him for continuing to shout at Sonechka, whereupon he stormed out of the salon.

Mary continued the attack, 'Living in Lara's luxurious home, how can you possibly appreciate the plight of the downtrodden Chinese. You bourgeois Russians deserve your fate. Before long you'll be forced to flee for your lives, just like all the other imperialist exploiters.'

Sonechka thought it unbelievable that Mary, the mild-mannered person who had been so good to her, could be so virulent. Nor could she believe that Mary shared Tai's fearsome hatred of foreigners.

She toyed with telling Lara about Tai and Mary's outbursts, but decided against it. Reflecting on what Tai had said, she could see why he had learnt Russian, the pathway to the Bolshevik paradise propounded by Lenin.

Sonechka was surprised to receive a letter from Olya, the Harbin acrobat. She wrote that next week she was coming with Roy, her American husband, to Shanghai. They would be there for three days before boarding a ship bound for America. She wanted to know where they might meet. Sonechka sent a telegraph suggesting the salon would be the best place.

When Olya entered the salon with Roy, a powerfully built, fresh-faced young man, she warmly embraced Sonechka. Sonechka's transformed appearance and *haute couture* job amazed Olya. While proudly showing Sonechka her wedding ring, Olya explained that Roy came from a farm in Ohio where they planned to live. She was looking forward to settling down and having a family.

She wondered whether Sonechka still intended joining her brother in America and fulfilling her dream of becoming a film actress there. Though Sonechka made light of her not being able to get to America, she envied Olya for her success in doing so.

Sasha's last letter had spelled out how difficult it had become for stateless Russians to enter America. Trying to console Sonechka, he wrote that she was probably better off in Shanghai, where she was well cared for and had rewarding work. He thought it unlikely, with her limited English, that she would find a comparable job in America. She was delighted to hear that he had fallen in love with the young woman he wrote of in a previous letter, Arlene, an arts student from San Francisco's Nob Hill.

Sonechka was concerned that she had not heard from Liza for some time. Perhaps the censors had destroyed her letters? Sonechka wondered whether her letters to Liza had met the same fate.

On Pentecost Sunday, Sonechka went to the Divine Liturgy. After the service the congregation was invited to have lunch in the *trapeza* (dining hall). Sonechka sat with two sisters, Nadya and Masha, from Harbin. Masha, who spoke English well, worked as a clerk in a warehouse and Nadya, a qualified dentist, worked as an assistant to an established Russian dentist. Like Sonechka they had been in Shanghai a year. Complimenting Sonechka on her fashionable clothes and hairstyle, they were not surprised to learn she worked as a model.

Sonechka found it refreshing to meet these two Russian women of her own age. Nadya and Masha's friendliness was infectious. Sonechka readily accepted their invitation to see where they lived. It was a Russian boarding house in Hongkou. Though sparsely furnished, the room that Nadya and

Masha shared on the second floor was clean and compact, reminiscent of the boarding house where Sonechka had stayed in Harbin. She said little about where she lived, and told Nadya and Masha they were fortunate to have found such a good boarding house. Sonechka realised that they were well off compared to many unemployed Russian exiles living nearby. Their landlady, who had fled from Irkutsk with her family during the Civil War, fed them well.

The afternoon passed quickly, making Sonechka loathe to leave her new-found friends.

CHAPTER THIRTY-THREE

One morning, Mary and Sonechka set out together by rickshaw to visit a client. They had not travelled far on Nanking Road when a sea of crazed protesters, shouting, gesticulating and brandishing placards, suddenly surrounded them. Flung out of the rickshaw, Sonechka fell on the ground, landing heavily on her back. Dazed, she tried to get up. Her rickshaw boy was nowhere to be seen. Desperate, she looked for Mary. Chinese, mainly youths, their eyes full of hate, screamed and spat at her. Terrified, she imagined herself being torn apart limb by limb. She had given up all hope when, above the bedlam, she heard gunfire. Her tormentors fled. Mary appeared as if from nowhere and helped Sonechka to her feet. After taking a few steps she assured Mary that she was not injured. Mary, who had hidden under the upturned rickshaw, explained that the rioters were Nationalist students and trade unionists demanding the expulsion of all foreigners from China.

One of Sonechka's attackers looked remarkably like Tai, Mary's boyfriend. But surely, Sonechka thought, she must be mistaken.

Lara, having heard the gunfire, and seeing the rampaging rioters, was greatly relieved when they both returned unscathed to the salon.

That evening, on hearing about Sonechka's ordeal, Gustav said, 'It is only a matter of time before the Chinese will evict all foreigners from China'.

Shanghailanders found it difficult to believe that such an outburst of hatred towards them had happened in their very midst. Protesters had been shot dead and others wounded by the International Settlement's British police. Chinese Nationalists commemorated the uprising by declaring it the revered May 30, 1925, Nanking Road Incident.

For the forthcoming ball, Mary and Sonechka worked late in the evenings to complete the intricate beading on Sonechka's calf-length delphinium-coloured chiffon and crepe de Chine evening frock.

All eyes turned in Sonechka's direction when she entered the drawing room for the pre-ball cocktails. Lara's English near-neighbours, Cynthia and

Gerald Parsons, and Duncan had been invited. Duncan, with a twinkle in his eye, gallantly raised his glass to his hostess and her delightful debutante.

For Sonechka the ball was memorable. The ballroom was tastefully decorated, two excellent orchestras, most of whose members were Russian, played and guests dressed in their finery enjoyed the food and wine. The conversation was light and entertaining. On the dance floor, enveloped in Duncan's embrace, Sonechka's cares melted away.

After the ball my mother felt confident enough to accept Cynthia Parsons' offer to teach her to play tennis. Even Lara thought it a good idea, maintaining it would allow her to meet more people. Cynthia's mother thought she should also learn to play croquet. According to her it was a game that not only tested one's wits, but also taught one how to deal with losses gracefully.

It surprised Sonechka that the Parsons spoke of England as 'home', despite both having been born in India and having lived there much of their lives. Cynthia had come to Shanghai from Bombay in 1922 and Alice, her widowed mother, followed her from Bombay the next year.

The tall and slender Cynthia paid scant attention to her appearance. However, when the occasion demanded it, she could make herself attractive. In view of Gerald's prominent position at the bank, Cynthia's life could have been one long party. Instead, she involved herself in numerous charities and good causes, just as she had done when part of Bombay's expatriate community. A member of the Church of England, Cynthia made no secret of her Christian faith being the driving force in her life.

Gerald Parsons held an important position at the newly built Hong Kong Shanghai Bank. With its magnificent Italianate dome, this splendid edifice dominated the Huangpu River frontage known as the Bund. It housed Shanghai's most powerful banking institution and financed much of China's exports and imports.

The morning after the ball, Vasily, Duncan's chauffeur, burst into the salon bearing an enormous basket of flowers. As he handed Sonechka an envelope he announced that these flowers and note were from Mr Kerr. He was to wait for her reply.

Delighted with the flowers, Sonechka read Duncan's brief note and told Vasily she would be pleased to accept Mr Kerr's dinner invitation.

On seeing the flowers, Lara exclaimed, 'Duncan is not wasting any time!'

That evening, sitting beside Duncan in his motor car, Sonechka was overwhelmed when he presented her with an attractively wrapped package, asking her to open it. She opened it to find an elegantly shaped bottle of

Coco Chanel's exotic perfume, No 5, which had recently taken the fashion world by storm, Sonechka was lost for words. Never before had she been given such an expensive perfume. Duncan told her that Ernest Beaux, Coco Chanel's perfumier who made Chanel No 5, was a White Russian.[8] As they were ushered through the restaurant, several men greeted Duncan, whereas their women companions pointedly looked away. Sonechka presumed that her distinctive Slavic features prompted them to snub her for being a stateless Russian ensnaring a wealthy eligible Englishman.

She sat at the table, pondering the icy reception the women in the restaurant had given her.

Later Duncan clasped Sonechka's hands in his. Looking into her eyes he said that he would be the most fortunate man in Shanghai should she agree to be his alone. Though she thought Duncan a charming, attentive and attractive man, it frightened her that he wanted to have her 'all for himself.' Speechless, all she could do was to stare at him through tear-filled eyes as he pleaded with her. She had no wish to be his mistress. Finally, realising the futility of his entreaties, Duncan apologised and begged to be forgiven for his forthright declaration of love. He hoped that one day she might reconsider his proposal.

When she arrived home, Lara beckoned Sonechka to join her in the drawing room. Putting on a brave face, she answered Lara's searching questions.

However, Lara, the seasoned observer of human nature, sensed that Sonechka wanted to be on her own. As they bid one another goodnight, Lara, embracing Sonechka affectionately, said she could see that Duncan, from the moment he set eyes on her in this very room, had been smitten.

Sonechka slept little that night. Though she had vowed that she would never be anyone's mistress, she could not help wondering what life with Duncan Kerr would be like.

At breakfast, noting that Sonechka was much more subdued than usual, Lara asked if she still wanted to attend the end-of-season summer cocktail party at the race club in two days. Sonechka maintained that she was looking forward to going, but her answers were not full of her usual enthusiasm. This made Lara ask her what had happened with Duncan the night before. Shedding her pretence, Sonechka told Lara about his proposal. It heartened her that Lara, who confessed that she never thought Duncan would become so besotted by her, understood her predicament.

The evening at the race club was to be a great success. Duncan behaved impeccably, so no one but Lara was aware of Sonechka's dilemma.

The main topic of conversation was the forthcoming holiday exodus from Shanghai's stifling summer heat. Alone on the veranda, Duncan again apologised for his hasty proposal. It distressed him that he had upset her. On the other hand, he remained hopeful that she would one day agree to be his constant companion. Soon he was going on business to Hong Kong, and would return at the end of September.

One of Lara's clients, who had a seaside resort not far from Shanghai, offered Lara her villa for the summer. Lara thought it would be good for Sonechka to go there. Besides the change of scenery and sea air, she could help Maria Nikolayevna look after the boisterous twins. Lara could spend only a week with them, since she had arranged to go on her annual buying trip to Harbin. Mary was left in charge of the salon.

CHAPTER THIRTY-FOUR

Duncan was forever in Sonechka's thoughts. She so wanted to be his one and only love, but how could she without being his mistress? Doubtless, many women in her situation would not hesitate to accept his proposal. She bitterly recalled her relationship with Nikolai. 'Oh, dear Lord,' she cried, 'why do I have to fall in love with men who either do not believe in marriage or can't marry?'

During the week that Lara was with them at the seaside, Sonechka learned more about Duncan. Lara pointed out that, although Duncan was married, he and his wife had been separated for some time. She refused to divorce him. An excellent horsewoman, she loved English country pursuits. She hated the East, particularly the humid, foul-smelling Shanghai. What's more she had little time for its expatriate community. Lara had met their two daughters when they spent several months with their father the year before. They were pleasant young women but, like their mother, disliked Shanghai.

Lara pitied Duncan. During the time she had known him, he had escorted a number of eligible women without any word of scandal. She mused that Duncan, the perfect English gentleman, seemed to have everything except a loving wife. She thought Sonechka should overlook the fact that he was a married man. After all, she would have a wonderful life, free of material worries, cared for by a man who adored her.

Sonechka received several newsy letters from Duncan. In them, he made no mention of their relationship. He looked forward to seeing her on his return.

Once back from the seaside, Sonechka resumed her friendship with Nadya and Masha, whom she invited for tea at Lara's. They were most impressed by the home and garden. Sonechka could not believe that it was only a year since she had arrived.

On his return to Shanghai, Duncan contacted Lara, telling her that Angus, his nephew, had arrived from England. Lara invited them both for dinner.

Sonechka was in two minds. Though she longed to see Duncan again she had no wish to continue tormenting him.

On first meeting Angus, Sonechka was surprised how much he resembled Duncan in both build and voice. Sitting opposite him, she was struck by how his mannerisms mirrored those of Duncan, seated beside her. She felt he could easily have been taken for his son. She was touched by the profuse tribute he paid her brother, Sasha, for having saved his father's life.

Though her English had improved considerably since arriving in Shanghai, Sonechka found it difficult to follow rapid English table talk. Had Duncan not acted as her interpreter, Sonechka would have understood little of the conservation.

Angus admired his uncle. He had followed him by gaining a Cambridge mechanical science degree and doing an apprenticeship in the family firm. An outstanding athlete, he gained Cambridge rugby and athletics blues.

Gustav, who had been intently observing Angus, added in a gruff voice that if he wanted excitement then he had certainly come to the right place. In his opinion, Shanghai was teetering on the edge of an abyss. He asked whether Angus had read about the recent riots and strikes in Shanghai.

'I read several articles on the subject in *The Times*. Nobody on the voyage seemed concerned, I might add. Anyway, I'm sure our navy and military 'chaps' will see off the 'Chinks'. After all, we licked the Kaiser's lot,' Angus quipped. There was silence after this statement.

To change the subject, Lara asked him, 'Did you fight in the war?'

'I didn't. That's the problem. I was raring to have a go at the ruddy Hun, when they called the whole bloody thing off. Can you believe it? I missed out by just a day!'

There was an uncomfortable silence again. Angus, realising his faux pas, said, 'Did you know that Duncan had what we in England call, "a good war".'

A "good war" made no sense to Sonechka. She deplored how the English looked upon war as an extension of the playing field. It dismayed her how they apparently discounted the ghastly consequences of war's indiscriminate slaughter and mutilation of those caught in its path.

'I thought Duncan might have done something special in the war, but what, I've no idea,' Lara said. She then asked Duncan, 'I know you're too modest to speak of your exploits. So do you mind if I ask Angus about them?'

'If you insist, I suppose not,' he replied.

'Uncle Duncan was one of the first tank officers. A dangerous assignment if ever there was one. It probably helped more than any other weapon to win the war. What's more, with his mechanical knowledge, several of his suggestions to improve the tank's performance were incorporated in later models.'

'Angus, you're wrong to make me out to be a hero,' Duncan said. 'Put simply, I'd become bored waiting for my cavalry brigade to be called into action. So, like many others, I saw the tank as a means to break the trench warfare stalemate. Looking back now, I believe the tank's advantage was more psychological. It terrified the Germans.'

Then Duncan asked Angus if he was planning to fly for a Chinese warlord, as he wrote in one of his letters. Duncan had heard that these aircraft were death traps, poorly serviced, with a dearth of spare parts.

Angus retorted that he had only been joking. Duncan smiled, shrugged his shoulders, and added that Angus would no doubt find more than enough to keep him amused in Shanghai. Gustav added that, for excitement, nothing exceeded the Paper Chase Hunt and he thought it would suit Angus admirably. When Angus agreed, Gustav warmed to him and an animated equestrian discussion ensued.

Throughout the evening Duncan's presence dominated Sonechka's thoughts. The imploring look in his eyes as they greeted one another dispelled any lingering doubts she had about his love for her. She felt that he must have sensed her continued determination not to be his mistress since, even when alone together on the balcony, he made no mention of the matter.

She could see that though Duncan and Angus shared many family traits, diplomacy was certainly not one of Angus's.

Unbeknown to Sonechka, Duncan organised a twenty-first birthday party for her at the Majestic Hotel. Sonechka, along with Gustav and Lara, joined Duncan, Angus and the Parsons at a table in the main restaurant. She was surprised to see, seated beside Angus, a strikingly good-looking young woman. As Lara predicted, Angus appeared much more interested in Shanghai's social life than working in the family business.

While the orchestra struck up the first few bars of 'Happy Birthday', Duncan placed an oblong velvet box in front of Sonechka. Vivid childhood memories flooded her mind, recalling her father's love of the family's Name Day celebrations. She opened the box and gasped in awe at its contents. There lay a long string of flawless pearls. Duncan clasped the pearls around her neck. Then Sonechka recalled what Glasha had said about gifts of pearls; that they signify tears when given by a man to his beloved.

As if Duncan's gift was not unsettling enough, Sonechka came face to face with English hostility towards her. While in the ladies' powder room she heard snippets of conversation from two English women.

In a voice dripping with venom, one of them said, 'Duncan must be mad escorting that Russian.'

The other woman quipped, 'I suppose, like most, she has no money. These prostitutes have trapped so many Shanghailanders. I just cannot understand how she trapped Duncan.'

So she was just another vampire. Sonechka struggled to regain her composure before she returned to the dining room.

On Saturday night Sonechka went alone to vespers. In a quiet, candlelit corner, she knelt down before the icon of the Mother of God, beseeching her help. While the choir chanted the evening psalms, she prayed for guidance. At the end of the service she joined the other worshippers to be blessed by the elderly bearded priest. As she bowed her head a feeling of serenity swept over her. In her heart, she knew that God in His wisdom would not forsake her.

The velvet box, containing Duncan's exquisite gift, prominently displayed on her dressing table, was a constant reminder for Sonechka of his unwavering love. Only now, after weeks of deliberation, was she able to give him an honest answer.

Pouring out her feelings for him on paper proved to be one of the most difficult things she had ever done. She knew that in his presence she would not have had the heart to rebuff his proposal. In her letter, she thanked him for all he had done for her and Sasha. She stressed her admiration for him and how it pained her to hurt him. Being the father of two daughters of her age, she hoped he would understand that her decision was based on her Christian belief in the sanctity of marriage. In returning the pearls, she trusted that he would not be offended, since she could not, in all honesty, keep them.

CHAPTER THIRTY-FIVE

Having heard so much about the Paper Chase Hunt, Sonechka looked forward to the opening meet early in November 1925. The whole event was intriguing; there were no foxes in Shanghai, instead the resourceful Paper Chase Hunt members got the Chinese to lay a paper trail for them. But irate Chinese farmers devised all sorts of fiendish stratagems to keep the riders off their land, making the course doubly dangerous. Most Chinese supported this action since they deplored the desecration of their ancestral burial sites by the 'white barbarians'. Besides the risk of being drenched by the creeks' fetid tidal waters, Sonechka marvelled how the riders negotiated bridges that were no wider than a paving stone. Why so many English women longed to ride in this exclusively male event surprised her.

On the day of the opening meet Sonechka went by car with Lara and Gustav to the end of Bubbling Well Road, at the western end of the International Settlement. Here the men mounted their ponies. Despite the bitter cold, no one seemed to complain except Lara, who refused to leave her car. Sonechka climbed out and joined a substantial crowd of spectators. She was relieved when Duncan, Angus and Gustav cleared the first water jump. Others were not so lucky.

Sonechka rejoined Lara in the car and Lara told her how Gustav had, on several occasions, arrived home soaked to the bone and stinking to high heaven; the creeks and pools he fell into were little better than open sewers.

Suddenly, Angus stood before them, bedraggled and covered in slimy mud. Water dripped from his dishevelled riding attire. Vasily came to his aid with a blanket and a flask of brandy, which Angus quaffed. Unperturbed, he made light of his tumble, maintaining that had his pony not bolted he would have remounted and carried on.

Towards the end of the race, Sonechka and Lara got out of the car to view the finish. That Gustav came third, by far his best performance yet, did not seem to mean much to Lara. She praised Duncan, who finished halfway down the field, for riding 'sensibly'. The risks that Gustav took in his determination to win alarmed her. She believed that Gustav's guilt for not having fought for Germany in the war accounted for his reckless riding. She did not appear to understand that for Gustav nothing could be better than for a German to win an equestrian event that the English considered their domain.

Once all the riders had been accounted for, the participants and their supporters returned to the race club for the post-hunt celebrations. The camaraderie of the English amazed Sonechka. She had never seen them so happy and relaxed. Gone were the renowned English 'stiff upper lip' and the 'disdainful withering stare'. Even Gustav joined in the merriment. They sang traditional hunting songs with tremendous verve and the day's winner was hoisted up on the bar.

Sonechka was relieved that although her relationship with Duncan had cooled, they remained good friends. On occasions he continued to escort her to functions with Lara and Gustav. Considering all that had happened, she was amazed he still gave her as much attention as ever.

In early December a number of leading fashion houses, including Lara's, donated dresses and outfits for auction at a tea dance and fashion show staged at the Astor Hotel. The proceeds were to go towards the care of destitute Russian children. A large gathering of prominent Shanghailanders attended, including Duncan's party. Not until the end of the auction did Sonechka realise that Angus had been outbid for one of the two dresses that she had modelled. The successful bidder, an American director of the British and American Tobacco Company, was one of Shanghai's wealthiest taipans. Sonechka assumed that Angus wanted the dress for Galina, the attractive young Russian woman who accompanied him.

After the fashion show Sonechka returned to Duncan's table. Angus, leaning towards her, whispered how divine she had looked modelling. With a wicked grin, he added that since the stunning model was not interested in his advances, the next best thing was to bid for the dress she wore. Turning to Galina he said that if 'that damn Yank' had not outbid him the dress would look glamorous on her. Ignoring Angus' risqué outburst, Sonechka asked Galina if she had visited the hotel before.

'I just love coming here,' she said beaming. 'I've met so many interesting people, mostly Americans. They tell me that this hotel is as good as its namesake in New York. Americans fascinate me. I'd like to live in America.'

As Angus escorted Galina on to the dance floor, Sonechka did not know what to make of her. Her choice of outfit was provocative – a scanty evening frock accentuating her voluptuous figure. No wonder Angus found this fair-haired, blue-eyed Russian so attractive. She wondered when and where they had met. Lara, having overheard their conversation, told her that Mary, who had been helping behind the scenes at the fashion show, had recognised Galina. Apparently, she was a high-class call girl in this hotel's exclusive night-club, where Tai had taken her dancing.

Duncan smiled and said, 'I don't know what you two are worried about. Angus is just a red-blooded young man with no ties.'

On returning to their table from the dance floor, Angus asked Sonechka for a dance. Before they even got out on to the dance floor, he blurted out how he had been waiting all afternoon for the moment when he could hold her in his arms. As his grip round her waist tightened, he continued his amorous utterances. Sonechka, trying to loosen his hold on her, changed the subject by asking him how long he had known Galina.

Angus had met her at a party given by one of Duncan's American clients not long after he arrived in Shanghai. Galina had fled from the Bolsheviks during the Civil War and lived in Harbin for several years before settling in Shanghai. She was a qualified pharmacist, living with her mother and aunt, both of whom she supported. He thought she spoke English rather well, albeit with an American accent. He felt sorry for her, having lost everything in fleeing from the Bolsheviks.

Sonechka asked if Angus knew which pharmacy Galina worked at. He understood that it was somewhere in Hongkou. She presumed Galina had acquired her accent from the free-spending American clients she met in her hostess role. Sonechka was relieved when Duncan, who was dancing with Galina, tapped Angus on the shoulder, and asked if he could dance with her.

Sonechka found out that Duncan was concerned that Galina would compromise Angus. From what Galina had said Duncan thought she had Angus wrapped around her little finger. Furthermore, Duncan found it difficult to believe that she was a qualified pharmacist. He told Sonechka that Vasily, his chauffeur, would try to discover more about Galina.

Within a week Vasily had established Galina's real identity. She was a partially trained pharmacist, having had to curtail her course because of the Civil War. Like him, she was a Cossack from Rostov-on-Don. She had married a fellow Cossack with whom she had fled to Vladivostok in 1920. Her husband, who lost an arm fighting the Bolsheviks during the Civil War, could not find a job. Like many disabled and unemployed White Army soldiers he began drinking heavily.

Galina then left him and came to Shanghai by boat from Vladivostok with thousands of other Russian refugees. On her arrival in Shanghai she had looked for any sort of work, but to no avail. So she became the mistress of a wealthy Chinese man. She realised that her looks could earn her a livelihood. Accordingly, she made inquiries and got a hostess job at the American-built Astor Hotel in Hongkou, just across Garden Bridge, near the Soviet consulate. The prospect of finding a rich American husband there appealed to her.

On hearing Galina's story, Sonechka could not help feeling sorry for her. She knew that, but for the grace of God, she might well have been forced to do something similar. She had heard several similar stories about destitute Russian women being forced to sell their bodies to survive. Duncan did not condemn Galina for what she did, but he thought he should let Angus know Galina's true situation.

At first Angus refused to believe that Galina had deceived him, but he came to resent being duped by her. Within a short while there was a noticeable change in his demeanour. He forsook Shanghai's fleshpots for work and flying. Sonechka believed that his days of rescuing duplicitous Russian maidens were not over. The subtle, and not so subtle, amorous advances he continued to pay Sonechka made her wonder whether he had really changed.

Though Lara conceded that Angus was still a bit 'rough around the edges', she thought he would eventually match his uncle in charm. Lara was exasperated that Sonechka could not see that Angus was very eligible.

'My dear Sonechka, who do you think you are?' Lara snapped one day. 'I have no doubt that there are countless Russian women here in Shanghai who at least would get to know Angus better before rejecting him.'

But Sonechka found Angus's frequent flippant remarks irritating. Most of all, she could never marry anyone who considered Imperial Russia, its culture and her Orthodox faith some sort of joke.

It did not take Sonechka long to realise that many of the people she met at Shanghai's endless round of parties and functions were bored with one another. Most disregarded the desperate plight of the city's millions of Chinese and the impoverished, stateless Russians.

Sonechka became resigned to being stranded in Shanghai. She knew Lara spoke from personal experience when she told her to pretend to love Angus so he would marry her. But Sonechka knew she would not be true to herself if she did that.

Letters from Sasha became few and far between. When he did write he had little to say except to emphasise how much better off she was working for

Lara than trying to find a comparable job in America. Accordingly, Sonechka knew it to be pointless pouring out her true feelings to him.

For many months she had had no word from Liza and Pavel. Fellow exiles in Shanghai told her that she should be wary of writing to relatives and friends in the Soviet Union. Several high ranking Soviet defectors who had fled to Shanghai confirmed what had long been suspected: the recipients of these letters, and their families, ran the risk of being imprisoned and even shot. Not knowing whether to write again, Sonechka put off writing to Liza until she heard from her.

Sonechka's Orthodox faith provided the solace she sought. She attended the Divine Liturgy on most Sundays. After the service, she enjoyed spending time with Nadya and Masha and their friends. It made her appreciate that her concerns were trivial compared to those of most people.

CHAPTER THIRTY-SIX

In mid-October 1926 fear gripped Shanghai. General Chiang Kai-shek's massive Chinese Nationalist Army slowly advanced towards the city from their headquarters in Guangzhou (Canton), 1600 km to the south. Chinese fighting one another in the Chinese sectors of the city and in the International Settlement's Hongkou district north of the Garden Bridge caused considerable damage. As these areas were not under the protection of the Shanghailanders' municipal police forces, many Russian residents fled to the safety of the French Concession or to the International Settlement south of the Garden Bridge.

European wives and children were urged by their respective concession authorities to return to their home countries. The Russian exiles were marooned. Few, if any, wanted to return to the Soviet Union.

Ironically, Chiang proved to be the saviour of General Glebov's Cossacks, who were still living aboard the vessels that brought them to Shanghai four years earlier. Desperate for trained military personnel to defend the foreign concessions, both municipal councils enrolled these Cossacks in the Shanghai Volunteer Corps (SVC). This enabled them to reside in Shanghai.

Duncan visited Gustav and Lara on a number of occasions to discuss the continuing crisis. Whereas Duncan was confident Shanghai's foreign concessions would not fall to the Chinese nationalists, Gustav thought otherwise.

'I just cannot understand why you will not accept that we are doomed,' Gustav said. 'How can we defeat a massive army equipped and officered by the Soviets? Our defence forces will be overwhelmed. It is frightening how easily Hankou (Wuhan) fell to the Nationalists and how its extra-territorial rights were revoked. That must convince you of the gravity of the situation.'

Sonechka did not know what to think. However, she was less worried than she might have been, as Duncan said that a good friend of his had assured him that Chiang would not attack the city's foreign concessions. Gustav thought this preposterous. He was sure the advancing Chinese Nationalist Army would be welcomed with open arms by Shanghai's hundreds of thousands of downtrodden Chinese. The number of Chinese Nationalist flags on display and the flood of leaflets demanding the expulsion of foreigners from the country confirmed this. He believed the Bolshevik activists were behind the strikes that had brought the city to a virtual standstill. In his opinion it would be a rerun of the Russian Revolution and Civil War – a bloodbath.

In late April, 1927, it was clear that the Chinese Nationalist Army would not attack Shanghai's foreign concessions. Instead a Communist-backed uprising in the Chinese parts of the city had been brutally suppressed by Chiang.

Sonechka was bewildered by the fact that Chiang, their would-be conqueror, had turned out to be their saviour. It took her some time to comprehend the complex machinations that saved them all from a probable bloodbath.

She was to learn later that Shanghai's notorious Green Gang and their Chinese business associates had secretly financed Chiang's successful bid for the leadership of the Chinese Nationalist Party on the death of its founder, Dr Sun Yat-sen. These Chinese feared that otherwise Borodin, the Soviet revolutionary and leading light in the Chinese Communist Party, would head the Chinese Nationalists. This would destroy their businesses and put their lives at risk.

Besides trading in opium, the Green Gang extorted money from the city's innumerable opium dens, brothels and gambling houses. Gustav suspected that the French Concession's municipal council had long been hand in glove with the Green Gang. But he was shocked to learn that the British and American *taipans* of the International Settlement condoned Chiang's treachery. Worse, both of the concessions' police forces, the Volunteer Corps and multinational military forces, helped the Green Gang's armed units and Chiang's anti-Communists. They stopped Chinese Communists and their sympathisers fleeing to the safety of the foreign concessions. What followed was a cold-blooded massacre and the macabre display of severed heads on spikes inside bamboo cages. These were suspended from telegraph poles.

Outraged, Gustav despaired of China, likening it to Bolshevik Russia – a hell on earth. He longed to return to a rejuvenated, powerful and orderly Germany.

During this period, Sonechka noted a distinct change in Mary's demeanour. She spoke little, and appeared to be in a trance at times. Sonechka asked Lara if Mary had any particular concerns. She was horrified to learn that Tai had been beheaded during the recent uprising in the Chinese sectors of Shanghai. Shanghai's Green Gang had interrogated Mary, accusing her of being a Communist activist in view of her close relationship with Tai. Had it not been for the intervention of the International Settlement's municipal police she felt she too could have been beheaded. The municipal police had evidence in their thick files that Tai was a fanatical Chinese Marxist-Leninist bent on world revolution.

Sonechka suspected it must have been Tai whom she saw in the crowd of rioters that attacked her during the May 30 Nanking Road incident.

CHAPTER THIRTY-SEVEN

After church, Sonechka often spent afternoons with Nadya and Masha's family. Their parents had recently fled from Harbin to Shanghai, where they set up a Russian delicatessen in Avenue Joffre. They had feared that the increasing Soviet presence in Harbin endangered their business and their lives. An acquaintance who returned to the Soviet Union had confirmed their worst fears. Convinced he would be so much better off living back there, he promised to send them photographs. Should his expectations be fulfilled, he would be photographed standing. The photograph he sent was of him lying down!

Harbin's White Russian community was being bombarded by Soviet propaganda. The Soviet Union now part owned the Chinese Eastern Railway, so those Russians who wanted to continue working there had to take out Soviet citizenship. Anti-Bolshevik Russians who did this were known as radishes, red on the outside and white inside.

On Sundays, Nadya and Masha's parents closed the shutters of their store downstairs. Upstairs, where they lived, they set up a table laden with perishable delicacies left over from the delicatessen. This was also the room where the parents slept, while the girls occupied an adjacent bedroom. Soon, other Russians who had no family joined them.

In the autumn of 1927 Masha got married. Her parents gave her the best wedding they could afford. Besides the bridesmaids, Sonechka and Nadya, there were six *shafera* (grooms), who took turns holding the two gold crowns above the bride and groom's heads during the wedding service. Alexei and Masha had been childhood sweethearts in Harbin, where he had trained as a mechanical engineer.

Sonechka and Nadya helped Masha into her ankle-length silk wedding dress, generously given by Lara. As Sonechka placed the tulle veil on Masha's head, a pang of profound sadness overcame her. Was she destined never to marry?

The reception was held at the local Russian Club. As Masha and Alexei entered the reception room, Masha's mother greeted them with the traditional bread and salt. Her father presented them with a *charochka* (traditional silver cup containing champagne) on a silver salver. Masha and Alexei both drank from the *charochka*, while the guests chanted: '*Pei do dna*' (drink to the bottom). Throughout the wedding reception there were frequent shouts of '*Gorko! Gorko! Gorko!*' (Bitter! Bitter! Bitter!), obliging the bridal couple to embrace and kiss one another.

During the wedding ceremony the bridal couple stood on a white cloth, which symbolised their purity before God. Later a lively discussion ensued trying to establish whether it was Masha or Alexei who had first stepped on the white cloth placed before the *analoi* (a high table with a sloping top on which an icon is placed). Tradition had it that whoever stepped on the cloth first became the undisputed head of the household.

Sonechka enjoyed the delicious food and Russian music from the orchestra. As the evening wore on, she was overcome by a profound sense of melancholia. These feelings occurred whenever she found herself in the midst of her Russian friends. She thought of Duncan and how he loved her and wanted to look after her, but could not marry her. She felt secure with him. But had he replaced her beloved father, she wondered?

Sonechka's heart skipped a beat on hearing the first strains of the ever-popular romantic ballad *Chrysanthemums*. She was transported to those happy days in Pavel's sitting room when she and Nikolai sang this song together. How she had yearned for Nikolai's approval and love. She wondered what her fate would have been had she remained with him and not fled from Russia. Her eyes filled with tears as she recalled the poignant words of the refrain:

The chrysanthemums in the garden have lost their flowers long ago.
But the love is still alive in my aching heart…

That night as she lay in bed she wondered what God's destiny had in store for her.

The next day Sonechka received a letter from Liza. On a single sheet she wrote:

My dear Sonechka,
I beg you to forget about us. We are all well. Please do not write again.
Your loving sister,
Liza.

In disbelief Sonechka stared at the stark two lines Liza wrote. Any thoughts she had that the lives of Liza's family might improve were dashed.

Sonechka now knew what was the reality of Stalin's widely proclaimed 'socialism in one country': the virtual imprisonment of its people. She dreaded to think what might happen to Liza's family, cut off from the outside world, with Stalin about to implement his Five-Year Plan to industrialise the country at breakneck speed.

She recalled at the time of Lenin's funeral that few people had picked Stalin to be his successor. Only now did she realise the significance of Stalin's glowing funeral tribute to Lenin, couched in Russian Orthodox eulogy terms, which Pavel read out from *Pravda* to her and Liza.

Stalin's manipulation of the minds of the masses, drawing on his Russian Orthodox seminary training, horrified Sonechka. Articles and letters in Shanghai's Russian press about the relentless persecution of Orthodox believers in the Soviet Union left Sonechka in no doubt that Stalin was the Antichrist.

Lara and Maria Nikolayevna sympathised with Sonechka's shattering news, whereas Gustav shrugged off Stalin's ruthless rule as being self-evident. Showing Sonechka scant sympathy, he claimed Stalin was an imperialist intent on dominating the world under the guise of a peace-loving socialist leader.

Sonechka was tormented by the thought of what might have happened to Liza and her family. Had her letters compromised them? She prayed that they would survive. She shuddered to think what Pavel's fate might be should his masquerade as a supporter of the Bolsheviks be revealed. What would happen to Liza and Sofia if he had been shot or imprisoned? Was Liza being truthful when she wrote, 'We are all well'?

Sonechka heard about and read many heart-rending stories of people being imprisoned or shot in the Soviet Union. But their hoped-for haven in Shanghai was a bitter disappointment for most. They were either ignored or despised by other foreigners. Bewitched by Comintern propaganda portraying a Soviet paradise in the making, some Russians were tempted to return to their Rodina (Motherland). This was a true reflection of their plight.

November 7, 1927, was the tenth anniversary of the Bolshevik Revolution. This led to some White Russians demonstrating in front of the Soviet Consulate. A youth group hired a Chinese barge on which they placed a coffin draped in black with two effigies on it. These effigies depicted a black leather-coated commissar pointing a sub-machinegun at a cowering figure clad in drab prison garb. The Soviets objected to the police, demanding that the coffin be removed, whereupon another barge was hired with a similar coffin and effigies. This barge was tied under the middle of the Garden Bridge in full view of the Soviet consulate throughout the day.

News spread that the Soviets were planning a celebration that night to mark the anniversary of the revolution. By nightfall thousands of Russians had descended upon the consulate. Their protests could be heard far and wide. In anger, some started hurling rocks at the windows of the consulate. Before long, most of the windows on the first and second floor were broken. In retaliation, the Soviets opened fire on the unarmed crowd. A number of people were wounded, two men seriously, and one, Yevgeny Bakhtin, died several days later. His funeral was attended by thousands of Russians.

Though Sonechka did not take part in this demonstration, she read about it in the *Shanghaiskaya Zarya* (*The Shanghai Dawn* daily newspaper). It was said that the Soviet consulate held detailed information on every Russian exile in Shanghai.

Despite Sonechka's protestations, Lara persisted in trying to convince her that she should at least give Angus the chance to dispel her poor opinion of him. She begged Sonechka to re-evaluate her situation and consider him as a possible husband, stressing that not only did he come from a good family, but he was wealthy. Also, by marrying him Sonechka would become a British subject.

Sonechka knew Lara hated the interminable philosophising about matters of the heart, so beloved by Russians. Lara's philosophy was simple – 'one got out of life what one put into it.' Hard work held her marriage together and ensured the success of her business. Feeling sorry for oneself was alien to Lara. It exasperated her that Sonechka seemed incapable of appreciating Angus as a suitor. She felt Sonechka might be forced to marry an impecunious fellow Russian. Moreover, married to Angus she would have Duncan as a guardian.

Sonechka knew that Duncan was the reason she could not accept Angus as a serious suitor. Angus would always be second best in her estimation. Although, she knew she could never love Angus, she decided to pursue her relationship with him, if only to placate Lara.

On getting to know Angus, Sonechka learned about his passion for aircraft and his dream of one day owning a fleet of them. He saw commercial aircraft surpassing ships in ferrying people long distances. Though Duncan and his father did not agree with his airline proposal, Angus hoped in time to convince them of its merits.

Sonechka conceded that Angus had some commendable qualities. He was an attentive companion and a good dancer. She particularly enjoyed dancing in the newly constructed French Concession's *Cercle Sportif*, also known as the French Club. The French claimed that their *Cercle Sportif* was the world's most luxurious leisure complex. Besides an Olympic-size heated indoor swimming pool and tennis courts, it had an elegant art deco staircase and exquisite stained glass windows.

Occasionally, several of Sonechka's Russian friends joined their party. Her best friend, Nadya, liked Angus and wondered why Sonechka did not consider him a serious suitor. Sonechka told her that, though she enjoyed being feted in Shanghai's finest venues, she had no thought of marriage. Besides, Angus had not proposed to her.

One afternoon while Sonechka and Mary were embroidering a beaded evening dress, Sonechka was surprised when Mary said that she had seen Angus on several occasions at the cabarets where she and her new boyfriend went dancing. On each occasion Angus was with a different Russian girl. Sonechka felt betrayed. Mary's revelation confirmed Sonechka's long-held reservations concerning Angus. He was an ardent womaniser and likely to remain so.

Late that summer Duncan announced he would be going to England for his eldest daughter's wedding. Before his departure, he gave a farewell cocktail party at his home. Besides Lara, Gustav and Sonechka, several of Shanghai's elite were present. Duncan, the perfect host, circulated among his guests making a point of chatting to everybody. Angus spent most of the evening at Sonechka's side prompting Duncan to proclaim, 'Wouldn't you agree that these two make a wonderful couple?'

Sonechka feared he might, at any moment, announce their engagement.

The night before his departure, Duncan invited Sonechka to dine with him. Reluctantly, she agreed. She knew this rendezvous would be difficult for both of them. She tried to keep the conversation as light as possible. However, within a short while, Duncan declared that his feelings for her had not changed and that her precarious stateless Russian status worried him.

Duncan told Sonechka that Angus was like a son to him and that he had the utmost confidence in his ability to head the family business in Shanghai. His dearest wish was for her to marry him. He saw her as 'an asset to the family' and he knew that Iain, his brother, would be delighted to have her as his daughter-in-law. Gently kissing her hand, he murmured, 'Since I can't marry you, I trust you will have Angus as your husband.'

Confiding in her, he said that he had decided not to return to Shanghai.

Sonechka had a sudden premonition that this would be the last time she would ever see Duncan. She had no wish for ill feelings to mar this precious time together. Her heart went out to him. Emotional turmoil overwhelmed her.

On parting in Lara's foyer, Duncan handed her an all-too-familiar oblong box, the gift of pearls she had returned to him. He begged her to accept them, as a token of his undying love.

Rushing upstairs she threw herself on her bed and began to weep. She wept for her broken heart and for Duncan's love.

CHAPTER THIRTY-EIGHT

Angus pursued Sonechka with some vigour. Once he even accompanied her to church. However, he was not impressed, describing the service as full of mumbo jumbo, idols and incense. Angus played rugby in winter and tennis or cricket in summer. Sonechka watched him play only one game of rugby. He was a member of an International Settlement team pitted against a team from the French Concession. After seeing how the players viciously attacked one another, she understood why Lara considered rugby barbaric. As for cricket, Lara found it incredibly boring, maintaining that one needed a good book and a chaise longue to pass the time. Though Sonechka tried to appreciate these English sporting obsessions, in the end she had to agree with Lara.

Once Sonechka and Angus went to watch greyhound racing at the Canidrome in the French Concession, near where Angus lived. The Canidrome accommodated up to fifty thousand spectators and had a restaurant, bar and ballroom overlooking the track. The Chinese were the majority of the spectators. They were there to bet and had little real interest in sleek, fleet-footed, Australian-bred greyhounds. However, the crowd was too noisy and the races too short for their liking.

The incredible amount of money gambled on the greyhounds was a bonanza for the French who levied a forty per cent tax on the revenue. Combined with the revenue from betting on the equally popular, and incredibly fast, Basque racquet and ball game of *Jai Alai* (pelota), staged nightly at a nearby specially constructed stadium, French charities received as much as two million dollars a year!

Sonechka was surprised when Angus invited her to dine with him at his home in the Cathay Mansions on New Year's Day. She had been there the previous evening for cocktails with a group of his friends before going on to the New Year's Eve Ball at the French Club. She wondered if she should go there on her own, but given his recent behaviour, she saw no reason to believe he would take advantage of her.

During dinner Angus boasted that the Cathay Mansions building was one of Shanghai's showpieces. Besides providing ample entertaining facilities for its residents, including the restaurant where they dined, the building had such innovations as central heating and air conditioning.

Sonechka enjoyed the dinner. However, as the evening wore on, she became concerned about the amount of wine Angus had drunk. They retired for coffee to his luxurious apartment. Angus surprised Sonechka when, after fumbling in his pocket, he handed her a small square red box. She was shocked when he mumbled drunkenly, 'Duncan thinks it's high time we got engaged. After all, the family already consider us betrothed.' When he slipped the emerald-cut diamond ring on her finger, Sonechka gasped at its sheer brilliance. Then, to her horror, he grabbed her and started unbuttoning her dress. Sonechka wrested herself from his clutches. She slapped his face. He fell to the floor at her feet. Momentarily mortified, she thought she must have killed him. Relief overwhelmed her when he moved, smiled sheepishly and tried to sit up, only to fall back in a drunken stupour.

Sonechka prised the ring off her finger, replaced it in the box and fled.

That night one *koshmar* (nightmare) followed another. Each ended with Duncan berating her as Angus's body lay motionless on the floor. Morning was a welcome relief.

That evening Sonechka went to vespers to ask God to give her the strength to start afresh. She felt guilty for not having been to church for some time. She knew it was the only place where she could commune properly with God. Standing there among the candle-illuminated icons with the sweet-smelling incense enveloping her senses a feeling of peace descended upon her. She knew she had been living an illusion in trying to accept Angus as a substitute for Duncan. By rejecting Angus she was severing her links with Duncan. Falling in love with Duncan had been a mistake, yet she had ignored what her intuition told her.

Sonechka now realised that Angus lusted after her, rather than loved her and that Duncan had been wrong to encourage Angus to marry her. She and Angus were not destined for each another. Yet she could not blame Duncan or Lara. They had done everything possible to help her – the destitute and stateless Russian exile.

Sonechka was relieved that when she next saw Angus he behaved as if nothing untoward had happened. Lara, on the other hand, found it difficult to accept her decision not to marry Angus.

In late January, Lara's mother, Maria Nikolayevna, fell ill. She lost her appetite and literally wasted away, dying just before Easter. For Lara it was an irreplaceable loss. Apart from a short period after her marriage, Lara and her mother had been inseparable. The boisterous ten-year-old twins greatly missed their grandmother, who had lavished affection on them. A pall of gloom descended on the household. Even Gustav, realising that the boys needed time to grieve, allowed them to forgo the rigorous scholastic and sporting regime he insisted they follow. Sonechka sorely missed Maria Nikolayevna, her last link to a cherished bygone age.

One evening not long after Maria Nikolayevna's death, a distraught Angus arrived unannounced at Lara's home. He had just received a most distressing cable from his father. Duncan was dead, killed in England in a hunting accident when his horse bolted and threw him. At first Sonechka could not believe it. As the horror slowly sunk in, numbness overtook her. How could Duncan be dead? She did not want to believe it. He was such a careful rider.

Once again, Sonechka relived the agony of losing a loved one. She felt guilty for not giving Duncan, who had treated her so well, the happiness he deserved. From their first meeting she had felt drawn to him. Her feelings had grown into great affection – surely a form of love. But for Duncan her and Sasha's lives might well have been very different, even disastrous. Duncan's world in Shanghai and England had beckoned her. Why had she chosen to reject it? After all, countless women would have been prepared to live with such an eligible man. Why was marriage so important to her?

Work at the salon helped heal both Lara and Sonechka's grief. The deaths created an even closer bond between them and Lara sometimes accompanied Sonechka to church. It helped restore the emptiness that Lara felt for the loss of her mother.

That August Lara did not make her annual trip to Harbin to replenish her stock of furs. Instead, she joined Sonechka and the boys in a rented villa at a seaside resort north of Shanghai. The sea air together with the tranquil setting proved invigorating.

Towards the end of the year Iain, Angus's father, decided to close the Shanghai branch of the family enterprise. Just before he returned to England, Angus invited Sonechka, Lara and Gustav to a farewell dinner party at the Cathay Mansions. Cynthia and Gerald Parsons were also present. For Sonechka it was an ordeal – she thought of Duncan and he was not there.

Soon after Angus's departure Gerald Parsons told Sonechka that Duncan had left her a small legacy. She marvelled how her ever-loving Duncan had provided for her, enabling her to have a degree of independence.

CHAPTER THIRTY-NINE

In 1929, after Duncan's death and Angus's departure, Sonechka became increasingly involved in Shanghai's White Russian community.

One of the highlights of the year was the Charity Masquerade Ball held at the Majestic Hotel in the week before the Great Lent, known as *Maslenitsa*.[9] In Imperial Russia great feasts of *blinis* (pancakes) were held. The blinis were piled high and eaten with *smetana* (sour cream), caviar, smoked salmon and herring washed down by copious quantities of vodka. Villages staged competitions to see who could eat the most *blinis*. Some even died from over-indulgence.

Dressed in traditional Russian costumes, Sonechka and Nadya served at the buffet table. Many families, including Nadya's parents, had prepared the food.

One of Lara's friends loaned Sonechka the costume of a *boyarina* (Russian noblewoman), which she had brought with her from Russia. It was a beautiful creation with a stunning headdress. Sonechka spent many hours restoring the damaged beading on this family heirloom. This labour of love proved well worthwhile. Sonechka looked stunning.

During the evening donated items were auctioned, including one of Lara's evening dresses, which Sonechka modelled. After the auction Sonechka changed back into her boyarina's costume and joined Nadya and their friends to dance.

Towards the end of the evening Sonechka decided to sit out the energetic polka and observe the merriment around her. Though she enjoyed the evening she could not help recalling happier times dancing with Duncan.

When the music stopped Sonechka noticed a well dressed gentleman making his way towards her table. Bowing formally, he introduced himself as Vladimir Emilyevich Rossi and asked her for the next dance. As their eyes met, Sonechka felt a delicious quiver run through her body. Enchanted, she wondered who this softly spoken Russian might be.

To the strains of Tchaikovsky's Polonaise, Vladimir escorted Sonechka on to the dance floor. She worried that she did not know the Polonaise well, but Vladimir dispelled her concerns by deftly guiding her through the elegant steps. Gliding blissfully to the music, Sonechka was transported back to Imperial Russia.

Soon Vladimir and Sonechka became engrossed in conversation as they learnt more about each other. Their intense tête-à-tête was broken only by Nadya and her boisterous friends rejoining them. Sonechka introduced Vladimir to them and tried not to show her annoyance at their return. On parting, Vladimir and Sonechka arranged to meet the next day.

Vladimir's immaculate manners and his attentiveness captivated Sonechka. She had never met a Russian like him. She then recalled something that Vera had said, many years ago – one knew instinctively when one met one's destiny.

After the church service the next day, Sonechka met Vladimir. It surprised Lara that Sonechka had not mentioned him to her. Realising that their rendezvous had been prearranged, Lara tactfully left them to spend the day together.

It was spring and blossoms were bursting from the plane trees lining the avenues of the French Concession. Walking arm and arm, Vladimir and Sonechka were oblivious to their surroundings; even the oppressive, foetid odours that permeated Shanghai.

Over a leisurely meal at a French café on Avenue Joffre, Sonechka learned that Vladimir had only recently arrived in Shanghai. Fluent in six languages he was working for the political department of the French Municipal Police. For the previous nine years Vladimir, like so many of his exiled countrymen, had lived a gypsy-like existence, moving from one country to another in search of a place to settle and work. In the aftermath of World War I, few countries welcomed Russians fleeing the Bolsheviks. All but a handful were destitute and stateless.

Sonechka admired Vladimir's dedication to Imperial Russia – honour and duty were paramount. But then the very foundations of his life had collapsed as they had for her. Yet Vladimir was determined to make a new beginning. So he took the momentous decision to travel halfway around the world to Shanghai.

The afternoon passed all too quickly. While escorting Sonechka home, Vladimir let slip how the night before he had watched her in awe, modelling at the ball's auction. Then, looking into her eyes, he murmured: 'Your charm and beauty graced the room.'

Sonechka was thrilled that Vladimir was so effusive. She was drawn to him; she had never felt like this for any other man. Though their Russian backgrounds were different, she knew they shared the same values.

On parting, Vladimir caressed her hand and whispered, '*Dushenka moya* (My little soul mate), this has been one of the happiest days of my life. Destiny has played many tricks on me. Only now do I know why I was brought to this place, of all places on earth.'

Sonechka's heart leapt with joy.

Lara had no need to question Sonechka about Vladimir. The radiant gleam in her eye told her everything. But she had reservations about this budding romance. She felt Sonechka was rushing into it without considering the consequences. After all, she thought the stateless and impoverished Vladimir had little to offer.

One evening, Vladimir proposed to Sonechka. Seeing the light on in Lara's drawing room she burst in to break the news. Lara was unmoved, still worried that Vladimir's wage would not allow Sonechka to lead the full life she felt she deserved. Sonechka retorted that their love and respect for one another far exceeded the pleasures of Shanghai. She mentioned that the small legacy Duncan had left her would enable them to buy a small apartment in the French Concession. Then they could live relatively well on what Vladimir earned.

Sonechka wrote to her brother, Sasha, about her forthcoming marriage, confident that he would approve.

The next week Sonechka and Vladimir invited Lara and Gustav for dinner to a restaurant in Avenue Joffre. Sonechka was relieved that Lara and Gustav kept their reservations about her forthcoming marriage to themselves. Thankfully the men got on well with one another from the beginning. Gustav complimented Vladimir for his fluent German. However, he could not understand why he chose to leave Europe and live in Shanghai. Surely anywhere else would be better.

With a wry smile, Vladimir said, 'Had I not come to Shanghai, I would never have met my darling Sonechka. Besides, in my opinion, socialists, communists and fascists are tearing Europe apart. I deplore how Germany is bent on revenge for the Versailles Treaty, as if there has not been enough killing in the world war. Europe seems, once again, set on the path of destruction. It depresses me that so many commentators and influential people in the West believe the lies spread by the Bolsheviks' Moscow-orchestrated worldwide propaganda organisation, the Comintern.'

Shaking his head in disgust, Gustav retorted, 'How can you possibly say that about fascism? It is remarkable the way Mussolini has invigorated Italy and what Hitler proposes doing for my country once he gains power will be wonderful too. The consensus politics of your democratic Russian Provisional Government proved useless against Lenin's October 1917 counter-revolution.'

Pausing for effect, he thundered, 'Only fascism can defeat communism.'

Realising it was pointless trying to convince Gustav that fascism and communism were equally evil, Vladimir discreetly changed the subject.

Sonechka was relieved that the rest of the evening passed pleasantly enough. She hoped that with time Lara would accept her decision to marry Vladimir. Nevertheless, she understood why the materialistic Lara, her confidante, should be apprehensive and worried about her.

The next morning Lara complimented Sonechka on how tactful Vladimir had been to sustain a discussion with Gustav. Gustav's reverence for Hitler sickened Lara, for she knew that Hitler believed the Slavs, including Russians, to be subhuman. Not only was Gustav insisting that the twins be sent to boarding school in Germany, but also that he would return to live in Germany if Hitler became chancellor. Lara told Sonechka that she had no intention of accompanying him, even though it would break her heart to be separated from the twins. She felt that Alexander might survive the rigours of a German boarding school, however for the aesthetic Peter it could be hell. Besides, she would not want to give up her business in Shanghai. Lara thanked God that her mother did not have to endure the breakup of her family.

Sonechka sympathised with Lara and tried to comfort her. Lara who seemed to have everything one could wish for in material terms, made Sonechka wonder whether her loveless marriage explained her reluctance to accept Sonechka's happiness.

During the next few weeks, Sonechka was caught up in making arrangements for her wedding. Gustav insisted on giving the bride away and Boris Aprelev, a colleague of Vladimir's at the French Municipal Police and a former Corps of Pages graduate, was to be the best man. Several other Russian men, friends of the bride and groom, were to hold the crowns above my parents' heads during the wedding ceremony.

Sonechka spent a lot of time looking for a suitable apartment, well aware that without Duncan's legacy they would never have been able to afford their own residence. She was relieved that Vladimir did not appear to resent Duncan's largesse.

Alone in her room the night before the wedding it saddened Sonechka to think about the people she would have liked to be present at the wedding to share her happiness. In her heart she would always carry the memory of all those dear ones. Each had been like a stepping stone. Without them she would never have got to Shanghai.

At 1.30pm, Sonechka, dressed in a cream ankle-length silk dress adorned by a long tulle and orange blossom headdress, arrived at the Russian Orthodox Church. Despite the absence of the bride and groom's families it was a joyous occasion. Gustav solemnly escorted Sonechka into the church foyer where the priest stood waiting with Vladimir. As the choir began singing the joyous refrain, 'Come, O Come, my Bride from Lebanon,' Vladimir and Sonechka exchanged nervous smiles as the priest blessed them and began the service, later leading them up to the middle of the church.

During the service the bridal couple stood on the traditional white square cloth placed before the *analoi*. The six *shafera* who stood behind them took turns holding the crowns above their heads. The sanctity of the surroundings, the flickering candles and the choir's magnificent singing filled the air. Closing her eyes Sonechka was transported back to her beloved Russia.

At the end of the service Sonechka and Vladimir stood on the steps of the iconostasis to greet the well-wishers, including her old friends, Cynthia, her mother and Gerald Parsons. Standing beside her husband, Sonechka knew this to be the happiest day of her life. The newlyweds were whisked away for a drive along the Bund, allowing time for the guests to make their way to the reception.

In her nervousness and carried away by the occasion, Sonechka could not recall who had first stepped onto the white cloth.

Vladimir took a fortnight's leave, allowing the couple to have their honeymoon at Qingdao, a seaside resort with silken sandy beaches, north of Shanghai. During those halcyon days they opened their hearts to one another. Finally they had found the solace each had craved. Sonechka knew that as long as Vladimir lived she would never be alone.

CHAPTER FORTY

Sonechka listened enthralled to Vladimir's reminiscing about his family and their sophisticated life in Imperial Russia. This so inspired her that, on their return to Shanghai, she recorded what Vladimir had told her.

Vladimir was born in St Petersburg in 1894 and brought up in the family's imposing yellow and white mansion overlooking the Moika canal, not far from the Winter Palace.

Vladimir's father, Dr Emil Karlovich Rossi, was also born in St Petersburg, in 1839. He studied medicine in Tallinn, the capital of Estonia. For distinguished service in the 1877–78 Russo-Turkish War, Emil was made a general and awarded the St Vladimir Cross. He later became the chief inspector of the Imperial Military Hospitals in the St Petersburg area. His office in the Admiralty faced the Winter Palace. He was directly responsible to Tsar Alexander III and subsequently to Nicholas II.

In 1890, the fifty-one-year-old Emil married Sofia Fyodorovna Rousseau. She was twenty-eight years his junior. He had not been married before, having devoted his life to the care of his deceased sister's five orphaned daughters. Only when his nieces were married did he consider matrimony. Even though Sonechka and Vladimir's families had lived in Russia for generations, they, like many nobles, were descended from foreigners who had intermarried.

It amused Sonechka how Vladimir's parents met one another.

Over the years Emil had been a frequent visitor and cherished friend to Mr and Mrs Rousseau, who would become Vladimir's grandparents. Sofia, the Rousseau's only daughter first met her husband-to-be when she was aged two, dressed in a white crinoline frock as she sat on Emil's knee playing with his pocket watch. The Rousseaus were a French Protestant family (Huguenots) who had fled persecution in France after the revocation of Edict of Nantes in 1685. They first settled in Poland where a member of the family was the Postmaster-General of Warsaw in the early 1800s. In the 1820s one of the Rousseaus went to St Petersburg, where he became a successful banker, enabling him to build the mansion on the Moika canal overlooking one of the city's beautiful bridges.

Besides playing chess with Mr Rousseau, Emil, a talented pianist, performed at their musical evenings. He often made up a four at bridge with his future mother-in-law, Dorothea.

Over the years Emil's nieces invited Sofia to their soirees and parties. However, the tyrannical Rousseau, who adored his only daughter, trusted no man except Emil to be alone with her. Rousseau chaperoned his daughter to every ball and dance, immediately taking her home if she was asked to dance more than once by the same man.

When she became gravely ill at the age of twenty-one, Emil was called to her bedside to treat her. They fell in love. Although Sofia's father admired and respected Emil, he insisted that he wait two years before marrying his daughter.

Emil and Sofia were given an eight-roomed apartment in addition to adjacent staff quarters on the first floor of the Rousseau family mansion overlooking the Moika canal. Sofia's parents occupied the remainder of this floor.

When Sofia, was expecting Vladimir, Emil asked Tsar Alexander III if he would give him the honour of being the godfather to their second child. The Tsar agreed. However, Alexander III died unexpectedly just before Vladimir's christening. When Nicholas II learned that his father was to have been Vladimir's godfather, he sent his best wishes and gave Sofia a Faberge brooch. The exquisite centre-piece featured the Romanov double-headed eagle studded with diamonds and a dainty watch pendant.

Dorothea von Meltzer, Vladimir's maternal grandmother had a great influence on the upbringing of Vladimir and Dora, his sister, two years his senior. Their grandmother introduced them to a world of fantasy with bedtime fairytales that she made up. Sometimes Emil joined these imaginary visits to strange lands. Vladimir affectionately recalled how Dorothea liked sitting in her favourite green velvet armchair overlooking the Moika, watching the world go by.

Dorothea's family, the von Meltzers, came from the Grand Duchy of Mecklenburg-Schwerin. They arrived in St Petersburg in the 1830s, where they set up a coach-making business. Soon their business had diversified into cabinet making. The von Meltzers became the leading manufacturers of furniture to the imperial court.

Though Vladimir and Dora had a privileged upbringing, Sofia, their mother insisted they adhere to a strict regime. First thing in the morning their

Russian *nyanya* (nanny) marched them to the bathroom where she supervised their ablutions and dressing. Earlier, Emil had taken his daily cold shower. They then joined their father for breakfast in the dining room. Emil drank tea from a crystal glass in a silver stand and ate toasted buns with honey, while the children had their *kasha* (a type of porridge) and drank the 'dreaded' warm milk, also from crystal glasses in their individual silver stands.

After breakfast their father walked the short distance to the Admiralty. Irrespective of the weather, including snow, the *nyanya* took Vladimir and Dora for their morning walk along the Moika embankment. On their return, they went to their playroom. When Dora turned seven, part of the playroom was converted into a classroom. While Vladimir learned to read and write, Dora had lessons in Russian and French, given by an aunt. When Vladimir was seven, a German tutor came daily. Their German was enhanced by speaking with their grandmother, Dorothea, in her mother tongue. Though these lessons were at first for Dora's benefit, Vladimir quickly showed an aptitude and liking for languages.

Their mother, Sofia, rose late. Regularly, at 11.30am, she would come into the classroom to check the children's progress. At 2pm the children joined their parents for lunch. Afterwards the *nyanya* took them for another walk. On their return they read and played until dinner at 6pm. Dorothea often joined them for the evening meal. Their father insisted that only Russian be spoken during mealtimes. Soon Vladimir and Dora were able to switch from one language to another with ease.

The Rossis enjoyed entertaining family and guests for dinner. From an early age the children were present. The meal was usually *zakuski* (hors d'oeuvres), soup served with *pirozhki* (stuffed oblong-shaped meat or vegetable pies), a meat or fish dish with potatoes and vegetables, and a dessert. On special occasions, Dora and Vladimir were allowed wine diluted with a lot of water. Not that this meant they could forgo their warm milk!

When Dora was nine, Sofia hired a pretty young French governess who proved to be frivolous. Paying more attention to her appearance than teaching the children ensured her speedy departure from the household. Mademoiselle Louise, who came highly recommended, replaced her. She had been a governess for the previous ten years with a family closely related to the Tsar. She insisted that, in her presence, Vladimir and Dora spoke only French to one another, even at play and during their daily walks. One of their favourite walks was along the Neva embankment in front of the Winter Palace. Here they caught glimpses of the royal children at play in the palace gardens or sitting by a window of the second floor, reading. Sometimes members of the royal family passed in their carriages.

Vladimir's reminisces of St Petersburg reminded Sonechka of how impressed she had been with the city's architecture. It astounded her to learn that Karlo Rossi, one of the city's greatest architects and town planners, was Vladimir's great-grandfather. Sonechka recalled the intriguing story of how the critics of Rossi's Admiralty Arch, with its chariot and charioteers, were proved wrong when it failed to collapse once the scaffolding came down.

Another of Vladimir's ancestors, Gertruda Rossi, the mother of Karlo Rossi, fascinated Sonechka. Of Italian origin, she was born in Munich in the late 1740s. The beautiful Gertruda studied dance in Italy. Her premiere performance at La Scala in Milan received great acclaim. Gertruda performed at many European courts, including the court of Louis XV at Versailles and at the court of St James in London. Catherine the Great's ambassador saw her dance in London and invited Gertruda to come to St Petersburg. Like other artists of that period, Gertruda depended on royal patronage to pursue her profession. In St Petersburg, besides Empress Catherine the Great being her patron, Gertruda became a mistress of Catherine's son and heir, the Grand Duke Paul, who later became Tsar Paul I. In 1775, Gertruda gave birth to a son whom she named Karlo. Mystery surrounds Karlo's paternity. At the time it was strongly rumoured that he was the illegitimate son of Grand Duke Paul.

In 1783, Gertruda returned to St Petersburg at the invitation of Grand Duke Paul to instruct his children, including the future Tsars Alexander I and Nicholas I, in dance. She arrived with her seven-year-old son, Karlo and Charles Le Pique, her French husband and dancing partner.

As the imperial court's principal architect for many years Karlo Rossi was the leading exponent of the classical period of architecture in European Russia. Besides coordinating the architecture of St Petersburg, he beautified the city with his classical ensembles – public buildings, palaces and parks. A bohemian, Karlo Rossi, who had twelve children by two wives, lived his life outside the fourteen rigid Table of Ranks decreed by Peter the Great. He died destitute in 1849 and was buried in a pauper's grave.

Vladimir thought it odd that his family never discussed the courtesan Gertruda Rossi nor Karlo, and his probable illegitimacy. In their eyes she was the 'skeleton in the closet', a non-person. Karlo Rossi was just one of the many artisans from Western and Central Europe who played a vital role in the creation of St Petersburg.

To escape Petersburg's oppressive heat and humidity, the Rossi family usually spent late May to early September at Merkuli, an estate just across the border on the Finnish coast. A childless uncle had bequeathed the beautiful Merkuli to Dorothea. The many visitors, family and friends who stayed in comfortably furnished cottages built on the property admired the splendid homestead nestling in a plethora of luscious flora. In the evenings a small orchestra played in an ornate bandstand. After an early dinner, the holiday-makers strolled in the gardens, serenaded by the musicians, while the children played with their cousins and friends. These idyllic summer holidays evoked lifelong cherished memories for Vladimir and Dora.

During the week Emil worked at the Admiralty. On most weekends he joined the family at Merkuli, commuting by train from the *Finlyandsky Vokzal* in St Petersburg.

Vladimir and Dora loved to roam and play in the great outdoors with their cousins, Vera, Vasya and Kolya, who were regular summer visitors. It was there, aged five, that Vladimir, dressed in a Cossack overcoat and *papakha* (Cossack hat), first learned to ride. On that day his love of the four-legged creature was born and before long grooming horses became a passion.

Sofia's delicate health benefited from 'taking the waters' at one or other of the fashionable German spas. She particularly liked Wiesbaden, where distant relatives lived. As the children grew older they accompanied her there. Vladimir recalled the Wiesbaden Spa's Kurhaus, set in a large park with a casino and an impressive bandstand. During the day while Sofia had her various treatments, including mud baths, the children followed their strict study routine supervised by Mlle Louise. Most afternoons they spent walking in the park, later taking afternoon tea with their mother. As a special treat they had a choice of one of the many delicious chocolate gateaux with lots of whipped cream.

There was great excitement when Emil and Sofia visited the World Trade Exhibition (*Exposition Universelle*) held in Paris in 1900. Dorothea's two broth-ers, the owners of the Meltzer Furniture Factory, were asked to design and supervise the construction of all the exhibits in the Kremlin-like Russian pavilion at the exhibition. It was the greatest-ever exhibition staged anywhere in the world, visited by over fifty million people over the seven months from April to November. Before returning to St Petersburg the Meltzer brothers received the *Legion d'Honneur* from the French government.

Vladimir recalled the many gifts their parents brought back with them for everyone in the household.

The exhibition was a great success for the Meltzer firm, confirming their status as St Petersburg's premiere interior decorators and furniture manufacturers. Royal commissions included the refurbishment of the Tsars' private dining and bedrooms in the Winter Palace and the Alexandrinsky Palace. In 1911 the Meltzers also furnished Tsar Nicholas II's newly built Livadia Palace in Yalta.

CHAPTER FORTY-ONE

Just before his ninth birthday, Vladimir passed the highly competitive examination for entry to the Corps of Pages. This was the elite imperial military academy housed in the Vorontsov Palace, an impressive red rococo building set in extensive gardens. It had been commissioned by Paul I. For ten years Vladimir proudly wore the uniform of long black trousers with a red stripe down each side, a coat decorated with gold trimmings and braid along with the regulation military cap. The six hundred Corps of Pages students were under the Tsar's personal supervision. Only the sons and grandsons of generals, or sons of officers killed in service, were eligible for entry. Most graduates made the army their career. The remainder vied for prestigious roles in the government and administration of the enormous empire.

Talented teachers taught the cadets a broad range of subjects, which included history, literature, mathematics, geography, politics and Russian, French, German and English. Besides riding, fencing and gymnastics lessons, they were instructed in woodwork and metalwork. At the graduation ceremony, on August 6, 1913, Vladimir received the traditional white enamelled cross, modelled on the white Maltese Cross.

That same year, the House of Romanov celebrated its tercentenary. Vladimir had the honour of being one of the equerries to her Royal Highness, the Grand Duchess Tatyana Nikolayevna, Tsar Nicholas II's second-oldest daughter. He escorted her to a number of the lavish state functions and balls. The graceful young duchess enchanted him, particularly when they danced the Polonaise together. Chuckling, Vladimir recalled how his disliked childhood dancing lessons proved invaluable.

The young Grand Duchess Tatyana would later be murdered with the rest of the imperial family in Yekaterinburg.

As a Horse Guards Grenadier officer, Vladimir fondly recalled carefree evenings spent in St Petersburg's Tsygan (gypsy) cafes and nightclubs where he learned, besides many other things, how to hold his liquor. Alas, with the declaration of war in August 1914, those halcyon days were short-lived. At the onset of hostilities, Vladimir's regiment fought to defend Serbia, which the Austro-Hungarians had invaded. As soon as the Germans entered the conflict, Russia suffered a series of devastating defeats. Wounded several times, Vladimir recovered quickly but many of his fellow officers were killed or seriously wounded.

In early 1918 Vladimir joined the newly formed Volunteer Army, later known as the White Army. For three years he fought in the Civil War against the Bolsheviks' Red Army.

Some time later, one of Vladimir's friends told Sonechka how highly regarded Vladimir had been by the men he commanded. They affectionately gave him the sobriquet of Rossia (Russia), a play on his Italian surname. This respect could well have saved his life, since many White officers were murdered by the soldiers under their command, incited by Bolshevik propaganda, paid for in part by the Germans, to overthrow all that Imperial Russia represented.

Sonechka remembered Vladimir's voice quivered with emotion in recalling the fate of his fellow White Army officers who were victims of a heinous deception. They believed it to be their duty to accept the Bolsheviks' inducement to fight in defence of 'Holy Mother Russia' against Poland. Furthermore, they understood the Corps of Pages graduate General Alexei Brusilov,[10] the renowned Imperial Russian and White Army general who had defected to the Bolsheviks during the Civil War, would command them. Hundreds of White Army officers believed that the Bolsheviks would honour the amnesty they offered to fight Poland. Instead, Trotsky declared the officers traitors and executed them.

In early November 1920, Vladimir was seriously wounded in one of the final battles at the Isthmus of Perekop in the Crimea. This was the last bastion of the White Army in European Russia. Miraculously, two Cossacks under his command rescued him from the battlefield, taking him, slung between their horses, to a makeshift field hospital where his multiple wounds, including a shattered cheekbone, were tended to. Delirious from blood poisoning, his life hung in the balance. Several days later a ship evacuated him to Constantinople (now Istanbul). Unconscious during the sea voyage from Sevastopol, he woke up lying on a stretcher on a beach at Constantinople. Hundreds of other wounded soldiers lay alongside him. Russian doctors there saved his life. A renowned St Petersburg surgeon reconstructed his shattered left cheek and broken legs.

Vladimir admired how, from early on in 1920, General von Wrangel's leadership had welded the demoralised White Army into a cohesive force, enabling a hundred thousand combatants and fifty thousand civilians to be evacuated from Sevastopol and other ports in the Crimea to Constantinople and countries bordering the Mediterranean. It was an astonishing accomplishment against apparently insurmountable odds. Otherwise these evacuees would have faced death at the hands of the vengeful Bolsheviks, the fate of most White Russians unable or unwilling to flee the Crimea. Vladimir maintained to Sonechka that had Wrangel been in command from early on in the Civil War, rather than General Denikin, the White Army might well have defeated the Bolsheviks in European Russia.

Though shocked by the unexpected death of his father during the year of the Romanov tercentenary celebrations, Vladimir thought it a blessing Emil had not lived to see the destruction of all he held dear. After Emil's death his wife Sofia sold the Merkuli estate in Finland. In 1915 she sold the Rousseau mansion on the Moika to the Russian Bank and invested the bulk of the monies in government bonds in support of the war against Germany. She wanted to be near Dora and her husband, Andrei, a naval officer stationed in the Crimea. She bought a substantial property adjacent to the orchard of the Livadia Palace in Yalta, overlooking the Black Sea. Sofia died from typhus in Novorossiysk in March 1920.

The many White Russian exiles who found sanctuary in Serbia had the Serbian king, a graduate of the Corps of Pages, to thank for their refuge. In gratitude for Imperial Russia fighting in defence of his country from the Austro-Hungarian invaders, the Serbian king did all he could to help the White Russians. Many were given public works jobs repairing the massive destruction of the country's infrastructure caused by the war. Nevertheless, life was extremely difficult for most of them.

Once Vladimir had recovered from his wounds, he left Constantinople for Serbia, where he stayed several weeks with Dora and her family. Had Dora not earned money embroidering silk lingerie for a *haute couture* salon in Belgrade, her family could have starved. Unable to afford to pay rent, they lived in an abandoned and broken down dwelling on the outskirts of the city where sheep sought shelter.

Though other Western and Central European countries accepted White Russian exiles they did not get the warm welcome they received from their fellow Slavs, the Serbs. Most found that they were ignored, verbally abused or attacked. Many exiles 'sat on their suitcases' believing the Soviets would be overthrown, allowing them to return to their beloved Motherland.

While in Serbia, Vladimir met three of his officer friends. Though warfare was the only profession they all knew well, they could sing and play musical instruments. So they formed a quartet to earn their keep, singing Russian folk songs and Tsygan (gypsy) melodies to the accompaniment of balalaikas and guitars. They had made these themselves, although a skilled gypsy musical instrument maker gave them invaluable advice. Gypsy music revived nostalgic memories for Vladimir, recalling happier days when he and fellow officers frequented St Petersburg's Tsygan cafes.

Unencumbered, they decided to go to Italy to try to earn a livelihood as a quartet.

The poverty in Italy appalled Vladimir, although he enjoyed the magnificent architecture of Rome and the northern cities, which had inspired Karlo Rossi. In Rome they stayed with two distant relations of Vladimir's who, to make ends meet, had converted the family villa into a guesthouse.

Venice reminded him of his stay there with the family in 1909, during their grand tour of Europe to celebrate his sister Dora's engagement to Andrei. Vladimir recalled how when he was sixteen his parents had entrusted him to chaperone the young couple when out and about. Being their constant companion was a thankless task, lessened by Andrei bribing him to make himself scarce, especially when the lovebirds took gondolier rides. Though dressed like the tall and slim Andrei, Vladimir was hard put to match his effortless nonchalance and savoir faire. Andrei was a suave gentleman who wore a well-cut cream linen suit, stiff white collar, tie, studs and a straw hat. He liked to stand admiring Italy's visual delights while leaning, ever so slightly, on an unfurled umbrella.

In 1922, Vladimir joined Dora and her family on the Côte d'Azur at Menton, near Nice. Besides being entitled to live in France, Vladimir received a small pension from the French government for wounds sustained fighting for the Allies against the powers allied to Germany. With so many Frenchman killed and seriously wounded in the war, Vladimir soon found a job driving trams in Nice. Having visited it before the revolution, he was familiar with the Cote d'Azur, once the playground of the imperial family, aristocracy and wealthy Russians. Now it was overwhelmingly a refuge for thousands of destitute and stateless White Russians who had fled from the Crimea.

Dora and her family were fortunate to find friends prepared to accommodate them at a modest charge, along with a number of other White Russian families, in one of their two heavily mortgaged villas overlooking the sea.

On Sundays the household joined other White Russian exiles at the Divine Liturgy in Nice's exquisite Russian Orthodox cathedral. This jewel of Russian Orthodox Church architecture, commissioned by Tsar Nicholas II, had been built between 1903 and 1912.

Dora's two children, Gleb, aged ten, and Katherine, aged eight, were weekly boarders at the newly established Russian school in Cannes, returning home by train in the weekends. A wealthy Russian woman had donated a large villa set in extensive grounds for the school. It held classrooms, dormitories and other amenities for the exiled Russian boy and girl pupils. Their ages ranged from seven to eighteen years. The school strictly followed the French state education curriculum. In addition, reinforced by the belief that their return to a liberated homeland was imminent, pre-revolutionary Russian literature, history and geography were taught.

After a year in the south of France, Vladimir was anxious to make use of his language skills. He moved to Paris where he found an editorial job in one of the numerous Russian publishing houses. However, the firm collapsed after a few months. He enjoyed editing, but it was a precarious occupation, with each of the several Russian publishing houses he subsequently worked for struggling to survive. Nor was he well paid. Hence he supplemented his income by joining the ranks of many of his fellow countrymen driving taxis in the evenings. Vladimir deplored how the Parisians had succumbed to the Comintern's distorted portrayal of the White Russian taxi drivers – they were either princes or grand dukes who deserved to suffer for having forced their peasants to work by flogging them. In fact, the great majority of White Russian taxi drivers in Paris had been middle class of modest means in Russia.

The Russian publishing houses that prospered in Paris were strongly suspected of receiving substantial financial assistance from the Soviet government through the Comintern's European headquarters in Berlin. Vladimir had no doubt that they were sophisticated fronts for pernicious Soviet propaganda. He could not work for such an organisation. So when he heard about a well paid tram driver's job in Lille, he decided to try his luck there.

Meanwhile, Dora found a job on the telephone exchange at the American Hospital in Paris, replacing a St Petersburg friend who was expecting a baby. Before long, Dora was offered the prestigious job of head receptionist at the hospital. With her fluent French, English and German, she dealt well with patient and visitor enquiries.

After about a year Vladimir decided to leave Lille. Though the money was good, he missed the vibrant, cosmopolitan life in Paris. The city was full of Russians who had fled the Soviets. They included the artistic cream of Russia. Among them were Sergei Diaghilev, the impresario of the *Ballets Russes*, the composer Igor Stravinsky, the painter Marc Chagall and the writer Ivan Bunin, who would win the Nobel Prize for Literature in 1933. Besides, Vladimir missed the camaraderie of his officer friends. There was also the friendship of a certain Russian lady he had known in St Petersburg.

Vladimir's decision to return to Paris turned out to be a good move because quite a few people, mainly rich Americans, wished to be driven throughout the length and breadth of France. With his fluent English and French, war service and knowledge of European history, he was eminently suited to fulfil the role of a limousine chauffeur and tour guide for these people. It was 1926, the height of *Les Annees Folles* (The Crazy/Foolish Years), when artists of every kind flocked from around the world to Paris. Others came to let their hair down. Some came to wash away the images of the slaughter and the maiming of millions in the World War and its appalling sequel, the Russian Revolution and Civil War. Tens of thousands of Americans, profiting from the strength of their dollar and wanting to be free of their country's puritanical legislation, particularly Prohibition, formed by far the largest proportion of these foreign fun-seekers.[11]

For several summers, Vladimir ferried mainly affluent Americans on guided tours throughout France. During the rest of the year he drove taxis in Paris. The contrast between the war-devastated north and east, and the remainder of France could not have been greater. The extent to which France had suffered was a revelation to Vladimir's American and English-speaking clients. The vast areas laid waste and cratered by innumerable shell holes transformed the countryside into a lunar landscape. Millions lay buried, millions more were handicapped and some grotesquely disfigured. For the French, who lost one and half times more men than Britain and her empire, this war really was the war to end all wars (*La der des ders*).

Sonechka wondered why Vladimir had decided to leave the beautiful and cultured Paris for the unknown Far East. After all, it meant forsaking his sister and her family, not to mention friends amongst the tens of thousands of fellow White Russian exiles living there. Smiling and taking her hand, Vladimir related how a series of opportune events had brought him to Shanghai.

Boris Aprelev, an officer friend of Vladimir's who lived in Shanghai, wrote to him suggesting that he should apply for one of the equestrian instructor jobs advertised by the International Concession's multinational Shanghai Volunteer Corps (SVC). Boris thought that Vladimir's equestrian and linguistic skills eminently suited him for this post. The prospect of once again working with horses rather than horsepower certainly appealed to Vladimir. However, he at first ruled it out because he did not have the money to pay for the sea voyage to Shanghai. Vladimir wistfully added, 'Here, *dushenka moya*, destiny intervened.'

Vladimir's good fortune began when Dora met an American couple at the hospital who came to see where the volunteer American Field Ambulance Service was founded. At the very beginning of the war, their only son was one of the first volunteers to enrol in the service. Like other American volunteers he set out for the front from the American Hospital driving the specially modified lightweight and versatile Ford truck. Sadly, he was killed in the course of duty.

When this American couple asked Dora if she could find them a limousine driver who spoke good English for a tour of the battlefields of France, she suggested Vladimir.

Vladimir and the American couple duly left Paris, initially visiting the Marne and then Verdun. Vladimir got on well with the couple. On several occasions they said he reminded them of their son. It astounded them that Vladimir had survived fighting first the Germans and then the Bolsheviks. They realised that he was no ordinary limousine driver. When he told them about the job offer in Shanghai, to his utter amazement, they offered to pay for his passage. He was forever grateful for this couple's extraordinary generosity.

Vladimir's family and friends bid him farewell from Paris's Gare de Lyon, where he took the train to Marseilles. From there he travelled by ship to Shanghai, on one of the French boats of the renowned *Compagnie des Messageries Maritimes* via the Suez Canal. This company had transported merchandise and passengers on this route for sixty years. Although he had been given considerably more money than the cost of a luxurious first-class passage, Vladimir opted to travel third class. Forewarned that third class was ghastly, Vladimir reasoned it could be no worse than the battlefields of Europe and Russia. Not only did he survive this supposed hardship – the lot of impoverished Europeans and Chinese travelling this route – but he had a tidy sum of money left over to start his new life in Shanghai.

On arriving in Shanghai, Vladimir could not believe that the job promised him by the International Settlement's Municipal Council had fallen through. As a stateless exile there was no one he could appeal to for redress. He later learned that, determined to save money, the municipal council had cut back its funding of the Shanghai Volunteer Corps. Also, with their ally General

Chiang Kai-shek now firmly in control of most of China, the council felt that neither rampaging warlords nor nationalists determined to expel them threatened the International Concession any longer. Though dismayed, Vladimir realised there was no going back. He must find a job in Shanghai. Once again his friend Boris Aprelev, who worked for the political section of the French Municipal Police, came to his rescue. Boris recommended Vladimir for a position to join him in this 'supremely well informed department'. As luck would have it, there was a vacancy for the linguist Vladimir.

CHAPTER FORTY-TWO

On their return to Shanghai, Vladimir and Sonechka took over their apartment in the French Concession. It was not far from the Municipal French Police headquarters where Vladimir worked. His job was to read and translate into French articles from British, German, Russian, Italian and Spanish newspapers, journals and magazines. He also made synopses in French of radio broadcasts that he listened to from countries around the world. He found the work stimulating and revealing.

After living so long at Lara's, Sonechka had to learn to organise her own household. She had a number one boy whose duties included shopping for food, cooking and waiting at table. There was Amah who did the cleaning, washing and other household chores. In the humid months of July and August, with temperatures averaging in the mid-30s, the servants proved indispensable. It was not unusual for Vladimir, who came home for lunch most days, to change his shirt and white linen suit. If he went out in the evening during these trying two months he would change again.

Several weeks after they moved into their apartment Sonechka invited Lara to lunch. They had not been together since the wedding. Noticing several photographs displayed on a bureau, Lara commented on one showing a dignified lady. It was Vladimir's mother. She was seated with a group of children dressed in French aristocratic costumes. Lounging at her feet was a small boy sporting a drooping moustache clothed as a Chinaman. It was Vladimir. Amused, Lara said, 'Who could possibly have imagined that this little boy would one day meet and marry you and live in Shanghai?'

Suspecting Lara still had reservations about Vladimir, Sonechka was pleased she thought him a charming gentleman. Sonechka knew that Lara expected him to be bitter for having lost not only wealth, but also his status in Imperial Russia. Sonechka confessed to her that in the presence of Vladimir's officer friends, she sometimes felt ill at ease. Lara told her that Europe's officer corps elites, irrespective of their nationality, all shared an air of self-confidence verging on arrogance. For Lara, Gustav, with his arrogance and petulance, was a caricature of a Prussian officer.

Sonechka was relieved that Vladimir had decided not to hunt; she did not want him to repeat Duncan's tragedy. Eventually Vladimir told her that in the Crimea, a gypsy soothsayer had read his palm. She had predicted that he would survive the war but that should he hunt in peace time he would fall and die. She added that he would travel across the world's great oceans and settle in a far off country. Not being superstitious, Vladimir discounted the gypsy's prediction. Only when he married my mother did he realise just how accurate her prophecies had been. Why then should he tempt fate?

Vladimir's greatest equestrian disappointment was failing to be selected as a reserve for the Imperial Russian equestrian team that competed in London in 1914. Captained by Colonel Rodzianko, this team won a number of events, including the King Edward VII Cup. It was the third time they had done so. The English were astonished, but they regarded the Russians with considerable suspicion, seeing them as members of a ruthless autocracy.

Sonechka and Vladimir enjoyed dancing at the *Cercle Sportif*, where he was a member by virtue of his job in the French Municipal Police. Its oval grand ballroom and beautiful stained glass elliptical ceiling lit from behind were magical. In Vladimir's arms Sonechka knew she was the happiest woman in the world.

Like most of their Shanghai friends, Sonechka and Vladimir were hardly affected by the 1929 Wall Street stock market crash. Millions of jobs were lost but in Shanghai most businesses continued to prosper. Shanghai's booming economy prompted some respected pundits to paint a rosy picture of the city's future. In 1931 the British business magazine *The Economist* predicted that by the end of the century Shanghai would be the world's most prosperous city.

Sonechka received regular letters from her brother, Sasha. The catastrophic 1929 stock market crash had not only destroyed his livelihood but also his marriage to Arlene. Her stock market investments were worthless and his portrait commissions ceased. He was desperate. Then by chance he got a job painting houses at Russian River, some 75 miles north of San Francisco. He decided to build a small holiday home here. It was to be his *dacha* (a Russian country house or villa), but while it met his needs, Arlene was not happy. She was a big city girl, and considered it a hovel. He wrote that at first he had missed her terribly but eventually the tranquillity of Russian River compensated for his loss.

A number of neighbours were Russian; some had emigrated before the revolution, others had fled during or after it. Sasha, like so many Russians, loved the countryside. Out of necessity he had become a handyman: a carpenter, bricklayer and plumber. Often he was paid in kind.

Dora, Vladimir's sister, also wrote regularly. She was enjoying her receptionist's job at the American Hospital of Paris, but her husband Andrei was unemployed. The hospital was within walking distance of their small two-roomed rented apartment in Clamart, where hundreds of White Russian families lived. Many of the men worked in the nearby Renault factory, where they were abused by French Communist workers.

Dora said that many of Paris' forty-five thousand Russians were starving. The reason was the reduction in the American aid that had for so long helped them, not just in France, but throughout Europe.

Preoccupied with their own problems, few French people or their government agencies helped the Russian exiles. In Dora's opinion, the French did not know, or care, that most Russian exiles were fighting to survive in Paris.

Drawing on what commentators described as the Great Depression, Vladimir realised he was lucky to be in Shanghai. His business escorting wealthy Americans around France would have shrivelled with the Depression. Vladimir and Sonechka never imagined that a world at peace could suffer such economic turmoil and that America would be so badly affected.

Sonechka recalled how bitterly disappointed she had been not to travel to America. Now she and Vladimir could not imagine anyone wanting to live there, at least according to the reports that Vladimir read, which described the social turmoil in the USA.

Early in 1930, Sonechka learnt that she was pregnant. She had never felt better. Vladimir was ecstatic about becoming a father. On July 30, Sonechka gave birth to a baby girl. She thanked God for sending her such a loving husband and a beautiful daughter, Margarita. Vladimir doted on her.

Though polite to Sonechka's Russian friends, Vladimir had little time for their mundane conversation. Sonechka usually saw them during the day. Masha's little boy, Shurik, was Margarita's age. While the children played together Sonechka and Masha chatted, enabling Sonechka to catch up with the latest gossip. Masha and her husband, Alexei, and their son, continued to live with her parents above the delicatessen – an unofficial Russian community centre.

Sonechka and Vladimir's circle of friends included Vladimir's Russian work colleagues at the French Municipal Police, several of whom were Corps of Pages graduates. They also met a number of Russians who had lived in Shanghai since before the world war. At first Sonechka found the wives of these former merchants, bankers and diplomats aloof, but for Vladimir's sake, she tried to keep up appearances in their presence.

Vladimir and Sonechka became particularly friendly with a Russian couple, Nikolai and Valentina Bibikov. Nikolai's business had brought them to Shanghai before the war. They lived in a large, detached home, surrounded by a garden, in the French Concession. Nikolai, who had retired, possessed a wonderful library of books and classical gramophone records. They were generous hosts and held musical soirees which Vladimir and Sonechka attended. Vladimir also liked playing chess with Nikolai. They would toss a coin to decide which of their favourite pieces would provide the background music.

Vladimir spent one evening a week playing chess at the Russian Officers' Club. In acknowledgement of his Cossack command towards the end of the Civil War, Shanghai's Don Cossacks made him an honorary member. Though he enjoyed the camaraderie of their lively reunions, they revived disturbing memories of the barbaric Civil War.

By comparison, his Corps of Pages reunions were sedate affairs. Nostalgia for a bygone age prevailed, enhanced on special occasions by choice wines and champagne.

Although aware that every country engaged in propaganda, Vladimir found that the surfeit produced by the Soviet Union exceeded the combined total of all the other countries he analysed. He hated the way they trumpeted the imminent collapse of capitalism while calling the Soviet Union a socialist paradise.

The arrest by the combined foreign concessions' police forces of the Comintern agents Hilaire Noulens and his wife in mid-1931 was regarded as a major defeat for the Soviet Union. Vladimir was upset that Madame Noulens was a St Petersburg aristocrat; her real name was Margarita Moiseyenko.

Hilaire Noulens was one of the many aliases used by Jakob Rudik, a Russian Jew. He had operated as the secretary-general of the Pan-Pacific Trade Union, based in Shanghai. In reality he headed a vast network of Comintern agents involved in espionage, kidnapping and assassinations throughout the Far East. Following his arrest, hundreds of other agents joined him in prison.

CHAPTER FORTY-THREE

In 1932 Shanghai turned out in force to welcome the legendary aviator Charles Lindbergh on his round-the-world trip in a flying boat. After visiting Shanghai, Lindbergh and his wife flew up the Yangtze to Wuhan. Here, because of the raging floods, their plane was severely damaged and they were hurled into the Yangtze's filthy water. The Chinese did not see how the Lindberghs could survive, but the Shanghailanders saw their miraculous escape as proof of the white man's invincibility.

Vladimir and Sonechka became increasingly concerned for their fellow White Russians in Manchuria. But those in power had little interest in what the Japanese were doing there; they'd forgotten the disastrous 1904–1905 Russo-Japanese war, when Japanese victory had encouraged Japanese expansion. Vladimir and Sonechka saw Japan as determined to build a mighty Asian empire.

They did not have to wait long for the Japanese to turn their attention to Shanghai. In late January 1932, four to five hundred Japanese marines attacked Chiang's Chinese Nationalist Nineteenth Route Army in Shanghai. The Chinese were dug in near the North railway station in Zhabei, on the northern outskirts of Hongkou. The Japanese maintained that their marines were defending thirty thousand fellow citizens living in Hongkou from the Chinese, who had recently killed several Japanese and were boycotting Japanese goods. This might have happened, but it was the only way the Chinese could protest against the way their people were mistreated during the Japanese occupation of Manchuria.

Within no time the battle escalated. The Nineteenth Route Army stood its ground, proving to be more formidable opponents than the Japanese had anticipated. This meant they had to deploy a much larger military force than they had thought necessary.

Shanghailanders considered the conflict an entertainment and, supported by the city's foreign press, wanted the Japanese to win. Chinese soldiers were depicted as a despicable and undisciplined rabble, incapable of beating the Japanese. Vladimir and Sonechka were sickened by the numbers of people watching this bloodbath from roof-top gardens and other vantage points. Shells arching over the International Settlement, fired from a Japanese flagship moored on the Huangpu, caused great excitement, as did Japanese bombers roaring overhead.

These shells and bombs targeted Zhabei, one of the most densely populated parts of Shanghai. The spectators gave no thought to what was happening to the hapless Chinese. To them it was like a giant fireworks display.

After several weeks the relatively poorly equipped but courageous Nineteenth Route Army slipped out of Shanghai, leaving the Japanese in control of the devastated Zhabei. Much of Hongkou was also damaged. Tens of thousands of Chinese had been killed or badly injured with hundreds of thousands made homeless. Their livelihoods had been destroyed. Many fled across Garden Bridge into the southern part of the International Settlement and into the French Concession. They settled wherever they could find a space – in the doorways of buildings or in parks. Those who remained in Zhabei and Hongkou risked torture and death at the hands of the Japanese. Little was known about the fate of the White Russians living in this war zone.

Some time later, under the terms of a peace treaty instigated by the British Foreign Office, the Japanese vacated Zhabei and reduced their military presence in Hongkou.

Within six months or so, the resourceful Chinese had largely reconstructed Zhabei. Similarly, Shanghai's businesses bounced back and boom times returned to the city.

During this time Sonechka received a disturbing letter from Nina Borisovna in Harbin. Since her stay at Nina's boarding house on her way to Shanghai in 1924 the two women had exchanged greeting cards at Easter.

In her letter Nina explained that she had been forced to house Japanese soldiers for the last few months. They were demanding and contemptuous. As a stateless White Russian she had no rights and, living on her own, had no one to protect her.

But despite her despair Nina was delighted to hear that Sonechka, like her married daughter, Natasha, had a child. In her opinion a marriage was incomplete without children. Sonechka remembered Nina's nephew, Grigory, who had so proudly showed her 'his' Harbin. Several years ago he had migrated to America where a company, impressed by his engineering expertise, employed him.

Having worked for several years for the French Municipal Police, Vladimir had no illusions about the widespread corruption and organised crime exercised in Shanghai. But at the insistence of France's Foreign Office in Paris, Jacques Meyrier, the new French consul-general, vowed to eradicate corruption in their administration and in the police.

This clean-up was prompted by the death of Edgar Koechlin, Meyrier's predecessor, and three other prominent persons who were poisoned by Ningbo mushrooms in March 1932. They all became ill after attending a banquet staged by the Chinese Green Gang boss, Big-Eared Du. This fateful dinner was in honour of the participants in Citroën's Beirut to Beijing motor vehicle endurance expedition.

Koechlin was a marked man after he tried to stop Du bribing members of the French Municipal Police. Vladimir joked to Sonechka that he was obviously not considered worth bribing! Despite the new consul's intent, Vladimir believed corruption would continue and the pitiless Du would remain supreme.

In effect Du, through his highly complex networks, controlled not just the Chinese sections of Shanghai, but also the French Concession and, in part, the International Settlement. It disgusted Vladimir that Du, who monopolised Shanghai's notorious opium trade, simultaneously headed the organisation appointed by the French to suppress it!

Vladimir and Sonechka enjoyed the famous people who visited Shanghai in the early 30s. One was Noel Coward who wrote his play *Private Lives* while in Shanghai.

In February 1933 the cruise ship *Empress of Britain* brought George Bernard Shaw to Shanghai. The renowned Anglo-Irish writer and socialist was an ardent advocate of Stalin's Union of Soviet Socialist Republics. Most of Shanghai's White Russians hated him because of what he had written and what he had said after a visit to the Soviet Union in 1931. Vladimir and Sonechka found Shaw's lavish praise of Stalin unbelievable: 'Jesus Christ has come down to earth. He is no longer an idol. People are gaining some sort of idea of what would have happen if he lived now.'[12] Many knew from personal experience that what Shaw said was a lie.

Nor did it help that prominent left-wing American journalists such as Harold Isaacs and Agnes Smedley formed part of Shaw's admiring entourage. Sonechka and Vladimir heard that enraged White Russians would confront Shaw during his visit. Andre Gide, Romain Rolland and Andre Malraux all supported the Bolsheviks. Shaw, Gide and Rolland won Nobel prizes for Literature, highlighting the powerful influence these writer-philosophers exerted on the western mind. Life for France's White Russians was more difficult than for their fellow exiles in Shanghai, where business, not politics, predominated.

Vladimir recalled how shocked the White Russians in Paris had been on learning of the unexpected death, in 1928, of New Zealander Dr Harold Williams, the foreign editor of *The Times*. The White Russians admired his lucid and learned accounts of their predicament and the brutal reality of the Bolshevik regime. A journalist in Russia from 1905 to 1919, only recently has Williams been acknowledged as the greatest witness of the Russian Revolution. No one of any consequence in the West understood Russia as well as this phenomenal linguist who spoke some fifty languages. Williams and Ariadna Tyrkova, his Russian wife, were regarded as the White Russians' greatest friends in the West. For many White Russians such support in the West was a tonic: so many prominent persons sang the praises of the Soviet Union. The Bolsheviks certainly knew Williams' worth. In 1919 their London representative Maxim Litvinov described Williams, who at the time was a journalist in the midst of civil war-torn Russia, as 'Russia's greatest enemy'.[13]

For Lara it was different. As soon as Hitler came to power in January 1933 Gustav left for Germany, taking the twins with him. Though free of Gustav's fascist diatribes, Lara hated being parted from her sons. As a mother, Sonechka sympathised with Lara and tried to console her.

The boys wrote regularly. Alexander's letters were full of enthusiasm for his new life. He got on well with his fellow pupils and he liked the Hitler Youth summer camp, with its energetic outdoor activities. However, Peter sorely missed his mother. He hated the rigours of boarding school and the Hitler Youth camp.

After the loss of her twins, Lara threw herself into expanding the salon, interspersed with trips to Singapore and Manila to replenish her salon stock. The sale of her home and subsequent refurbishment of the Cathay Mansion's apartment kept her occupied. Lara was a perfectionist in such matters, whether it be detail on a frock, or a sofa cushion.

Although Sonechka was busy with her life as wife and mother, she had missed Lara's companionship. They often reflected on the memories of those close to them who had died.

Lara confessed how cross she had been when Sonechka rejected Angus Kerr's proposal of marriage. Now she admired Sonechka's determination to marry for love. She regretted not heeding her mother's advice to get to know Gustav better before marrying him. Gustav's wealth and the prospect of travel beguiled her. Until fascism became an obsession for Gustav, she felt the twins made their marriage tolerable.

CHAPTER FORTY-FOUR

Margarita was a beautiful child. Lara, her godmother, who lamented not having a daughter of her own, enjoyed helping Sonechka with Margarita's wardrobe. Lara saw Princess Elizabeth and her sister Margarita Rose as ideal role models. Chuckling proudly, Vladimir said his daughter's wardrobe was as good as that of the British princesses.

Early in their marriage Vladimir started collecting literary classics in several languages. He enjoyed browsing in the secondhand bookshops in Avenue Joffre. One of his first purchases was a book of Pushkin's poems published in St Petersburg before the revolution. At bedtime Vladimir read Russian and English fairytales to Margarita. Her favourite stories were *Beauty and the Beast* and *Rapunzel* from the beautifully illustrated English *Blue Fairy Book*.

Vladimir liked to reminisce about his own happy childhood and how he and his sister Dora looked forward to their bedtime stories. He wanted to instil in Margarita the same love of books that had enriched his life.

As she grew older Vladimir introduced her to Russian and English classics. He was pleased that learning came easily for her.

Listening in the evenings to the repartee of the two people she loved, Sonechka's mind often wandered to her beloved Alushta. Her eyes brimming with tears, she recalled the pungent aroma of her father's cigarette, mingled with the sweet scent of roses. She pictured Anastasia seated at the piano playing a duet with Liza, while Aunt Olya sat gently rocking and humming a tune.

Vladimir, conscious of the faraway look in his wife's eyes, understood how much she missed her family. He knew that Sonechka often reread Liza's very brief letter begging her to forget them. He wondered what fate had befallen them. Had Pavel and Liza perished like so many in Stalin's purges? Or were they languishing in a Siberian gulag? Was their daughter, Sofia, one of Russia's countless millions of orphans or had she too died?

Some time later Lara endorsed what Vladimir had to say about the Nazis' hatred of the Jews. She quoted from a letter written by Alexander. He told her that his form master, a highly decorated war veteran, had his spiked leather helmet prominently on display in the classroom. But he made the Jewish pupils sit apart from the others, because he believed the Jews had cost Germany its victory in the war. He also warned the boys that since the Jews were everywhere, they must be on their guard against them.

Sonechka was delighted to hear about Wolfgang, the new man in Lara's life. Lara had first met him a year earlier at the German club. She found his sensitivity a refreshing contrast to Gustav's arrogance. Wolfgang had fought for a year with the Austro-Hungarians on the Eastern Front. Then the Russians took him prisoner. During his two years imprisonment he learned to speak Russian, the mother tongue of his maternal grandmother. The war's senselessness destroyed Wolfgang's belief in armies. In 1929, with the Nazis fighting the Communists, Wolfgang accepted a job in Shanghai. Unlike Berlin, the Germans he got to know in Shanghai were not obsessed with politics.

On their first outing both women were relieved that Vladimir and Wolfgang got on well with each other. The conversation soon turned to the recent Shanghai visit by the controversial White Russian Count Anastasi Vonsiatsky. Vladimir knew about him. His story was extraordinary, even when compared with others who had fled the Bolsheviks.

A penniless White Army officer, Vonsiatsky, masquerading as a count, escaped to Paris. There, while working as a curtain puller at the *Folies Bergère*, he met Marion Ream. She had inherited part of the estate left by her wealthy father, who had made a fortune dealing in wheat and pork. Marion was one of the many American volunteers helping in Europe after the war. A passionate person, she saw the handsome Vonsiatsky, who was half her age, as someone on whom she could lavish her largesse and love. After their marriage they went to live in America.

Vonsiatsky came to Shanghai to rally support for an attack on the Soviet Union. In his official capacity, Vladimir attended one of these rallies. He listened in disbelief as Vonsiatsky, together with Konstantin Rodzayevsky, a fanatical fascist, told how they could recruit a hundred and fifty thousand Russians worldwide to their cause. Vladimir knew this to be an impossible figure.

These two fascists were not only unrepresentative of the great majority of the diaspora, but also differed markedly from one another. Whereas Konstantin Rodzayevsky led a precarious existence in Harbin, Vonsiatsky, an American citizen, enjoyed the life of a Connecticut squire on his wife's farm. With a number of fellow fascists, including one of his sisters and her husband, Vonsiatsky planned worldwide propaganda campaigns while turtles with swastikas painted on their backs patrolled the perimeter of their property. Vonsiatsky's proposed White Russian fascist force was a fiasco; only a handful of Shanghai's White Russians supported him. (Whereas Rodzayevsky was a fervent anti-Semite, Vonsiatsky was not. His first wife was Jewish and when he fell seriously ill in Shanghai a Jewish doctor treated him. There is strong circumstantial evidence that Rodzayevsky had tried to poison Vonsiatsky.)

Subsequently, light-hearted conversation prevailed and Vladimir and Wolfgang arranged to play a game of chess.

CHAPTER FORTY-FIVE

As they were ostracised by others in Shanghai, White Russians formed their own organisations in an effort to help the less fortunate. One of these was the Russian Military Union (ex-Army and Navy servicemen), which helped with accommodation, soup kitchens and the search for work. The American Red Cross, besides giving a considerable sum of money to the Russian sister organisation, fully funded a much-needed medical dispensary unit. In due course it became the Russian Hospital, staffed by Russian doctors and nurses. Russian Orthodox Church organisations also strove to help the Russian-speaking peoples.

During the early 1930s, however, some Russians, including Sonechka and Vladimir, became concerned about the dissension within the Shanghai Russian Orthodox church, which soon spread to the wider community in Shanghai.

They hoped that the new Bishop, John Maximovich, would end this disunity. He arrived in late 1934 from Serbia to take up this appointment. Most Orthodox believers thought the slightly built, hunchbacked Bishop John, who spoke with a slight lisp, was an improbable saviour. They did not believe that he had graduated from a military academy in Poltava and studied law in Kharkov. During the Civil War he fled to Serbia. In Serbia he attended the Bitol Orthodox seminary. On graduating with distinction he was appointed an instructor there.

Bishop John received a wonderful testimonial from Metropolitan Anthony (Khrapovitsky), the founder of the Russian Orthodox Church outside Russia (ROCOR), when he dispatched young Bishop John to China.

The metropolitan wrote: 'I am sending you Bishop John as my soul, as my heart; this little, frail man almost a child in appearance, is something of a miracle of ascetic firmness and strictness in our time of spiritual paralysis.'

It soon became obvious not only to Sonechka, but to many others, that Bishop John was someone special. The unassuming sparrow-like Bishop John wore the simplest of clerical clothing and sandals. He often gave away his sandals to the needy. With his boundless energy he restored harmony to the Russian community. He gained respect by helping wherever help was needed irrespective of status, faith or religion. Before long he had established cordial relations with the Serb, Greek and Ukrainian Orthodox believers in his diocese.

The selfless Bishop John involved himself in virtually every émigré organisation. He was the inspiration and driving force for the construction of churches, a hospital, an asylum for the mentally ill, an orphanage, a home for the elderly, and a community dining hall. In essence, his enthusiasm and tireless work created a social welfare and spiritual network that provided care and sustenance for many of Shanghai's Russian refugees, especially the sick and poverty-stricken.

Soon after his arrival in Shanghai, Bishop John consecrated an impressive new cathedral dedicated to the Mother of God. It held two thousand standing worshippers, there being no pews in these churches.

Sonechka and Vladimir were taken aback when Bishop John, in one of his first sermons, admonished the congregation for neglecting the many Russian street children in Shanghai. He called upon the Russian women present to help him organise a refuge for these children. This became known as the Orphanage of St Tikhon of Zadonsk.[14]

Sonechka immediately became involved. It was a cause close to her heart. The desperate plight of these children appalled her. Soon the initial handful of children at the orphanage rose to more than a hundred. Though most of the children's parents had either abandoned them or died, some were too poor to bring them up. A number of the orphans were Eurasians born of Russian mothers and Chinese fathers. Sonechka recalled how Bishop John once brought back a little girl whom he 'bought' from a Chinese man for a bottle of vodka.

Painful memories flooded back of the emaciated dead bodies of children she had helped collect from the streets in Simferopol while working for the Cheka. She was afraid that Sofia, her niece, could well be in the same situation in Soviet Russia.

Sonechka joined a number of other Russian women whom Bishop John called his *Damy Patronesy* (Lady Patronesses of the orphanage). Besides helping in the orphanage, they organised various fundraising activities.

Sonechka admired the way Bishop John treated everyone with equal respect and did not pass judgement. He maintained that, 'one cannot preach the gospel without manifesting love in one's deeds', and, 'concerning the salvation of men's souls, one needed to remember that people also had bodily needs which clamour for attention'.

Not everyone held Bishop John in high regard. Lara, for instance, considered his church services interminably long and objected to not being permitted to wear rouge on her lips when kissing the cross at the end of the liturgy. In part, Sonechka sympathised with Lara. However, like Vladimir, she was amazed at how Bishop John had united the fractious and dispirited Orthodox community in Shanghai. They felt that the good he was doing far outweighed any criticism of him.

Knowing how Stalin, following Lenin's lead, was brutally suppressing all religions and beliefs other than the Marxist-Leninist creed, Sonechka and Vladimir appreciated being able to worship freely in Shanghai. They thought it evil that Stalin's knowledge of the Russian mind had been gained from his Russian Orthodox seminary training. For Stalin ensured Marxism-Leninism had its own saints, martyrs and devils, with Lenin its first Messiah.

Margarita, a bright little girl, started private lessons with a Russian teacher, Lyudmila Mikhailovna, who taught her to read and write in Russian, English and French. Margarita enjoyed reciting the poems Lyudmila taught her in these languages.

When she was older Margarita attended a Russian Orthodox Church school on Saturdays. Many Russian children attended these schools, where they were taught Russian grammar, literature, history, geography and foreign languages. Some of their teachers had held prestigious teaching positions in Imperial Russia, Harbin and Tianjin. A priest instructed them in the fundamentals of the Orthodox faith.

On Sundays, Sonechka, Vladimir and Margarita attended the Divine Liturgy.

Sonechka was pleased that Gerald and Cynthia Parsons got on well with Vladimir. On several occasions Gerald, who was a long-standing member of the exclusive British all-male Shanghai Club, invited Vladimir to accompany him there. Vladimir knew that the only Russian member of this elite club was George Sapozhnikov (pseudonym 'Sapajou'), the brilliant political cartoonist of the prestigious British-owned *North China Daily News* (affectionately known as the 'Old Lady of the Bund'). Sapajou's often humorous cartoons gave one a unique insight into the astonishing complexities of life in cosmopolitan Shanghai.

But Cynthia and Gerald were soon to return 'home' to England. Cynthia longed to be near her married daughters and grandchildren. Cynthia's mother had already returned to England.

Gerald told them he was pleased to retire. 'I'm sick and tired of living a lie. I hate people's propensity for avarice in Shanghai. A line in Shakespeare's *King John* says it all: 'Bell, book and candle, shall not drive me back/when gold and silver becks me to come on.'

Gerald hated the free market, which was so brutal and unconstrained. The *taipans* who had created it were predominately British and American, although there were also a number of wealthy Iraqi Jewish businessmen, including Sir Victor Sassoon. For Gerald, the International Settlement was proof that the free market was a monster. He mused that the *taipans'* substantial charitable donations were more to do with salving their consciences than a genuine concern for Shanghai's impoverished masses. He believed that for the populace to accept capitalism's market economy it should operate under certain constraints, ideally within a Christian moral framework.

At home later that evening, Sonechka and Vladimir reflected on Gerald's insights. Drawing on his knowledge of Shanghai, Vladimir concluded, 'It's all very well for Gerald to feel guilty for having made his fortune from banking, but I wonder whether he would be so philosophical had he lost it all. From early on I realised that morality and money make for poor bedfellows. Shanghai is like Renaissance Florence, an amalgam of criminality, finance and religion. It is grotesque how Stalin, the former Orthodox seminarian and bank robber, has managed in a matter of mere years to outdo the most monstrous absolute power seekers in Renaissance Italy.'

CHAPTER FORTY-SIX

In 1936 Sonechka and Vladimir joined hundreds of their compatriots to hear the Russian base Fyodor Shalyapin sing the unforgettable Boris Godunov arias. Together with the Bibikovs, they also went to a recital by Arthur Rubinstein. It was one of the highlights of the year for Vladimir and Nikolai who, for long afterwards, discussed Rubinstein's memorable concert while listening to his records as they played chess.

In the mid-1930s Shanghai attracted artists from all over the world. These included famous actors, opera singers and ballerinas. Shanghai usurped Depression-ridden Paris as the cultural crossroads of the world. White Russians played an important role in this rich cosmopolitan mix of artistic talent. Russian operas, ballets, orchestras, singers, musicians and writers matched the quality of their much better known Russian counterparts in 1920s Paris. More than half of the members of the Shanghai Symphony Orchestra were Russian and Shanghai published more Russian newspapers, journals and books than Paris.

Sonechka and Vladimir admired the White Russian journalist Captain V.D. Zhiganov, who gave a balanced perspective on the innumerable contentious issues that faced the Russian-speaking community in Shanghai. In 1936 he single-handedly compiled and self-published an immense album of photos and stories entitled 'Russians in Shanghai'.

In stark contrast to the stereotypical portrayal of Shanghai's Russians as being prostitutes, bodyguards and good-for-nothings, his album showed them as an enterprising and resourceful people. Zhiganov showed how, against almost impossible odds, the Russians created vibrant communities. These included manufacturing, retailing, schools, hospitals, higher educational establishments, places of worship and a wide range of sporting, recreational and cultural activities.

In the summer of 1936, Vladimir took his long service entitlement. He had nine months paid leave for the six years he had worked for the French

Municipal Police. Unable to afford the fare to go to France to see Dora and her family, they rented a house at a popular seaside resort on the outskirts of Dalian, two days north of Shanghai by sea.

A sizeable White Russian exile community lived there. There were several Russian Orthodox churches as well as Russian schools and clubs. Grigory Semyonov, the fearsome Cossack *Ataman* (leader), had his headquarters there and a large number of Cossacks remained loyal to him.

Nearby was the former Imperial Russian possession, Port Arthur, a poignant reminder of the torpedo boat attack in early 1904 (the Pearl Harbour of its day). Several Russian warships were sunk, initiating the fateful Russo-Japanese war.

During that summer, several of their Russian friends sent their daughters to stay with them. Vladimir, recalling his wonderful childhood summer holidays on their Merkuli estate, became a gracious host. Apart from daily walks, swimming in the sea and sunbathing on the rocky foreshore, Vladimir enjoyed organising outings and entertainments to amuse his charges. Several girls had a Name Day to celebrate during that summer. A cake was baked and a special dish prepared to mark these celebrations. Vladimir did his best to buy 'just the right gift' for the celebrant.

For Sonechka this holiday proved onerous. Besides having to cook on a primitive kitchen stove, she had little help with the washing and cleaning. Even so, by the end of her holiday she felt rejuvenated and ready to face life again in bustling Shanghai.

Galina, one of the older girls who came to stay with them, was a pupil at the prestigious Sacred Heart, the Roman Catholic Convent School for girls in the French Concession. Sonechka and Vladimir hoped that Margarita would go there.

They made approaches and Vladimir's charm, along with Margarita's command of French and English convinced the dignified Reverend Mother Fitzgerald to accept her. Aged seven, Margarita commenced her formal education in the preparatory department. Margarita and Galina were the only Russian Orthodox pupils at the school.

CHAPTER FORTY-SEVEN

Vladimir and Sonechka were alarmed by newsreels of the 1936 Berlin Olympic Games and films such as Leni Riefenstahl's, 'Triumph of the Will', that glorified Nazi Germany and idolised Hitler and Hermann Goering. Vladimir admired Churchill and deplored the way the appeasers labelled him a vicious warmonger. He found it difficult to believe that the British could discount the threat posed by Goering's Luftwaffe. Vladimir suspected that Churchill's credibility suffered from the support he gave King Edward VIII in his decision to marry Wallis Simpson, who had lived in Shanghai in the 1920s.

From what Vladimir read of the continuing rearmament in Japan, and the build up of her forces in Manchukuo (the former Manchuria), it seemed inevitable they would attack China.

This happened in July 1937. Japanese troops swept over the northern half of China, capturing Beijing and Tianjin. On 12 August, they mounted a concerted attack on the several million Chinese living in greater Shanghai adjacent to the foreign concessions defended by Chiang's Nationalist army. The guns of twenty Japanese warships stationed on the Huangpu River shelled Shanghai's Chinese sections.

At home with Margarita, Sonechka heard two enormous explosions. They rushed outside and saw a mix of smoke and flames billowing high into the sky. The waterfront end of Nanking Road was the focal point of the fire. Two more huge explosions which sent smoke and flames leaping into the air smothered the International Settlement and parts of the French Concession.

Since the police headquarters where Vladimir worked were located some distance from the explosions, Sonechka thought that he would not be in danger. Even so, she worried until a messenger delivered a note telling her that Vladimir was safe. But she also was worried about Lara whose salon was close to the explosions.

Later that afternoon, a distraught Lara arrived at Sonechka's apartment. The windows of her salon facing Nanking Road had been blown out, but neither she nor her two clients had been injured. But she was horrified by the blood, body parts and debris that littered Nanking Road. To make matters worse, she had recently received a letter from her son, Alexander. He wanted to train as a Luftwaffe pilot and join the elite Condor Legion fighting for Franco in the Spanish Civil War. She was shattered. In view of what she had just seen, she did not know how he could consider being part of an air force that attacked and killed civilians, as had happened in the Spanish city of Guernica.

Later they learned that one bomb had hit the Palace Hotel, and the other, the Cathay Hotel at the junction of Nanking Road and the Bund. Chinese pilots, flying American Northrop fighters, dropped these bombs and two others on the Great World, a popular multi-storey Chinese entertainment complex near the French Concession boundary.

In all, a thousand people were killed and about the same number were injured. Chinese Nationalists insisted that their aircraft off-loaded these bombs fleeing from heavy Japanese gunfire. Others believed that the Chinese hoped to get the British and the Americans to side with them in fighting the Japanese. This was a remote possibility. The British and Americans were both firmly against intervention in what they considered other people's wars. Sonechka wondered where it was safe and where they could go. From what Sasha had written it did not appear that the United States offered a safe haven. The likelihood of Vladimir getting any sort of job there was remote. She and Vladimir reluctantly concluded that trying to get there was out of the question. Moreover they did not like the American's rigorous isolationist policy reflected by their wish to have nothing to do with the rest of the world, particularly Europe.

Finally, after two months, a truce ended the Shanghai conflict. Chiang's army, which had fought heroically against the vastly superior Japanese military machine, had lost two hundred thousand men.

The momentous autumn 1937 Battle of Shanghai scattered thousands of desperate, destitute Chinese. Many of them sought refuge in both foreign concessions. No one seemed to know, or for that matter care, how many Chinese civilians had been killed or injured. Was it tens or hundreds of thousands? Had it not been for the remarkable Father Jacquinot de Besange, many more Chinese would have died.

The Japanese took total control of Hongkou, the former northern section of the International Settlement. It was 'Little Tokyo'. Thousands of Japanese lived cheek by jowl with hundreds of thousands of Chinese. The Japanese stationed guards on Garden Bridge, the sole entry point from Hongkou to the International Settlement south of Suzhou Creek. If the Chinese failed to prostrate themselves before the guards they were badly beaten. Some were killed.

Shanghailanders also had to show obsequious respect to the 'Sons of the Rising Sun'. If not, they would be struck by a rifle butt or worse.

No one knew how many White Russians remained in Zhabei and Hongkou or the number killed during the 1937 battle.

The Japanese controlled the Chinese Municipality of Greater Shanghai through their dreaded military police, the Kempei Tei, and gangsters working with the puppet regime, headed by the Chinese turncoat Wang Jingwei. They also dominated the formerly ill-defined Western Extension of the foreign concessions where Lara, Gustav, Sonechka and Duncan Kerr had lived. The Western Extension rapidly became known as the 'Badlands'. The Japanese occupied many gracious residences where they established – gambling centres, opium dens and houses for prostitutes. Besides the financial return it was an important part of a deliberate policy to demoralise the Chinese.

The Rape of Nanking – in which so many Chinese, particularly the women and children were tortured, raped and killed – demonstrated the Japanese attitude toward the Chinese: they were vermin to be exterminated.

The autumn Battle of Shanghai badly affected the foreign residents. They were no longer spectators. Hundreds had been killed or injured by the bombs that fell on them so unexpectedly on August 13. Most foreign companies advised their employees to send their wives and families home.

Sonechka and Vladimir were alarmed when they heard that some émigré families had taken out Soviet citizenship, believing that if they returned to the Soviet Union they would have a better life. Sonechka understood why they wanted to leave Shanghai, but was baffled as to why they chose the Soviet Union.

But these people were influenced by Comintern propagandists working for the newly created Repatriation Union of Russian Returnees. They beguiled them with a wonderful picture of life in the Soviet paradise. The anti-Soviet French consul-general refused to allow this Soviet organisation to be located in his concession, but the International Settlement authorities allowed them to establish themselves there. Vladimir believed that the British and American *taipans*, who controlled the International Settlement, would agree to anything provided their businesses did not suffer.

Dora's letters from Paris made for equally depressing reading. France was wracked by irreconcilable divisions threatening to tear her apart.

Even the phlegmatic Vladimir, who accessed multiple worldwide sources of information, found the contradictions and unexpected consequences astonishing at times. Not least Stalin's notorious show trials, at which Lenin's dedicated comrades were condemned to death or imprisoned. No latter-day Bonaparte was going to usurp Stalin.

Just prior to the Munich Agreement in late September 1938 Vladimir read in the French press that hundreds of thousands of people had fled Paris during that week. They feared the Luftwaffe would annihilate Paris and its inhabitants. For White Russians like Vladimir's sister, Dora, there was no refuge.

CHAPTER FORTY-EIGHT

A letter from Sasha explained that his situation was unchanged. President Roosevelt's charm and guile was all that prevented American politics erupting into open conflict. Sasha told them that new migrants, no matter what their nationality, were shunned. He was lucky. He had been in America so long he could pass as a local.

Lara's booming salon business reflected the Shanghailanders 'live for the moment' mentality. If they saw trouble ahead they buried it amidst their gaiety.

Apart from a brief note about the sale of their Shanghai home, Lara had not heard from Gustav since his return to Germany over five years ago. In a recent letter, Alexander told her Gustav had been appointed to a prestigious Nazi Party position but gave no details. He was still waiting to join the Luftwaffe and he believed it would be next month.

Peter, Alexander's twin brother, never mentioned his father. He longed for his Shanghai youth and hoped to do an arts course.

Wolfgang, who now lived with Lara in her Cathay Mansions apartment, told Sonechka and Vladimir about the number of German Jews he had met who had fled to Shanghai. Though most did not practise their Jewish faith they were still attacked by the Nazis. They maintained that some of their brethren, provided they renounced their Jewish roots, had been given honorary Aryan status if the Nazis considered their expertise or skills indispensable. (Field Marshall Erhard Milch, the effective head of the Luftwaffe during World War II, being arguably the most notable.[15])

When Hitler's forces invaded Czechoslovakia in March 1939, Vladimir saw war in Europe as inevitable. However, like nearly everyone else, he failed to predict the astonishing Non-Aggression Pact (August 1939) signed by von Ribbentrop, the Nazis' foreign minister, and Molotov, his Soviet counterpart, to divide up Poland.

On September 1, 1939, the Nazis invaded Poland on the trumped up charge of a Polish attack on Germany. On September 17, the Soviets subjected the Poles in the eastern half of their country to an equally horrendous ordeal.

It was beginning to dawn on the foreigners in Shanghai that their lives hung by a thread. The final straw was the withdrawal of all but a handful of Shanghai's European troops, to defend their people at home.

Dora wrote that the French were terrified the Germans would invade. After the Germans' blitzkrieg in Poland many began to question the wisdom of their country's reliance on the Maginot Line to protect them. What if the Germans circumvented it by invading France through Holland and Belgium?

Even more worrying was the defeatism that pervaded the country. The left-wingers blamed fascists for France's despair and the right-wingers believed the socialists and Communists to be responsible.

Dora dreaded to think what might happen to her son, Gleb, marooned on the Maginot Line awaiting the German onslaught. It did not help that her normally gregarious husband, Andrei, had become morose, immersing himself in his memoirs and émigré meetings. At least her job at the American hospital seemed secure.

For Vladimir, trying to predict Germany's next move defied analysis. Stalin's imperial ambitions were clear. Having ravaged the eastern part of Poland, he tried to conquer Finland, but failed. The Finns lost territory but the Soviets had shown that their army was not ready to fight even a small country; the cream of their armed forces had been executed by Stalin. It was a lesson not lost on Hitler.

Lara was dismayed when the Soviets seized her beloved Estonia. To make matters worse, Wolfgang had just lost his job.

Commiserating with Wolfgang and Lara one evening, Sonechka likened their situation to shipwrecked survivors washed up on a hostile island surrounded by shark-invested waters.

The astonishing contradictions Vladimir identified in the course of his job made him wonder how anyone could possibly make sense of it all. Though he knew that Lindbergh was a great admirer of Nazi Germany, it was a revelation that Henry Ford, the motor vehicle manufacturing magnate, was an avid anti-Semite. Fittingly, both men received the Nazi's highest award for foreigners, the Service Award of the German Eagle.

Having failed to fathom war-torn Europe, Vladimir turned his attention to China. With half the country occupied by the thinly stretched Japanese forces opposed by a tenuous alliance between General Chiang's nationalists and Mao's Communist forces, Vladimir found China as confusing as Europe.

He could see from the Soviet perspective that they wanted Chiang, despite his hatred of Communism, to tie down the Japanese, who might otherwise invade Siberia and seize its rich natural resources. The Soviets knew that their protégé, Mao, was not strong enough to do this on his own, Vladimir was baffled why Chiang's vastly superior Nationalist Army had not destroyed Mao and his beleaguered supporters.[16]

At the orphanage, Sonechka marvelled how Bishop John coped with the pastoral and social demands. Together with the other 'lady patronesses' she helped raise funds for the ever increasing number of orphans and abandoned children. The parents of many of these children were destitute Russians made redundant by the downturn in the city's economy. The non-judgmental Bishop John did everything possible to help the distressed with no thought of his own well-being. That he did not collapse from exhaustion or fall seriously ill from eating next to nothing, and being sparsely clad in the depths of Shanghai's bitter winters, amazed everyone.

CHAPTER FORTY-NINE

It took the Germans only six weeks to defeat the French; Vladimir's French colleagues were devastated. Their enraged rhetorical questions rent the air. How could two million of their soldiers possibly have surrendered to the Germans? What about the vaunted French armoured divisions and aircraft that matched the German military in number and quality? What was the French officer corps doing? Were they all fascists? Did the socialists and communists convince the rank and file to lay down their arms in the belief that it was a capitalist war in which they would be the hapless sacrificial victims? What had happened to French grandeur?

For Vladimir it was a rerun of the heated recriminations he had heard so often in Paris in the aftermath of the Bolshevik victory. He knew it was futile to apportion blame for a defeat. If he had not lived in France, he would never have believed it was such a divided country.

As the war in Europe continued, Sonechka and Vladimir spent many evenings discussing how it might affect them in Shanghai. The depth of hostility between the French and English surprised Sonechka.

Perhaps fortunately for Vladimir and Sonechka, Vichy France, not General Charles de Gaulle's Free French government-in-exile in Britain, remained in charge of the French Concession in Shanghai. Otherwise they might have been interned.

The concessions' police forces broke up an ugly brawl between French and British sailors. But for their intervention, the French would have shot British sailors in retaliation for the more than one thousand of their fellow sailors killed or drowned at Mers-el-Kebir by Britain's Royal Navy. Fearful the French Fleet would fall into the hands of the Germans, Churchill authorised this attack.

Vladimir deplored the eighty-five-year-old Petain's governance of Vichy France. Petain declared De Gaulle a traitor and condemned him to death in absentia. He also accused De Gaulle of helping the British to take France's prized overseas possessions.

Another Frenchman, Colonel Rene Fonck, a famous World War I air ace, claimed that some 200 French pilots were prepared to join him in battling the British. Vladimir saw this as indicative of the popular support for Petain's regime.

When Lara learned that many Luftwaffe pilots were killed in the Battle of Britain, she feared her twenty-year-old son Alexander could be one of them. She was also afraid he might have been killed earlier in Poland. In his last letter, written just before Hitler invaded Poland, he said how excited he was to have qualified as a Luftwaffe fighter pilot. Lara had not heard from Peter, whom she imagined had been conscripted into the army. Worried, she contacted the German consulate in Shanghai but they could not help her.

In late November, Vladimir received a distressing letter from Dora. The Germans had captured Gleb, her soldier son, on the Maginot Line and he was imprisoned with two million other Frenchmen. She continued working at the American hospital.

By late 1940 around twenty thousand Jews had found sanctuary in Shanghai. They joined the city's other victim diaspora, the White Russians, in the port of last resort.[17] Some enlivened both foreign concessions with their entrepreneurial skills and artistic talents, but for most life was a desperate struggle. They had arrived with nothing but the clothes on their back, a few meagre belongings and little money. Without the shelter and food provided for them by the city's Jews, particularly Sir Victor Sassoon, many would have died.

Operation Barbarossa, Hitler's invasion of the Soviet Union which began on June 22, 1941, tore Shanghai's Russian-speaking community apart. Some saw the Germans as liberators of their country from the hated Bolshevik regime. Others applied for Soviet citizenship at Shanghai's Repatriation Union of Russian Emigrants, to fight for their Motherland.

Sonechka and Vladimir were caught between these two extremes. That other Russians could not see their predicament in this way, and chose to support one or other of these totalitarian regimes worried them. They understood the beguiling power of Soviet propaganda. It had increased considerably in Shanghai since Stalin's recent neutrality pact with Japan, allowing the Comintern a virtual free hand in the city.

The White Russian journalist Zhiganov, who advised a neutral stance, had written a pamphlet entitled 'In Defence of the Motherland'. He pointed out that Russians supporting Hitler were wrong. For Hitler had said the Slavs were subhuman and planned to work them to death.

Shanghai's disparate Russian community was in real danger. The Russian

Emigrants Committee had been powerless since the Japanese, along with their Chinese collaborators, took effective control in early 1939. When Charles Meltzer, its respected head, refused to hand over its funds to the Japanese, they murdered him. The White Russian lawyer, Nikolai Ivanov, took over the committee, but he also was murdered just a year later.

But the Japanese left Bishop John and his fellow priests alone. This was because Bishop John made a resolute stand to ensure his parishioners could practise their faith. To Sonechka's relief Vladimir kept his promise to lie low. Like his Russian colleagues in the Municipal Police Department, he had signed the oath of allegiance to Marshall Petain issued by Cosme, the pro-Vichy ambassador to China based in Beijing.

Support for de Gaulle's Free French, though initially strong at the French Club, petered out when the Vichy French Concession authorities arrested several well known Gaullist activists. Vladimir sympathised with de Gaulle, but not to the extent that he would proclaim his cause. He knew that for his family to survive he had no alternative other than to swear allegiance to his employer, Vichy France. Vladimir felt he had done enough fighting for several lifetimes and had no wish to become embroiled in another conflict.

Defeat appeared inevitable for the Soviet Union. After just four months the Germans were poised to take Leningrad and Moscow. Their blitzkrieg tactics proved as devastatingly effective in Russia as they had been in Poland and Western Europe. Vladimir and his political section colleagues found it difficult to believe Operation Barbarossa had been such a surprise to the Soviets.

During this time Sonechka's heart went out to her sister, Liza, her husband, Pavel, and their daughter, Sofia. She wondered if they were still alive and living in Leningrad. She prayed for their safety.

However, the reports Vladimir and his colleagues were getting from Comintern sources in Shanghai and elsewhere showed the Soviets were not beaten. Some Allied commentators were saying that the winter would prove to be Hitler's nemesis, as it had been for Napoleon. By early November there were reports of inadequately clad German troops freezing to death and their vehicles and tanks being unable to function because of the intense cold – minus 40 degrees and below.

Vladimir had no doubt that the war would have been over had the Germans befriended the millions of Russians who initially welcomed them. However, instead of liberating his people from the horrors of Stalinism, the Germans inflicted a reign of terror on them.

Vladimir understood that the Soviets were putting up unexpectedly stiff resistance and stalling the German advance, not just at Leningrad, but on several other fronts. This change in fortune was due to Stalin heeding reports, provided by the Comintern operative Richard Sorge based in Tokyo, that the Japanese would attack America and not the Soviet Union. Consequently Stalin countered the German onslaught by calling on many well-equipped mechanised winter divisions, stationed on the Sino-Russian border to counter the long expected Japanese attack.

In a recent letter Sasha wrote how the United States economy had picked up since America had become a major supplier of military equipment and materials to Britain. As a result he had no difficulty getting painting contracts for factories and associated buildings. Having read the recently published *The Grapes of Wrath*, by John Steinbeck, Sasha felt he understood why so many Californians welcomed rearmament. The hordes of destitute and starving 'dust bowl farmers' who had fled there, had got jobs.

Dora's letters were brief. Sonechka and Vladimir wondered whether she feared they could be censored. She had not heard from Katherine for some time and Gleb continued to languish in a German prisoner-of-war camp. The American Hospital reception job seemed to be her sole solace.

CHAPTER FIFTY

Within hours of their attack on Pearl Harbour on December 8, 1941, the Japanese occupied Shanghai's International Settlement. Practically all the allied armed forces had left and the mainly Russian-manned Volunteer Corps was not mobilised. There was only a brief exchange of gunfire, when the Japanese boarded a British naval vessel, the *Petrel*, moored opposite the French Bund.

Because the French authorities had adhered to Marshall Petain's collaboration decree, the Japanese maintained they had no need to occupy the French Concession. However, despite this declaration, Japanese military and civilian personnel became much more conspicuous. Sonechka and Vladimir quickly learnt how to be deferential to the Japanese. At the French Club their overbearing behaviour became so bad that the couple ceased going. The escalating club costs, driven up by inflation, also led Vladimir to relinquish his membership.

At least he and Sonechka did not have to wear armbands identifying their nationality as did the British, Americans and those people in Shanghai whose countries were fighting the Axis forces. The armbands were marked 'B' for British, and 'A' for American.

As war engulfed the world after Pearl Harbour, Shanghai was now at the crossroads of this momentous conflict. The worldwide events that Vladimir read about and heard on the radio defied reason. The old adage that truth is the first victim of war applied as a flood of propaganda from all sides bombarded the airwaves and printed word. Musing on this point, Vladimir wondered how the British felt about their erstwhile staunch ally, the Japanese, now being their imperious conqueror. After all, Britain had done more than any other country to enable Japan to become a modern industrial nation.

It was a terrible shock for the six thousand British marooned in Shanghai at the mercy of the Japanese. They could not believe that the Japanese had sunk the battleship the *Prince of Wales* and the cruiser *Repulse*, the pride of their Southeast Asian fleet. Vladimir likened this British complacency to that of Imperial Russia's self-confidence at the outset of the 1904–1905 Russo-Japanese war.

The arrival in Shanghai of the notorious Gestapo Colonel Josef Meisinger, known as the 'butcher of Warsaw', worried Wolfgang since his maternal grandmother was Jewish. Vladimir reassured him that the Japanese, grateful for the very considerable financial help given them by Jewish bankers, would not allow Meisinger to exterminate Shanghai's Jews.

Also, the Nazi's rabid racial supremacy policy alarmed the Japanese, despite Hitler calling them honorary Aryans. Vladimir pointed out that at that time Vichy France accepted Christians with Jewish forebears such as Wolfgang.

Wolfgang's confrontation with a Japanese soldier on duty at Garden Bridge made them all realise how precarious life had become. The soldier examined Wolfgang's passport and papers and found everything in order. However, before allowing him to pass, the soldier snarled and thrust his bayonet, just centimetres from Wolfgang's face.

The Japanese forced all those Jews who had arrived in the city after 1937 to live in a restricted part of Hongkou, north of Suzhou Creek in the International Settlement. For the few who were comfortably settled in areas like the French Concession, this was an unimaginable ordeal. In the grotesquely over-crowded ghetto, some families lived in a single room with no running water and the stinking 'honey bucket'. Many White Russians had long endured similar living conditions in Shanghai.

The Jews' fate would have been even worse had Meisinger had his way. However, the Japanese ignored his repeated demands that Shanghai's Jews be exterminated. The infuriated Meisinger was powerless in the face of the control exercised by the Japanese in Shanghai. The Japanese treated German citizens little better than citizens of Allied nations and seized German businesses and properties.

Meanwhile, because of escalating inflation, Sonechka and Vladimir found it difficult to make ends meet. They were forced to sell their apartment. They received a lot less for it than they had hoped. Through Masha, Sonechka found temporary accommodation in a well-run Russian boarding house in the French Concession near Margarita's school.

Over the last ten years she and Vladimir had enjoyed collecting many beautiful things. Sonechka decided to supplement Vladimir's inflation-ravaged wage by selling some of their furniture, antiques and curios. Lara helped her by storing some of their items in her basement storeroom at the Cathay Mansions.

Although, at first appalled that a wife of his should trade on the streets with hawkers, especially Chinese, Vladimir soon realised that Sonechka's hitherto hidden talent paid dividends. He jested that he never knew from one day to the next what he might find sold in their two small, cluttered rented rooms.

Amah had returned to her village to take care of her ailing, elderly parents and being in a boarding house meant they could no longer employ a boy.

The Japanese demanded that all Russians be part of one organisation, the Russian Emigrants Committee. The Ukrainians vigorously opposed this order. They insisted they were a nation in exile, a people intent on casting off hundreds of years of Imperial Russian rule. The remainder, including the Jewish Russians, acquiesced to this Japanese demand.

The leeway given by the Japanese to the Comintern in Shanghai infuriated the Germans, Japan's Axis ally. Shanghai's Soviet broadcasts and newspaper reports vehemently refuted German accounts of the bitter war fought in the Soviet Union.

In despair, Sonechka and Vladimir concluded that Shanghai was a madhouse defying analysis. At least Vladimir did not have to evaluate what he heard and read, just translate it into French for his Vichy superiors to interpret.

The revelations concerning collaboration with the Japanese never ceased to surprise Sonechka. By the same token, in the case of Lara, she realised that her acquiescence to Japanese rule was a question of survival. The sad reality was that confronting the Japanese and their collaborators meant starvation or worse.

Lara's clientele changed dramatically. A number were the mistresses of Axis personnel – Japanese, Italian and German – with some even the mistresses of Soviet men. The gall of these mistresses, including several Russians, appalled Lara. Though the Japanese men accompanying their mistresses treated her with contempt, they did not quibble about her charges. When appropriate, she said she was Estonian to dispel the idea she was German. But usually Lara said little to her clients for fear of antagonising them, although sometimes she nearly erupted in anger when they boasted they could get anything they wanted from the black market. Lara bemoaned that she had to clothe these harlots in order to survive.

The notorious Big Eared Du and his fellow Green Gang gangsters had long ago fled the city for Chongqing, the capital of Chiang's Nationalist government. However, equally ruthless Chinese gangsters had replaced them.

Hand in glove with the Japanese in every conceivable criminal activity, they made a great deal of money out of Shanghai's millions of destitute Chinese and others in desperate straits, including the Russians.

Vladimir knew that Shanghai was full of spies and collaborators. Comintern agents, with their zealous belief in the victory of the world's proletariat, were the most dedicated. Many other agents consorted with criminals and acted for personal gain. It shocked Vladimir that the Kailin Mines in the north of China, owned and managed by Britons, continued to operate well into the war years, because its product was vital to the Japanese steel industry. Vladimir saw it as yet another example of the British placing commerce ahead of everything else.

During the siege of Leningrad the city experienced its coldest winter for one hundred years in 1941–42. Sonechka constantly worried about Liza and her family, should they still be alive and living there.

One night Sonechka had a most disturbing dream: she saw a grief-stricken Liza standing motionless, sobbing, as she stared into the depths of a Leningrad canal.

On waking, Sonechka knew in her heart that her loved ones must be dead.

CHAPTER FIFTY-ONE

The world war meant Sonechka could no longer write to Sasha nor could Vladimir correspond with his sister, Dora.

Following events closely from the limited information he had access to, Vladimir knew the Japanese had achieved a series of victories. In no time their forces swept through Southeast Asia, capturing Singapore in mid-February 1942. Indonesia was taken from the Dutch soon after.

A model student, Margarita, aged eleven, did so well at the convent that she skipped a year. Vladimir, her home tutor, took a great interest in her success. Having sold their piano, Margarita now played the violin. To further economise Vladimir acquired two secondhand bicycles. He rode one to work; the other one was for Margarita. Vladimir accompanied her in the mornings. En route they passed the statue of Pushkin. The Russian community had erected it in 1937, to commemorate the 100th anniversary of the writer's death.

On her way to and from school, Margarita was horrified by what she saw. Dead bodies often lay on the side of the road and emaciated people sifted through rotting garbage searching desperately for food.

It was with mixed emotions that Sonechka greeted the news she was pregnant. The joy of having another child vied with the realisation that it would be a terrible world for a baby. Vladimir could not contain his delight. For several days he became the doting father-to-be, discounting the desperate times in which they lived. Then the reality of their situation made him morose, but his normal optimism soon returned.

Sonechka prayed that at her age, and in their straitened situation, she would carry her child to full term. Would they have enough food to nurture it? She was due in October and was worried that the baby's vulnerable first six months would be during Shanghai's worst weather. The Japanese had already ripped out all the radiators in their boarding house. They were sent to Japan to be used in their armaments industry. Now they had only a single kerosene heater. Would this give enough warmth for the baby to survive?

In addition to her trading activities, Sonechka was determined to find a more suitable home before the baby's birth.

From early in her pregnancy, the asthma that had troubled Sonechka for several years miraculously disappeared. On the other hand in the latter stages of pregnancy her legs became swollen, and this made it difficult for her to cope with the oppressive humid heat. In her quest to find an apartment Sonechka walked far and wide, constantly praying to the Mother of God for help.

In mid-August her luck turned. Sonechka was walking towards the end of Avenue Petain on the outskirts of the French Concession. She approached two newly built, large apartment blocks and heard a heated discussion. Near the entrance of the Georgia Apartment building, a group of Chinese were arguing with two Japanese soldiers. Suddenly, one of the Japanese soldiers turned and pointed at her heavily pregnant stomach. He exclaimed that she could have the apartment in dispute. Only the previous day, she had asked the tall red-turbaned Sikh standing at the entrance if there were any vacancies. Somehow her request had been remembered.

Apparently, that morning, a family had vacated one of the ground floor apartments. These Japanese men evidently held pregnant women in high esteem. So when they saw her they decided that she should have the apartment. Sonechka's new home had two rooms, a tiny kitchen and a bathroom – the greatest thrill of all. Sonechka was elated. Her prayers had been heard. Now her baby would have a proper home.

And there was another pleasant surprise. Soon after moving into their apartment, their Amah appeared at the door clutching a small bundle of tattered belongings. Beaming and nodding at Sonechka's pregnant stomach she said: 'I stay, Missy.'

Amah told Sonechka that her village had been destroyed by the Japanese. Her family had either been killed or had died of hunger. In desperation, Amah returned to Shanghai. Seeking solace she went to the Chinese Buddhist Joss Amah (holy woman and clairvoyant) at the temple. The Joss Amah told her that her Russian 'Missy' (Sonechka) was pregnant. She warned her that 'Missy' could not afford her. Even so she should go and help her.

Imagine Vladimir's surprise, that night, when returning home late from playing chess, he stumbled over Amah's sleeping body in their narrow entrance hall. Amah made the entrance hall her part of the apartment. Every night at nine, she rolled out the blue cotton quilt on which she slept. Visitors soon learned to step over her. On waking she boiled water in the kettle and proceeded to the bathroom for her daily 'cat wash'.

Sonechka thanked God for sending Amah to them. She would be invaluable in the dismal days ahead.

Sonechka was touched when several of their friends' wives knitted woolly garments and blankets for the baby's trousseau. In exchange for his treasured carved jade chess set, Vladimir managed to get another kerosene heater.

Once Sonechka's birth pains started, Vladimir rushed her to the Russian Hospital where, several hours later, early in the morning of October 16, she gave birth to me, Olga. Sonechka could not get over how easy the birth had been. She was delighted when the doctor and nurse told her the newborn child was healthy. Sitting in the waiting room, Vladimir was overjoyed. It seemed an eternity to him before the staff allowed him to see his wife and new child. He embraced Sonechka passionately and later presented her with a bouquet of flowers.

On leaving the hospital that morning, Vladimir met Bishop John, who congratulated him on the birth of a healthy daughter and asked if they had decided on her name? Dumbfounded, Vladimir murmured that, as yet, they had not. Without hesitation the Bishop said, 'As your name is Vladimir, your daughter should be called Olga.'[18] Bowing slightly, the Bishop departed to visit a patient in the hospital.

Vladimir was continually amazed at how this simple man of God, in his threadbare clerical attire and flimsy sandals, was so dedicated to his parishioners.

CHAPTER FIFTY-TWO

Once home Sonechka was terrified Olga would get a chest infection as soon as the weather turned cold. Fortunately, it was a relatively mild autumn.

Anna, Boris Aprelev's wife and godmother to Olga, gave her some antique lace. Sonechka hand-sewed this into Olga's christening robe.

It reminded Vladimir of Dora's 'lace saga'. Fleeing from Sevastopol just ahead of the Bolsheviks in 1920, the family grabbed a chest of memorabilia. It contained antique lace, a small amount of silver and some family photographs (a number are shown in this book). It was not what they wanted. They had mistaken this chest for the one filled with valuables, which remained on the quayside.

Olga's christening took place in their apartment on the feast of St Nicholas, 19 December. Vladimir asked his friend Nikolai Bibikov to be Olga's godfather. By then the bitterly cold weather had set in. During the ceremony the priest immersed the naked Olga three times in water, after which Anna quickly wrapped her in a large white towel. Lara and several of their close friends stayed to celebrate the occasion. In true Russian tradition they all brought some food and Bibikov supplied champagne to toast the health of his goddaughter.

Sonechka's worst fears were realised when Olga became seriously ill in late March. She developed chickenpox. After several days the doctors said they could do nothing to save her. Sensing Sonechka's utter despair, Amah offered to go to the temple to seek the Joss Amah's advice. She was known throughout Shanghai for her wisdom and healing powers. As she left Sonechka pushed an oblong jewellery box into her hands. 'That's the payment if she can save my baby,' she said.

Standing at the back of the jostling temple crowd, Amah was astonished when the Joss Amah beckoned her to come forward.

Knowing that Sonechka worshipped a different god, the Joss Amah said she understood why 'Missy' could not come to her in person. However, she believed Sonechka to be a good woman and wanted to help her baby. Then Joss Amah handed Amah the recipe of a potion to be given frequently to the baby. In return, Amah handed 'the wise one' the oblong box. It contained Duncan's pearls.

Within a week Olga recovered. Overwhelmed with relief, Sonechka believed that God chose the Joss Amah to save her precious daughter's life.

News of the German defeat at Stalingrad at the beginning of 1943 was celebrated by Vladimir and Sonechka. Vladimir thought it ironic that Hitler, so confident of capturing Stalingrad, had planned a triumphant parade in Berlin to celebrate Fascism's conquest of Communism.

Vladimir felt that Stalin's decision to reopen the churches and his directive to have an aircraft circling Moscow with a bishop blessing the city with the Icon of the Mother of God were masterstrokes. From that moment the Russians put aside their hatred of Stalin's regime and fought for Mother Russia. Vladimir thought that if Stalin had not permitted this Orthodox religious revival, both Stalingrad and Moscow would have fallen to the Germans. But he also recognised that the militant atheist Stalin was using the Russian Orthodox Church for his own ends.

Regretfully some Shanghai Russians believed Stalin to be a changed person and were determined to return and fight for their Motherland. Sonechka and Vladimir's ground-floor neighbours, another Russian family, illustrated the tragic consequences of accepting this propaganda. Igor, the husband, took out Soviet citizenship and returned to the Soviet Union, despite his wife's desperate protests. She never heard from him again and was left alone to fend for their child.

Sonechka and Vladimir knew Stalin would never allow a Western-type democracy to develop. He was paranoid about holding power and anyone who might in anyway offer a challenge was to be liquidated.

Sonechka and Vladimir realised that those brought up after their families had escaped from Russia found this difficult to imagine. Those who had a better knowledge tried to enlighten those wanting to return to the Soviet Union, but Comintern propaganda was often stronger. Shanghai Russians living in dreadful conditions were mesmerised by the promise of the paradise the Soviets were purportedly creating.

During the first few months of 1943 the Japanese rounded up the remaining citizens of the allied nations and interned them. Some were pupils at Margarita's school so her class was reduced to five: three Russians, one Chinese and one Irish-American.

In June, the Japanese handed control of both foreign concessions to the Chinese collaborator Wang. It was just 100 years since the British took legal possession of the land that subsequently became the International Settlement. For the proud British this was the ultimate indignity. For the Japanese, it was a statement that they had finally defeated white colonialism in Asia.

Life became increasingly difficult for the Rossi family. Vladimir even gave up smoking. Sonechka saw this as a blessing since she felt it contributed to his nasty chest cough and could harm Olga's health. Amah only just managed to get enough food. How she got it, and where, Sonechka never really knew, though she had her suspicions. Aware that the Chinese eat anything on legs, and anything that flies, she learnt not to ask questions. Sonechka took care that all food was properly cleaned and if possible boiled. On hearing that the greyhounds had disappeared from Canidrome, it crossed Vladimir's mind he could have, unwittingly, sampled one. Where else Vladimir's meat came from did not bear consideration; given his love of horses he would have been horrified if that was what he had eaten.

Out of necessity even Vladimir became entrepreneurial. He struck a deal with two former Russian engineers who had a small butcher's shop on Avenue Joffre. On Saturday mornings Vladimir and Margarita delivered this meat throughout Shanghai on their laden bicycles. They sold the meat to their friends, colleagues and anyone else they could persuade to buy. Their payment depended on the amount they sold and ranged from several chops to a side of bacon. A side of bacon meant that they had enough meat for a week or more and the bones made a tasty soup. The ever-resourceful Sonechka learned to heat the lard, which she then mixed with an egg yolk. They used it as a spread, pretending it was butter.

Sonechka and Vladimir continually avoided the gaze of the short-tempered Japanese, who so easily took offence. A woman walking alone at night risked being raped by drunken Japanese soldiers.

The poorer quarters were cluttered with uncollected stinking garbage and 'honey buckets' full of human excreta. Dead bodies were often seen on the side of the road.

The city was lifeless apart from the nightclubs and cabarets where citizens of Axis nations, the Japanese, Germans and Italians, cavorted with a bewildering assortment of collaborators, crooks and gangsters drawn from many different nationalities. Amidst this gloom and squalor the lively Olga was a ray of sunshine in their dismal, insecure lives.

Another joy was the Bibikovs' Sunday afternoon music recitals. Here they listened to the works of Rachmaninov and Mendelsson. Both were banned in the countries where they were born. How such wonderful music could be declared anti-socialist by the Soviets in the case of Rachmaninov, and in the case of Mendelsson racially contaminated by the Nazis, defied reason.

CHAPTER FIFTY-THREE

While eating their evening meal Sonechka and Vladimir were startled by loud knocking. Vladimir warily opened the door. A smartly dressed Japanese officer strode inside, brushing him aside. Without a word he laid the envelope on the table, then, bowing slightly, he turned and departed.

The letter demanded that they vacate their apartment in two days. No reason was given. Only the day before Vladimir had heard how the Japanese had evicted a fellow Russian officer's family from their apartment. The family shifted into a garage.

Sonechka was mortified. How would they manage? Would Olga survive the winter? Having heard the Japanese were requisitioning apartment buildings like theirs to store ammunition, she knew only a miracle would save them. They might just as well have been interned like the British, she thought.

Throughout the night she prayed to the Mother of God. By dawn she knew what she had to do.

As soon as Vladimir and Margarita left the apartment, Sonechka and Amah flooded it by blocking the toilet. Sonechka sent Amah to tell the other ground-floor tenants to do likewise. Within no time an agitated Japanese official burst into the building. Aghast at the sight before him, he asked if such flooding had happened before. The tenants said that it was a frequent occurrence because of Shanghai's notoriously bad sewage system.

This being the case the Japanese authorities decided to allow them to remain in their apartments. However, it was a Faustian bargain. The floors above them were stacked with ammunition and anti-aircraft artillery pieces were placed on the roof. With this arsenal above them, all the residents dreaded the prospect of the Americans bombing Shanghai.

By 1944 the world war had turned in favour of the Allies. While welcoming this news, the reality was that Sonechka and Vladimir's lives got progressively worse. At work Vladimir never knew whether he would be paid in money or in kind. Sometimes he got sacks of anthracite, which they stored behind a curtained-off corner of their living room. This was a multi-purpose room where Sonechka and Vladimir slept on a divan, the family ate their meals, Margarita did her homework and guests were received.

During the bitterly cold winter weather the anthracite proved to be a prized commodity as they bartered it for food and other necessities. With inflation, money became worthless. By now everyone they knew was forced to barter or sell what they could to survive. The family increasingly relied on Sonechka's bargaining skills; these amazed Vladimir.

Sonechka persuaded Lara, who was now finding life difficult, to part with her hoard of precious silk fabrics. By cutting the fabric into dress lengths Sonechka found ways to exchange them for whatever she could get. At one desperate time, Sonechka even sold her precious gold wedding ring to buy milk for Olga.

After the Japanese banned rickshaws, most people had to walk or cycle. The trams were jammed with Chinese who all seemed to carry goods for trade. Vladimir, Sonechka and Margarita only used them occasionally. Other Chinese used ingenious methods to get around the city. They watched whole families riding around on overburdened wheelbarrows or bicycles. The father peddled the bicycle with the mother sitting side-saddle on the frame and their babies in the handlebar baskets. Their worldly goods would be packed precariously behind the father.

Somehow the Russian orphanage managed to clothe and feed the many children it cared for. Sonechka often wondered how they survived. Though she could no longer give them money she did what she could. Bishop John believed that come what may God would continue to help them.

Vladimir found events in the city bewildering. When Italy capitulated to the Allies in early September 1943, Shanghai's Italians were rounded up by the Japanese, their erstwhile Axis allies, and imprisoned. A week or so later, Mussolini, who had been snatched by the Germans from Allied captivity, declared that Italy remained at war. Then those Shanghai Italians who supported him were freed from prison!

Now that the Allies were winning the war, Vladimir discovered that the Frenchmen with whom he worked declared they had supported de Gaulle and his Free French movement from the beginning. They flatly denied being hostile to Britain in her hour of need and that they had wanted a German not a British Europe.

CHAPTER FIFTY-FOUR

Soon after the Allies launched their invasion of France on June 6, 1944, (D-Day), American bombers began flying over Shanghai. This gave Sonechka and Vladimir nightmares. They prayed that their residential area would be spared from being bombed. Sonechka worried that Vladimir and Margarita might be killed in a bombing raid while cycling on the outskirts of the foreign concessions on their Saturday meat round.

Not having heard from Dora for several years, Vladimir was now concerned for her safety should Paris become a major battleground. However, he thought it unlikely that she had been bombed since she lived and worked in residential parts of the city. He pitied the poor Russians who worked at the Renault factory and lived nearby. It had been a target for British bombers since early on in the war. He was very relieved when the Germans offered little resistance to the Allied liberation of Paris, on August 25, 1944.

There was enormous speculation among Shanghai's White Russians as to what would happen to them once the Americans occupied their city. Would they be considered allies or enemies? Sonechka and Vladimir hoped they would be seen as neutrals.

Despite the constant presence of American aircraft in the skies over Shanghai, and a decree that property owners dig trenches in their streets, the Japanese still claimed they were winning the war.

Sonechka and Vladimir were delighted when they heard that Germany had surrendered, unconditionally, to the allies on May 7, 1945.

However, their relief was short lived. Terrible rumours swept Shanghai of what their fate might be. Some believed that America's mighty European bomber force would be diverted to carpet bomb Shanghai. Others thought the Japanese would use them as human shields in their battle to the death with the Americans.

The intense cold during the last winter of the war badly affected Vladimir's chest. This was made worse by the frequent gas, electricity and water cuts.

The shortage of food together with the strict curfews added to the family's problems.

To make their plight worse, Vladimir lost his job after the collapse of Petain's regime. Sustained by her faith, Sonechka felt confident God would continue to protect her family.

With his rational western mind, Vladimir wrestled with the reality of their situation on the one hand, and on the other, like Sonechka, the belief that God would save them.

Though Lara closed her salon, she decided not to sell it. Ever the optimist, she dismissed the possibility that her premises would be bombed. Instead, she looked forward to Shanghai's free-spending Americans outfitting their lady friends in her creations.

Wolfgang kept in the background, determined not to attract Japanese attention. He feared they would treat him as an enemy now that Germany had surrendered.

As if this was not bad enough, Shanghai's White Russians were fearful that the Soviets would declare war on Japan and, in league with Mao's Communists, invade Japanese occupied northern China, including Shanghai. With nowhere to flee to, the White Russians would be in real danger of being declared 'traitors to the socialist cause' and executed or imprisoned.

Ugly uprisings by Vietnamese troops, who made up by far the bulk of the French Concession's garrison, also threatened the lives of Vladimir and his family. These Vietnamese were incited to rebel by militant nationalists agitating for their country's independence. Shanghai's demoralised and disillusioned French resented de Gaulle's decision to retain control of French Indochina, yet do nothing about regaining control of the French Concession from the Chinese.

The death of Louis Fabre, the widely respected, long-standing head of the French Concession's police force, under whom Vladimir had worked, exemplified the plight of the French after the collapse of Petain's Vichy regime. Some said Fabre committed suicide, driven by guilt for not standing up to the Japanese. Others believed that a radical Free French group had declared Fabre a traitor and executed him.

CHAPTER FIFTY-FIVE

Sonechka and Vladimir were horrified by the destruction caused by the atomic bombs the Americans had dropped on Nagasaki and Hiroshima. Despite their suffering at the hands of the Japanese, they did not believe any civilian population deserved that punishment.

Their joy at being freed from fears of American bombing was mixed with suspicion of a Sino-Soviet alliance. Stalin had declared war on Japan just before it capitulated. His forces, fighting alongside Mao's Communists, swept through Manchuria. Many Russians living there fled to Shanghai. They were sure that those who stayed in Manchuria must have taken out Soviet citizenship, but in reality many of them were transported back to the Soviet Union on their way to the gulag.

To Sonechka and Vladimir's amazement, for several weeks after Japan capitulated, the Japanese continued to control Shanghai. The war had ended so abruptly that it took the Americans some time to mobilise their occupation force, so they and the Chinese Nationalists tacitly accepted this situation, hoping it would help retain order. In the interim, the Chinese Nationalists and Communists fought openly. This made the city more dangerous than ever.

After the war, Vladimir became a committee member of the Russian Emigrants Association. Sonechka attended all the open meetings, which were presided over by the Cossack Colonel Grigory Bologov. Many speakers expressed concern about their future. They were alarmed by the widely reported fate of forty-five thousand Cossacks and their families, many of whom had been born abroad. They had just heard that in June 1945, British soldiers brutally repatriated these Cossacks from their camp in Linz, Austria to the Soviet zone. Here they were either shot or sent to gulags.

Many at the meeting feared that if the British could do this to the Cossacks, all Russians living abroad could suffer a similar fate under the repatriation terms of the Yalta Agreement (February 1945).

Bologov promised that the committee's executive would do their utmost to ensure that the Americans would not forcibly repatriate those in Shanghai who had opposed Stalin. The executive was also empowered to find countries prepared to grant asylum to these Russians living in Shanghai.

Meanwhile, the Shanghai-based Soviet propaganda machine worked overtime to glorify Stalin, the brilliance of his leadership in defeating fascism and in creating a wonderful socialist state. This was music to the ears of many Russians, but not to Bishop John who refused to pay allegiance to the Moscow Patriarch. Bishop John had learnt the fate of many of the White Russians who returned to the Soviet Union.

One such victim was the fascist Konstantin Rodzayevsky, who had for so long led the Russian Fascist Union from Harbin. In a confessional letter to Stalin he pleaded the error of his ways, saying that it was now his fervent desire to participate fully in the 'victory of radiant Stalinist ideas'. Like so many other returnees he was shot.

Sonechka was thrilled to learn that Sasha, her brother, had applied for an affidavit for all of them to enter America. He seemed in good spirits. During the war he had been an army reservist as he continued to work as a painter. For the first time in years, the family's future looked less bleak.

In the meantime Sonechka and Vladimir struggled to survive. Vladimir's increasing shortness of breath and coughing bouts were a constant worry. She wanted him to see a doctor but he thought it unnecessary.

The arrival of the fresh-faced and fun-loving American servicemen in Shanghai, determined to put the horrors of warfare behind them, galvanised the city. As Lara had predicted, her salon prospered as they lavished money on outfits for their newly acquired lady friends, some of whom were Russian.

Vladimir was able to get a job with the American occupation forces as a dispatch driver for their military police and their standard of living improved. With his fluent English and knowledge of Shanghai, Vladimir was soon placed in charge of the dispatch drivers, many of whom were multilingual Europeans. Their office was in one of the gracious racecourse buildings erected by the British. It had been occupied by the Japanese during the war, and was now requisitioned by the Americans.

Vladimir worked mainly the afternoon and evening shifts. When he stepped in for absent drivers, he would not return home until well after midnight. In the depths of winter, Sonechka and Margarita would wait up for him, huddled round the kerosene heater trying to keep warm while sipping hot water, pretending it was tea. On one occasion he returned home so late that they had long gone to bed. He woke Sonechka up and was beaming from ear to ear. He had met a new dispatch driver, a Viennese Jewish professor, with whom he discussed music and art until dawn.

Once Vladimir began to work for the Americans, he and Margarita ceased their Saturday morning meat rounds. Because of the air raids and curfews during the occupation, the family attended the small neighbouring Russian Orthodox Church. This continued after the war and each Saturday Margarita attended the *Zakon Bozhi* (religious instruction) class there, often accompanied by the exuberant four-year-old Olga.

On Saturday mornings the nuns at the Russian Orthodox convent baked the *prosphora* (holy bread) to be used for the Sunday Liturgy's Holy Communion. This holy bread was delivered to Russian Orthodox churches throughout Shanghai. To ensure that I did not disrupt the lesson, Father Peter devised a ploy using the holy bread. Provided I was a good girl and sat quietly, he would give me several of these freshly baked *prosphoras*. With great relish I ate them one after another.

Vladimir heard from Dora. He was overjoyed to learn that she and her children had survived the war. The hospital had retained its independence by joining the Red Cross, the flag of which it flew. It intrigued Dora how the hospital manager, until very nearly the end of the war, managed to fill the hospital beds with patients of every nationality except German. Like most Russians, Dora had kept her head down, not wanting to provoke the Germans. Some sided with the Nazis while others defied them. Two White Russians who worked at the prestigious Paris de l'Homme formed France's first anti-German intelligence gathering network at a time when active resistance to the occupiers was miniscule. Five months later they were caught and executed by the Germans.

Dora was soon to leave Paris to visit her son, Gleb, in Germany. He had been a prisoner there since very early in the war. She would be staying with cousins in Marburg, near Frankfurt.

CHAPTER FIFTY-SIX

Anxious to know what had happened to Liza, Pavel and Sofia, who might still be alive in the Soviet Union, Vladimir contacted the International Red Cross. They could find no record of their whereabouts. Had they been executed by Stalin as 'enemies of the people'; sent to a gulag; frozen or starved to death or killed by the Germans during the Siege of Leningrad?

Lara was devastated to learn that both her sons had died fighting on the Russian front. Lara blamed herself for their deaths. She was tormented that she had done so little to prevent Gustav taking them there. Gustav's fate was unknown.

Vladimir was surprised when Dora told him that their cousin Vera, whom he remembered from summers at Merkuli, had survived the Soviet capture of Berlin. She had lived there since the mid-20s when she moved from Japan with Ernst, her husband, a professor of Oriental Languages at the Humboldt University in the Soviet zone of the city. They lived in the American sector and he commuted daily to the university by train.

In 1946 Dora was working in the American zone with the United Nations Relief and Rehabilitation Agency (UNRRA). Her proficiency in four languages was a useful skill as they sorted out the countless refugees and Nazi sympathisers. The devastated towns and cities she visited stunned her. Hardly a habitable building was left standing; they were replaced by a sea of rubble stretching as far as the eye could see. Here she dealt with thousands of displaced persons (DPs) from Central and Eastern Europe. They were fleeing from the Soviets and desperately needed food and shelter. Even more disturbing was the ghastly condition of skeleton-like former concentration camp inmates.

The fate of the Rossi's now lay in the hands of Chiang, whose bitter rivalry with Mao was tearing China apart. Vladimir considered them both unprincipled and ruthless. Chiang ingratiated himself with the Americans by marrying Mayling, the daughter of Charlie Soong, the fabulously wealthy American-educated Chinese banker. It also helped that Chiang became a Christian, baptised by

American Methodist missionaries. The Americans saw Chiang as their man to prevent China falling from their grasp and becoming Communist.

Russian shopkeepers and businessmen hated the protection money demanded by Chiang's Blueshirts. They were fascists in all but name. Their charges were even higher than those made by the thugs who had worked for the Green Gang boss Big-Eared Du before the war or by collaborator Wang during the Japanese occupation. The Blueshirts forced many Chinese out of business on the pretext that they had actively collaborated with the Japanese. Chiang and several other powerful families took control of these businesses, which masqueraded as legitimate state enterprises, although Chiang and his supporters took all the profits. The exorbitant rental and protection monies Lara paid to the Blueshirts meant she could barely afford to keep her business going.

Most of the American aid – tens of millions of dollars worth – given to Chiang ended up in the black market and profited Chiang's cronies. Vladimir was not surprised so many Chinese turned to Mao's Communists despite the risk of being executed by Chiang's Blueshirts. These executions were carried out on the streets in full view of the public.

Both Mao and Chiang saw the Chinese people as an amorphous mass that they could manipulate and murder as they pleased. The knowledge Chiang acquired from the Soviets when he lived in Moscow in the early 1920s and while a student at a Japanese military academy before World War I prepared him for his ruthless role. Chiang showed no interest in the White Russians. They came to realise that their only hope was to be granted asylum in a democratic country. But despite Colonel Bologov's best efforts not a single country was prepared to consider their pleas.

In May 1947, at the annual general meeting of the Russian Emigrants Association, Bologov made a splendid speech. He vigorously attacked a United Nations' proposal that they should remain in Shanghai under a Chinese Communist regime. During his speech, Bologov got thunderous applause from the two thousand five hundred people present when he pounded his fist on the table before him, exclaiming, 'We can be broken, but not bent.'

Archbishop John (he was made an archbishop in June 1946) and other Orthodox priests, including Father Nikodim, attended this meeting hoping to hear that a safe haven had been found for the stateless Russians stranded in Shanghai. It was rumoured that the Americans might evacuate a number of Russians to a former military base in the Philippines. Many were confused about how long Shanghai would be able to resist the Communists. Most knew that the Nationalists were now a spent force.

CHAPTER FIFTY-SEVEN

Despite increasing shortness of breath and loss of weight, Vladimir was adamant that the doctors could do nothing for him. Once the Americans got their own drivers and staff, he lost his dispatch job. However, knowing that the family relied on his wage to survive, the Americans gave him a job as a night watchman at the American Forces complex. Now he had to walk about in all weathers.

Sonechka dreaded to think what the coming winter could do to him.

In June 1947, Margarita graduated first in her class at Sacred Heart Convent. Vladimir, Sonechka and Olga attended the prize giving ceremony where Mother Fitzgerald presented Margarita with her certificate. Although proud of his eldest daughter's achievements Vladimir was worried about the future of his family. Would his poor health prevent them getting to America?

To help support the family and unable to afford the tuition fees at the *Aurore Universite*,[19] Margarita decided to get a job. Irene, a Russian girl she knew, who worked as a cashier at the American PX Club, got Margarita an interview with the officer in charge.

At the interview, Margarita, dressed in a smart navy suit Sonechka had made, felt ill at ease as the American officer looked her up and down.

After a long pause, he quipped, 'Irene has told me about you. You're top of your class and she says your English is very good. Well, you're certainly not the usual Russian girl who wants to work here. My boys like a bit of glamour, Betty Gable stuff. But if you cut those pigtails and wear a bit of lipstick, the cashier job's yours.'

'Thank you, sir, I'll do my very best. When would you like me to start?'

'We're very busy. Right away, I'd say.'

Meanwhile, the Rossi family anxiously awaited word from the American consulate concerning their application to settle in America, which the International Relief Organisation (IRO) – a branch of the United Nations – was handling.

In early November, Vladimir fell ill with a high temperature. He then became delirious. He was rushed to the Russian Hospital, where they found he had contracted typhus. Once in hospital they found he had severe anaemia, which was attributed to a stomach ulcer.

Sonechka stayed at Vladimir's hospital bedside praying to God to spare her beloved. Without him, how could she go on living? Father Nikodim visited him daily and Archbishop John came several times. After ten days Vladimir was much improved and was due to return home.

Sonechka was elated that God had heard her prayers.

That night a Russian nurse on duty persuaded Sonechka to go home for some much-needed rest. Though she was apprehensive about leaving Vladimir, he reassured her, '*Dushenka moya*, don't worry about me now that I am so much better. You've been here for days and nights on end. You know I'll be home soon. Go and have a good night's sleep.'

Bending to kiss Vladimir goodnight, Sonechka made the sign of the cross over him. He lovingly stroked her cheek and gently whispered, 'Sonechka, meeting you was the best thing that ever happened to me. Kiss my darling girls for me.'

That night, November 25, 1947, Vladimir died.

His sudden death decimated Sonechka and Margarita. Sonechka was convinced he had been poisoned by one of the Russian hospital staff. The patient in the next bed to him told her that Vladimir had started choking immediately after being given something to drink. The staff then hastily wheeled him out of the ward.

By now it was widely known that Shanghai swarmed with Soviet agents. Desperate to return to their *Rodina* (Motherland), many White Russians in China, some twenty thousand, had applied for Soviet citizenship. Furthermore Sonechka knew that some would-be 'returnees' to the Soviet Union worked at the hospital. She wondered whether Vladimir's incisive criticisms of the Soviet regime made at Bologov's Emigrants' Association meetings had attracted the Soviets' attention. She also thought that he could have been targeted for dissuading those who sought his advice about returning to the Soviet Union. Since his death certificate stated unequivocally that he had died of typhus, Sonechka knew it to be pointless pursuing the matter. As a stateless Russian, in an anarchic city on the verge of collapse, she counted for nothing.

Margarita was now the family's sole breadwinner. Though she was paid in American dollars they were not legal tender in Shanghai. With inflation rife, exchanging them for Chinese money meant she got only a fraction of their value. The next morning she went to work. It was payday and they needed the money for the funeral. Grief-stricken, with tears staining her face, she reported to the office. The understanding officer-in-charge arranged for a motorcycle driver to take her about that day.

Bewildered, I could not comprehend what had happened to my *papochka* (daddy). Why had he gone away without kissing me goodbye? Where was this heaven place they kept on talking about? And why could I not go and see him there? I expected him to reappear at any moment, especially at bedtime, when he had read Russian fairytales to me.

The evening before the funeral, Vladimir's open coffin, draped with the Russian Imperial flag, was placed in the middle of the cathedral. Standing at the head of the coffin, Father Nikodim read the vigil for the dead, with Sonechka and Margarita standing beside Vladimir, holding lighted candles.

The next morning Archbishop John conducted the Divine Liturgy followed by the funeral service. The overwhelming smell of flowers adorning the coffin would always remain a poignant memory for me. Standing throughout the long service, Sonechka and her orphaned daughters were tragic figures who brought tears to the eyes of many packing the cathedral to pay their last respects.

Sonechka was overwhelmed by the wonderful tributes paid to Vladimir, including those from people she barely knew. Lara, Father Nikodim and Archbishop John could not have been more supportive. Later, Father Nikodim painted a portrait of Vladimir in his Imperial Horse Guard's uniform.[20] He presented it to Sonechka as a token of his admiration for her husband.[21]

Sonechka reflected on how Vladimir had stayed true to his upbringing; underpinning everything he did was his belief in the need to show honour, duty and loyalty to the Tsar. Russia had lost a loyal imperial servant and patriot.

Equally important was his belief in God, without which he felt he would have become cynical and disillusioned. It distressed him that so many in Europe had succumbed either to communism or fascism. He abhorred both these fiendish ideologies, foremost for forsaking a forgiving and loving Christian God.

Vladimir's extraordinary life, from riches and status in Imperial Russia, to losing everything in the Russian Revolution and Civil War, then exile in France, and statelessness in Shanghai, taught him an enormous amount. He was able to use this in his job with the French Municipal Police.

Sonechka marvelled how well Vladimir, so steeped in European culture and with only a little Russian blood, understood the Slavic mind and soul. He was truly Russian at heart.

CHAPTER FIFTY-EIGHT

Ten days after Vladimir's funeral, Sonechka, Margarita and Olga were summoned to the American consulate to discuss their application for entry to America. This was the beginning of a lengthy process.

Running late that morning, my mother decided we should take the tram as far as the Bund and then walk the rest of the way to the consulate. As we were about to board the tram, I started screaming and stamping my feet, 'No! No! No! I don't want to get on it!' I was usually an obedient child and it annoyed my mother and sister that I had chosen today, of all days, to be naughty. But I was adamant. So the tram left without us and we took a rickshaw. On rounding the corner we saw the tram that we had nearly taken had overturned. Several people lay injured on the ground. There was broken glass everywhere.

My mother was sure my guardian angel had saved us.

Sonechka was worried. She heard a rumour that the American immigration authorities had decided that all Russians born in China were 'Chinese'. If this was true, her children would be refused entry to America.

But when they appeared before the consul he told them that his country would welcome them. He pointed out that Sasha's undertaking to house them helped their application since the last thing America wanted was more destitute refugees. Sonechka went home delighted; the first hurdle had been overcome.

It was, however, just the beginning of their quest to leave China. Next they had to pass the medical examinations. Then they required clearance certificates from the Chinese Nationalist authorities. And, they had to be classified as stateless by the IRO in order to qualify to enter America.

All three passed their medical examinations, but perhaps the biggest hurdle was to now find someone who was prepared to buy their apartment. Otherwise Sonechka would not have the money to pay for their fare to America.

The Chinese Nationalist authorities had finally removed the ammunition and anti-aircraft artillery pieces from their apartment block. She presumed they needed them to fight Mao's Soviet-backed forces. Within no time the apartments above them were occupied by Chinese and Soviet families. Since many Chinese Nationalists had fled Shanghai going to Hong Kong or Taiwan, Sonechka was sure the new Chinese occupants were Communists.

She had to sell the apartment to someone who would pay her in American dollars; they could only pay for the boat tickets in this currency. Marked hyperinflation made Chiang's Nationalist government's currency worthless and this made the situation worse.

After several fruitless weeks of looking for a buyer, Sonechka was at her wit's end. One morning Amah startled her by announcing that a Russian man wanted to buy the apartment. Sonechka's initial elation soon turned to apprehension for she knew that only a Soviet would want to buy a Shanghai property.

The Maoist Communist army was rapidly advancing south. Chiang's once mighty Nationalist army was demoralised and many were defecting to Mao.

When Sonechka asked Amah how she had found out about the Russian who wanted to buy the apartment, she just smiled and said friends told her about him. Since questioning her further proved futile, and Sonechka was desperate, she decided to take a chance and meet this prospective buyer.

Ilya arrived next day and, after exchanging a few pleasantries, offered Sonechka what she considered to be a good price. It was more than enough to pay for their passage to America. Ilya was in charge of the accounts of an American firm with an American bank account in California and hence could pay her in US dollars. Sonechka could not believe her luck. Overwhelmed, but suppressing her surprise, she asked Ilya to return the next day when she would let him know whether she accepted his offer.

Sonechka spent the intervening twenty-four hours worrying about selling the apartment to this mysterious Russian. Judging by his general demeanour, she thought he behaved like a gentleman. But was this a ruse she wondered? Might he not show his true colours when it came to paying her? She thought he might be a former White officer blackmailed into fighting for the Bolsheviks by threats. But surely if this was so, he would have been killed in one of the purges.

By the time Ilya returned the next day, Sonechka had decided to proceed with the sale. Not wanting to appear desperate, she adopted a nonchalant take it or leave it attitude with him. To her amazement he agreed to the terms she had stipulated: half paid to the shipping company in America and the other half in three days when he took possession of the apartment.

Once again Sonechka was tormented by doubt. What if Ilya returned accompanied by thugs, demanding the down payment back, and forcibly evicting her and the girls? On the other hand, Sonechka believed Ilya was an honest person.

Fearful of what the Soviet and Chinese occupants of the building might do if they suspected she was about to vacate her apartment, Sonechka, Margarita and Amah surreptitiously took turns to shift their personal belongings to Lara's apartment over the next two days.

As promised, Ilya returned and paid the balance of the amount owing. As Sonechka handed him the keys to the apartment, he said to her, 'It's obvious that you find me disconcerting. Don't worry, I've met your type before. Because I'm courteous you conclude that I can't be a Soviet.'

Startled, Sonechka retorted, 'Haven't you taken enough from us already without trying to read and control our minds?'

Ilya sighed and replied, 'You Whites are a lost people, wallowing in the memories of an imagined golden age which you were too stupid to realise was rotten to the core. No doubt you still believe in the fantasy of a Christian God and the fatuous promise of a wonderful life in the hereafter. Well, I can tell you that the new Soviet man and woman no longer believe that nonsense. We know that Marxist-Leninism will one day create a socialist paradise here on earth. We are living in the future not the past.'

Thinking of how the moderate, consensus-seeking Vladimir might have handled this outburst of Soviet-speak, Sonechka said, 'You're entitled to your opinion provided you'll accept that we can agree to disagree.'

'That's not possible for the simple reason that our scientific Marxist-Leninist principles provide all the answers to life's great questions. It amazes me how you Whites can still believe in a Christian God. A fat lot of good he has done for you. Just look at your situation – uprooted and fleeing to the capitalist West. You should have stayed in Russia and helped create our socialist paradise. Instead, you chose to leave. By rights you're a traitor. Mark my words though, after the final collapse of capitalism you'll see the light and be desperate to return to socialist Russia,' he declared, his eyes sparkling.

Sonechka, refusing to be provoked, left the apartment and headed for Lara's. As she went out the door she said, 'This has been a happy home. I hope you'll enjoy it.'

CHAPTER FIFTY-NINE

During the two weeks before their departure, Margarita continued to work for the Americans while Olga was well cared for by her adoring Amah.

Enjoying the relative safety and luxury of Lara's apartment, Sonechka recalled how, 24 years earlier, Lara had befriended her after she fled from the Soviet Union. Once again Lara was providing a sanctuary in her hour of need. Sonechka mused how she had spent more than half her life in Shanghai, perhaps the world's most exotic city.

Sonechka, Margarita and Lara attended the Russian Emigrants Association meetings but found pessimism pervaded the proceedings. They were incensed by the gall of Dr Low, the representative of the Chinese Communist party in Geneva. In an interview with the international press, he maintained that a Communist regime would not be a threat to their people, the White Russians, because the Chinese Communists were benevolent. The world's ready acceptance of Dr Low's word convinced Sonechka that only those who had lived under the Communist yoke knew its true face. The White Russians feared the free world would continue to ignore their anguished cry for a refuge from the Chinese Communists.

To get the precious exit stamp on their documents from the Chinese Nationalists, Sonechka needed a business owner to vouch for them. Only then could she obtain their tickets. Fortunately, Lara's salon was still viable.

In mid-September a Chinese Nationalist official came to Lara's salon regarding the family's application for exit visas. Seated in one of Lara's gilded chairs he berated Sonechka, 'Why do you want to leave Shanghai? Haven't we given you a sanctuary when no one else wanted you? You're ungrateful White Russian trash.' He carried on in this vein for several minutes. Then for sometime they sat in silence, which was only broken by the official's sighs. Having already paid for his services Sonechka knew he expected her to give him a bribe. She hoped he would get sick of waiting and go before she had to pay him.

Suddenly he stood up, muttered something under his breath and stamped their documents.

The next day Sonechka bought tickets to America on the *General Gordon*, which was scheduled to leave Shanghai towards the end of the month. She wondered whether this ship was named after 'Chinese' General Gordon, whom Duncan told her had saved Shanghai's foreign concessions from the Taiping rebels in the mid-nineteenth century. She thought it ironic that this vessel commemorating Gordon should be facilitating the flight of foreigners from the city he had secured for them.

Having got this far Sonechka assumed that the IRO would be a mere formality. To get there they walked along the frenetically busy Bund. For me this was an adventure into a world I rarely saw. I was fascinated by the count-less sampans and other vessels vying with one another for space as the coolies, bent double, scurried about like ants loading and unloading their cargo.

They crossed the Garden Bridge that straddled Suzhou Creek, to get to IRO's United Nations offices, which were very close to the Soviet consulate.

They joined dozens of other applicants in the IRO waiting room in full view of the officials. They tried to make themselves as comfortable as pos-sible on one of the hard benches. They were to spend several hours there. Olga wiled away the time playing with the other children while Sonechka and Margarita chatted to other White Russians. Sonechka recalled leaving Moscow. The situation was so similar and once again she was at the mercy of officialdom playing on the apprehension of the hapless applicants. At least in Shanghai there was no shouting and verbal abuse hurled at them.

After several hours an impassive, uniformed official beckoned them for-ward. Without a word, or eye contact, he waved them to the two chairs in front of his desk. The exhausted Olga fell asleep on Margarita's lap. Sonechka gave him their documents, which included the tickets for America. The of-ficial proceeded to meticulously scrutinise their papers. He then opened a drawer in his desk and placed them in it. They were told to go back into the waiting room.

As the day drew to a close, a sense of helplessness overcame Sonechka. Why had they been singled out for this torture? What was wrong with the papers that until now appeared to be in order?

'Oh, dear God, please don't abandon us now,' she cried to herself.

When the official finally beckoned them he spoke to Sonechka in fluent Russian. In an accusatory tone, he wanted to know why she and her daugh-ters wanted to go to America. Unruffled by this sudden outburst, Sonechka told him how she longed to be reunited with her brother, Sasha, whom she had not seen for thirty years. She now realised that her interrogator was a Communist official working for the multinational-staffed IRO. Here was yet another Marxist-Leninist ideologue, purportedly disdainful of money, waiting for a bribe.

While Sonechka wondered how much longer this farce would continue, Olga smiled bewitchingly at the official. To Sonechka's amazement, his face lit up and patting Olga on the head, he spoke tenderly to her. 'You've been a very good little girl today.' He then opened the drawer, took out their papers, stamped them and returned them to Sonechka. Without saying a word he waved them dismissively towards the door. Sonechka, clutching hold of Olga's hand, fled with Margarita from the building.

On crossing the Garden Bridge, Sonechka purchased some bananas from a street hawker. Sitting down, on one of the benches in the adjacent small park, Sonechka marvelled at their good fortune. She looked at her precocious little girl whose exuberance and love of life had apparently saved the day. She thought it wonderful that Olga could be so blissfully unaware of the existence of evil in the world.

One of the saddest tasks before they left Shanghai was to visit Vladimir's grave for the last time. Father Nikodim, who accompanied them to the cemetery, conducted the final *Panikhida* (memorial service) at the graveside.

The weekly ritual of visiting and tending to Vladimir's grave had given Sonechka and her girls a purpose in their lives. Now there would be a void. With heavy hearts they bid Vladimir a final farewell.

On their last evening, Lara confessed to Sonechka that she envied her for having such wonderful memories of Vladimir. She compared them to her feelings for Gustav, whom she presumed was dead. Wolfgang was a broken man, ashamed of the Germany he had once loved. He found it unbelievable that his people had ravaged Europe, systematically exterminating some many millions.

Sonechka was most upset about leaving Lara behind. Lara had been like a sister to her. Sonechka promised her that once they got to America she would do her utmost to help her get there.

Amah, who had come to Sonechka in her hour of need, pleaded with Sonechka to take her with them. Who would look after the little one, she implored? Sonechka knew that Amah had not only saved Olga's life but had helped them survive the Japanese occupation. She was part of the family. How could Sonechka leave this devoted servant? It was heart-rending for her to think what Amah's fate might be. However it was not possible to take her, since America strictly prohibited destitute Chinese entering their country.

Sonechka reflected how her life had long been filled with bidding farewell to people whom she loved. Once again she was travelling to an unknown destination, but this time she was not alone. What would the future hold for them? She mused that one day her girls might even see the mighty Mississippi River, her childhood dream.

Before going to bed that night, Sonechka had one more problem to resolve: where to hide the dollar notes from the apartment sale. She knew that Chinese Nationalist officials carried out stringent searches on passengers about to board the vessel. They were looking for foreign currency: in particular, American dollars.

CHAPTER SIXTY

It was a cool, damp October day when Sonechka and her daughters boarded the overcrowded *General Gordon,* a former troopship now carrying hundreds of civilians. The Chinese Nationalist officials, to her great relief, did not find the hundred dollar notes hidden in her box camera. She had wound the money round the film spool, which she replaced in the camera and then covered with a strip of film.

Sonechka took a last lingering look at the city where she had spent more than half her life. The majestic buildings on the Bund, which had dominated not just Shanghai but much of China for so long, had lost none of their grandeur, even though most of their owners had left. She marvelled how this extraordinary city had for a century harboured people of practically every race, religion, ideology and political persuasion. It was a crossroads of the world where anyone could reside. She found it difficult to believe that Shanghai was now about to fall into the hands of Mao's Communists and become cut off from the rest of the world.

As Shanghai disappeared from view, Sonechka recalled how Duncan had entertained her at the city's most prestigious and luxurious venues. She admired the way he tried to comprehend her culture and the depths of the Russian mind despite the limitations of his rational English perspective. She recalled that fateful evening when she had met Vladimir and how worried she had been when he asked her to dance the Polonaise. His self-assurance and knowledge of the world made sense of much of what otherwise would have been incomprehensible to her. Now she was leaving all this behind. She would only have memories to sustain her in the lonely days ahead. No, she must stop dwelling in the past and look to the future.

If only Vladimir could be here with them. Oh, how she missed him. He was not only the love of her life but her best friend. He understood her so well. She had no doubt that Archbishop John and his fellow priests would continue to shepherd and console thousands of fellow Russians stranded in Shanghai.

She prayed that a sanctuary would soon be found for them all, especially Lara and Wolfgang. Sonechka thanked God for delivering her family from the horrors of the approaching Red tide.

Sonechka, Margarita and Olga clambered cautiously down the steep stairs, with their narrow steps, to the dimly lit cabin where they would be sleeping and spending most of the voyage. A sea of three-tiered narrow bunks, with people of all ages milling round them, confronted the family. Sonechka was worried about how they would live here. Margarita occupied the top bunk, Olga the middle and Sonechka the lower one.

Sonechka and Margarita were surprised to see several familiar faces among the many Russians in their section of the ship. They realised that, fearful of what the Soviet agents might do, they were not the only ones to keep their plans secret. Most of their compatriots had lived in Shanghai for many years, but others came from elsewhere in China. What did America have in store for them?

A number of Russians Sonechka met were frightened that the Americans would consider them closet Communists, especially if they had taken out Soviet citizenship. By now, there was a virtual state of war between the two superpowers over the Soviets' decision to blockade Berlin.

The general pardon for the stateless White Russians by Stalin (June 14, 1946), convinced many doubters that they should return to their Motherland where they were promised a warm welcome. They believed that Stalin, despite the millions that he had killed, had been changed by the war. Those Russian Orthodox faithful who succumbed to Stalin's enticements believed that God forgave him once he opened the churches and restored the Patriarchate. However, once it became suspected that the Soviets wrought vengeance on their fellow White Russian returnees many renounced their Soviet citizenship and sought sanctuary in America and elsewhere. Sonechka could not believe the lengths the Soviets where prepared to go to in order to lure her people to their deaths or purgatory in the gulags.[22]

During the day Sonechka put on a brave face in front of her daughters. However, the ship's incessant engine noise meant they never knew that their mother cried herself to sleep most nights, grieving for Vladimir. Margarita pined for her doting father; I could not believe that I would never see my *papochka* again. For me the voyage was an exciting adventure. I enjoyed playing with the handful of children of my age. The highlight of the voyage was a birthday party for one of my playmates. Besides a scrumptious cake there was an assortment of delicious cookies.

The former troopship's amenities were basic. The door-less toilets and showers meant that anyone using them could be seen by passers-by, including members of the crew. The family liked sneaking up on to the out-of-bounds higher decks. There they sat huddled together relishing the fresh air. On several occasions friendly sailors gave them fresh oranges and fried chicken. Margarita, who suffered from severe sea sickness, especially appreciated these treats since she ate little of the stodgy porridge and other barely palatable food provided.

On approaching San Francisco, Sonechka could not believe that, at long last, she was about to be reunited with her brother Sasha and that finally she would be fulfilling her cherished childhood dream of going to America.

In her darker moments Sonechka felt rootless, wondering whether her flight from Russia, which had taken her nearly round the world would ever end. Her idyllic upbringing in the Crimea seemed unreal. On the last evening before leaving Leningrad for Moscow, Pavel had predicted that her wanderlust would be cured once she got to the border town of Chita.

Well, she had proved them all wrong.

Sonechka recalled a dream she had the night before leaving Moscow on June 2, 1924.

She was on a hillside overlooking Pavel's Crimean estate hanging out washing on what seemed to be an endless clothesline. Pavel, standing beside her, exclaimed, 'Sonechka, why are you hanging out all those dirty clothes?'

Startled, Sonechka began to take the washing off the line, whereupon Pavel said, 'Don't worry, Sonechka. Here, hang these up instead.'

Having done this, Sonechka looked back at the line and saw just three pristine white geese hanging in a row.

'So, that's what it meant,' Sonechka sighed. 'The dirty clothes were those I left behind – they had been sullied and then destroyed by the Soviets.'

Now Sonechka and her daughters were free to start a new life in America, which would preserve many of their cherished traditional Russian values.

EPILOGUE

Sonechka's American dream was finally realised when we arrived in San Francisco on October 6, 1948.

I recall my mother's poignant reunion with her brother, my uncle Sasha. Having not seen him for thirty years, she could not stop crying. That same day we motored up to Russian River to stay at his *dacha*. Shortly afterwards my mother found work as a housemaid cleaning luxury suites at the St Francis Hotel in San Francisco. Over the years Sonechka had a number of other jobs, including as a seamstress in a clothing factory and assembling radio components. Margarita became a trainee hospital laboratory technician and studied at night school.

In 1951, Sasha helped Dora, my father's sister, gain entry to America. She lived with us for several years in San Francisco. Dora, who adored my father, had nearly as great an influence on my upbringing as did my mother and sister. Besides having her written memoirs, Dora told me many memorable stories about my father and their childhood in St Petersburg and at Merkuli, the family estate in Finland.

In 1951 Lara arrived in San Francisco, facilitated by an affidavit provided by Sasha. For eighteen months she had been living on the remote, cyclone-ridden, tropical island of Tubabao in the Philippines. With some four thousand others, who were overwhelmingly White Russians, including the Tikhon Zadonsk orphanage, Lara was evacuated to Tubabao from Shanghai by the IRO. Wolfgang had died the year before in Shanghai. The ingenuity and determination of these marooned people created a viable community out of virtually nothing in the jungle.

In 1952 Archbishop John of Shanghai enabled most of these refugees to gain entry to America, Australia and Latin America. Had he not lobbied American politicians on their behalf, including sitting on the steps of Congress, Washington DC, for days on end, these refugees would certainly have remained on Tubabao for much longer. (Archbishop John died in 1966 and was canonised in 1994 – Saint John, the Wonder Worker of Shanghai and San Francisco.)

Several years later Lara married a Russian in San Francisco. She became a successful floral painter and had several exhibitions. She died in the mid-1980s.

In 1953 Margarita married Alex and went to live on his ranch in Colorado. I spent several wonderful summers with them.

In the mid-1950s Dora went to work in Palo Alto, after which my mother and I lived in many rented one-bedroom apartments in the San Francisco's Haight-Ashbury district. These frequent moves were, in part, due to my mother's belief that Soviet agents were on her trail.

During my schooling I had only one American friend. Senator Joseph McCarthy's vehement anti-communist crusade meant that most Americans made no distinction between White and Red Russians. Consequently I was brought up in a very close-knit White Russian community. At home we spoke Russian, ate Russian food, and attended Russian Orthodox Church services. We went to Russian plays and concerts given by Russian musicians at the Russian Centre. I enjoyed the Russian summer scout camps in Yosemite National Park and at Lake Tahoe.

For six years I attended the Catholic St Agnes School in Ashbury Street and later, because of our frequent moves, three different high schools. Two afternoons a week, from 4–6 pm, and every Saturday morning, I went to the Russian Church School in Fulton Street. Besides religious instruction we were taught Russian grammar, literature, pre-revolutionary Russian history and geography.

In 1960, on graduating from High School, aged seventeen I went to Europe with Aunt Dora. We crossed America on the Greyhound Bus and boarded a ship in New York, bound for Hamburg. We visited Vera, Dora's cousin and childhood playmate in West Berlin. Vera's two brothers, Vasya and Kolya, were killed fighting for Imperial Russia in World War I. Vera and her husband had survived the allied bombing and fall of Berlin. We then visited other relatives in Marburg, Wiesbaden, Frankfurt and Rome.

We arrived in Paris in mid-September to stay with Dora's daughter, my cousin Katherine and her family. Paris was magical. I wanted to stay there. My cousin found me an au pair job with a French family. The following year I attended a year's *Civilisation Francaise* course for foreigners at the Sorbonne. I lived in a Catholic student hostel in the Latin Quarter. It was during the height of the Algerian uprising, when civil war so nearly erupted in France. One night a plastic-type bomb destroyed part of the adjacent Moroccan hotel.

Apart from the little money I got from babysitting jobs, my mother continued to support me financially. Having completed the Sorbonne course I was supposed to return home to America.

However, destiny intervened. Through Dora's friends I got a job on the telephone exchange at the American Hospital of Paris. I replaced a Russian lady who was retiring after forty years. She was the very same lady whom Dora had replaced forty years earlier when she took maternity leave. Two weeks after starting this job, I met John, a New Zealand intern at the hospital. It was a whirlwind romance. We were married six months later in the Russian Orthodox cathedral of St Alexander Nevsky in Paris. My mother was ill and unable to attend our wedding, however, Margarita and Alex came. Alex gave me away. After a brief honeymoon in the Loire Valley, John and I went to live in England, where John continued his post-graduate medical studies.

Sadly, Sasha, who had done so much for us, died in San Francisco in late 1963. My mother came to live with us in England from 1965 to 1967 and Dora visited us there in 1966. By then we had two children. When we left for New Zealand in early 1967, my mother returned to America. She later came to live with us in Auckland, New Zealand, for two years. She returned to San Francisco in 1970 to help Margarita and her family. In 1971 Sonechka met and married Prince Alexander Massalsky-Surin. He had recently come to live in America. Dora had known him and his family in St Petersburg.

John and I returned to England in the summer of 1974, when John was appointed consultant rheumatologist at Bedford Hospital. That August my darling mother, who had sacrificed so much for me, died of a stroke. Several weeks later Aunt Dora died. They are buried beside one another in the Serbian Orthodox cemetery in San Francisco.

I was very close to my mother, especially after my sister married. Sonechka desperately missed Vladimir, my father. Her faith in God gave her some solace. She told me that one of my father's greatest wishes was to take her and his girls to Europe. In his memory, she was determined that I should fulfill this dream.

Unfortunately I was unable to attend either my mother or Aunt Dora's funerals. John and I had just moved to England and I had no one to look after him or our three children.

I dedicate this book to the memory of my mother, Sonechka, my father, Vladimir, and my Aunt Dora who have made me what I am today.

GLOSSARY

Analoi	A high, sloping table on which an icon is placed.
Bagmen	City dwellers who went to the countryside to exchange clothes and valuables for food, 1921–1922.
Barynya	Madam.
Banya	Steam bath.
Bozhenka	A diminutive of God.
Bozhe moi!	Dear God!
Burzhui	Bourgeois.
Cheka	Lenin's secret police (forerunner of the KGB).
Comintern	Communist International.
Dacha	A Russian country house or villa.
Dedushka	Grandfather, or sometimes simply an old man.
Gimnasia	A high school preparing students for university.
IRO	International Relief Organisation.
Julian calendar	Still used by the Russian Orthodox church: 13 days behind the Gregorian Calendar.
Kasha	Literally porridge, but usually referring to buckwheat.
Kelya	A cell used by hermit monks.
Komsomol	The Bolshevik youth organisation.
Koshmar	Nightmare.
Koshmary	Nightmares.
Kulich	A cylindrical Easter yeast cake.
Krendel	A yeast cake made with eggs, milk, honey, raisins and nuts.
Khristos Voskrese	Christ is Risen.
Kvartira	An apartment.
Kvas	A low alcohol homemade drink made of fermented breadcrumbs.
Lampada	Oil lamp usually hanging in front of an Icon.

Lazaret	Hospital.
Lubyanka	Moscow's dreaded prison headquarters.
Mamochka	Diminutive of mother.
Maslenitsa	Derived from *maslo*, Russian for butter.
NEP	New Economic Policy.
Nepman, Nepmen	Traders who took up the commercial opportunities offered under the New Economic Policy.
Nyanya	Children's nanny.
Panikhida	Funeral service.
Papochka, papa	Father.
Parastas	A vigil service for the dead.
Paskha	Easter.
paskha	Easter curd cheese dessert.
Pechka	A large stove used as much for heating as for cooking.
Pirogi	A pie.
Pomeshchik	A landowner.
Prosphora	Church bread used for communion.
Rodina	Motherland.
Sarafan	A smock worn by peasants.
Selo	Village.
Taipan	A foreign businessman or a trader in China.
Tovarish	Comrade.
Traktir	A bar.
Valenki	Thick felt boots.
Vokzal	A railway station.
Zhidi	Yids (slang for Jews).
Zimny Dvoretz	Winter Palace.

ENDNOTES

1　In her book, published in 2004, *The Port of Last Resort*, Marcia Ristaino states that Shanghai's Slavic community 'have thus far apparently resisted any temptation to revisit their generally difficult and sometimes tragic Shanghai experiences'.

2　The Great Lent is the most important Lent in the Russian Orthodox Church calendar.

3　In creating the Cheka, Lenin drew on his knowledge of the French revolution, enhanced by living in Paris in the early 1900s. Like the fanatical French revolutionary Robespierre, Lenin believed that single party rule could only be achieved by perpetual terror and the law of suspects.

4　The Prussian Willi Munzenberg, a friend of Lenin's in Zurich, headed the Comintern (Communist International), based initially in Berlin and from 1933 in Paris. In his book *The Red Millionaire. A Political Biography of Willi Munzenberg, Moscow's Secret Propaganda Tsar in the West*, Sean McMeekin reveals the enormous influence this organisation successfully exerted worldwide in the promotion of the Soviet Union and communism. Whereas the communist parliamentarian Munzenberg's Reichstag adversary Joseph Goebbels is a household name for perfecting the art of propaganda, Munzenberg remains a virtual unknown. Yet Goebells envied Munzenberg's propaganda skills. McMeekin maintains that Munzenberg lived the life of a millionaire from the seemingly limitless funding provided by Moscow.

5　*Vokzal* is derived from the English word Vauxhall. It was the name given to the railway stations built by British engineers (mainly Scotsmen) who constructed much of Imperial Russia's massive railway system.

6　Gibbes later became a Russian Orthodox priest: Father Nicholas. He returned to England in 1934, living in London and subsequently Oxford. Postwar he became involved in a bitter split within Oxford's Russian Orthodox Church, which he helped found, Father Nicholas sided with those Russians who transferred their allegiance to the Moscow Patriarchate. He died in London in 1961. The authors of this book, Olga and John, along with Olga's mother Sonechka, attended this church regularly while living in England in the mid-1960s.

7　In 1934 more people lived in Shanghai's French Concession than in Lyon (France's second largest city): 480,000 Chinese, 2,300 French and 19,000 foreigners, of whom 10,000 were Russians. The 30,000 former Imperial Russian citizens and their offspring constituted by far the greatest number of caucasians living in all of Shanghai. These Russians outnumbered the British by three to one!

8　The Moscow born White Russian Ernest Beaux was perfumer to Tsar Nicholas II. Commissioned by Coco Chanel, Beaux created Chanel No 5, the world's first artificial perfume, at Grasse in 1920. Besides Coco Chanel's close working relationship with Beaux, she had an affair with the Grand Duke Dimitri Pavolich, one of the Russian aristocrats involved in the assassination of Rasputin. The composer Igor Stravinsky was another White Russian with whom she was closely associated in Paris. Though it is uncertain whether she had an affair with Stravinsky, it is said that she made a man of him!

9   The word *Maslenitsa* is derived from *maslo*, Russian for butter. Western Christians celebrate the week before Lent as Mardi Gras or Shrove Tuesday (Pancake Day).

10 General Alexis Brusilov, a devout Russian Orthodox believer, died in Moscow in 1926 while under house arrest. He had become disillusioned with the regime he did so much to sustain by fighting for the Red Army. Belatedly he realised that instead of the promised people's paradise, a hell on earth had been foisted on his beloved Mother Russia. He exemplifies the tragic fate of those idealistic Russians who the Bolsheviks enlisted to their cause in the belief that their country was on the verge of an exciting and enlightened new beginning.

11 In his novel *The Great Gatsby*, F. Scott Fitzgerald catches the essence of this period, not just in Paris, but in any era. Fitzgerald wrote this work while living in France, including Paris, in the mid-1920s. *The Great Gatsby* shows how one can self-destruct, as did Scott Fitzgerald, striving to achieve absolute fame, absolute wealth and the absolute erotic experience.

12 Ferguson, Niall, *The War of the World*, London, 2007.

13 Alston, Charlotte, *Russia's Greatest Enemy? Harold Williams and the Russian Revolution*, London, 2007.

14 The Orphanage of Saint Tikhon of Zadonsk, for the fifteen years of its existence, cared for some three thousand children.

15 Rigg, Bryan, *Hitler's Jewish Soldiers: The Untold Story of Nazi Racial Laws and Men of Jewish Descent In the German Military*, Kansas, 2002.

16 Jung Chang and Jon Halliday, in *Mao – The Unknown Story* (London, 2005), maintain that the Soviet Union blackmailed Chiang Kai-shek by threatening to kill Chiang's son, who lived in Moscow, should Chiang defeat Mao.

17 Ristaino, Marcia Reynders, *Port of Last Resort: The Diaspora Communities of Shanghai*, America, 2004.

18 The Russian Orthodox Princess Olga was the grandmother of Grand Prince Vladimir, the founder of Russian Orthodoxy in 988, when Russia became a Christian country. They were both canonised by the Russian Orthodox Church for bringing Christianity to Russia.

19 *Aurore Universitie*, founded by the Jesuits, was renowned throughout China.

20 Father Nikodim was an iconographer who painted most of the icons adorning the cathedral consecrated by Bishop John in 1934. This building still stands today, but bereft of its cupola's gold crosses. They disappeared during the Cultural Revolution. Also, during the Cultural Revolution, all the cathedral's icons were obliterated by whitewash and the graves desecrated in the Bubbling Well Road cemetery where my father Vladimir was buried. Father Nikodim was evacuated from Shanghai to the Philippine island of Tubabao. Subsequently he went to Argentina.

21 I have this portrait of my father, painted by Father Nikodim, hanging in our dining room.

22 The 1999 French film *Est-Ouest* (East West), starring among others Catherine Deneuve, depicts the cruel fate of those White Russians who returned to their imagined welcoming Motherland. Nearly everyone was either shot on arrival at the port of Odessa or sent to the gulag.

BIBLIOGRAPHY

RUSSIA

Alston, Charlotte, *Russia's Greatest Enemy? Harold Williams and the Russian Revolution*, Tauris Academic Studies, London, 2007.

Applebaum, Anne, *Gulag: A History of the Soviet Camps*, Allen Lane The Penguin Press, Great Britain, 2003.

Figes, Orlando, *A People's Tragedy: the Russian Revolution 1891–1924*, Pimlico, London, 1996.

Figes, Orlando, *Natasha's Dance: A Cultural History of Russia*, Penguin Books, London, 2003.

Montefiore, Simon, Sebag, *Stalin: The Court of the Red Tsar*, Weidenfeld & Nicholson, London, 2003.

Ovsianikov, Yury, *Velikie Zodchiin (Great Architects) Trezini, Rastrelli, Rossi*, Publishers for the Russian Federation, St. Petersburg, 1996.

Pitcher, Harvey, *Witnesses of the Russian Revolution*, Swallow House, London, 2001.

Studemeister, Alexander, *History of the Meltzer Family*, self-published, California, 1988 (translation of the German text published in 1963).

RUSSIAN DIASPORA FRANCE

Johnston, Robert H., *New Mecca, New Babylon: Paris and the Russian Exiles 1920–1945*, Queen's University Press, Kingston, 1988.

Jevakhoff, Alexandre, *Les Russes Blancs*, Talandier, Paris, 2007.

Menegaldo, Helene, *Les Russes a Paris*, Les Editions Autrement, Paris, 1998.

Struve, Nikita, *Soixante-dix ans d'emigration russe 1919–1989*, Libraire Artheme Fayard, Paris, 1996.

RUSSIAN DIASPORA CHINA

Bologoff, G.K., *Shanghai: A Historical Note 25 Years Ago*, from the Russian newspaper *Russian Life*, 23 December 1973 (translated by Peter and Kyra Tatarinoff, Sydney, Australia, 1999).

Dong, Stella, *Shanghai: The Rise and Fall of a Decadent City*, HarperCollins USA, 2001.

Brossollet, Guy, *Les Francais De Shanghai 1849–1949*, Belin, Paris, 1999.

Jiganoff, V.D., *Russians in Shanghai*, self-published, Shanghai, 1936.

Jobert, Veronique, *Les Rapatries Russes de Chine*, Paris, 2003.

Johnston, Tess & Erh, Deke, *Frenchtown Shanghai: Western Architecture In Shanghai's Old French Concession*, Old China Hand Press, Hong Kong, 2000.

Lukianov, Valery, *Lantern of Grace (Saint John of Shanghai & San Francisco)*, Diocese of Western America of the Russian Orthodox Church Outside of Russia, San Francisco, 2004.

Ristaino, Marcia Reynders, *Port of Last Resort: The Diaspora Communities of Shanghai*, Stanford University Press, USA, 2004.

Sergeant, Harriet, *Shanghai*, Jonathan Cape, London, 1991.

Wasserstein, Bernard, *Secret War in Shanghai: Treachery, Subversion and Collaboration in the Second World War*, Profile Books Ltd, London, 1998.

GENERAL

Benaugh, Christine, *An Englishman in the Court of the Tsar: The Spiritual Journey of Charles Sydney Gibbes*, Conciliar Press Ben Lomond, California, 2000.

Brendon, Piers, *The Dark Valley: A Panorama of the 1930s*, Random House, New York, 2002.

Chang Jung and Jon Halliday, *Mao: The Unknown Story*, Jonathan Cape, London, 2005.

Fedorova, Nina, *The Family*, Little, Brown & Company, Boston, 1940.

Ferguson, Niall, *The War of the World*, Penguin Books, London, 2007.

Hingley, Ronald, *The Russian Mind*, The Bodley Head Ltd, London, 1978.

Ilyin, Olga, *White Road: A Russian Odyssey 1919–1923*, Holt, Rinehart and Winston, New York, 1984.

Kelly, David, *The Ruling Few or The Human Background to Diplomacy*, Hollis & Carter, London, 1952.

Koch, Stephan, *Double Lives: Spies and Writers in the Secret War of Ideas Against the West*, Free Press a Division of Macmillan Inc, New York, 1994.

McMeekin, Sean, *The Red Millionaire: A Political Biography of Willi Munzenberg Moscow's Secret Propaganda Tsar in the West*, Yale University Press, London, 2003.

Paxton, Robert, *Vichy France: Old Guard And New Order*, Allen Lane, New York, 2001.

Pecnard, Melincia, *American Hospital of Paris*, L'Aventure d'un siecle, le cherche midi, Paris, 2006.

Rigg, Bryan, *Hitler's Jewish Soldiers: The Untold Story of Nazi Racial Laws and Men of Jewish Descent In the German Military*, Modern War Studies, University of Kansas, Kansas, 2002.

Robinson, Paul, *The White Army In Exile, 1920–1941*, Oxford Clarendon Press, London, 2002.

Rodzianko, Paul, *Tattered Banners: An Autobiography*, Seeley Service & Co. Ltd, London, 1939.

Stephan, John, *The Russian Fascists: Tragedy and Farce in Exile*, Harper & Row, New York, 1973.

Tyrkova-Williams, *Cheerful Giver: The Life of Harold Williams*, Peter Davies, UK, 1935.